A CENTURY OF HERO-WORSHIP

Eric Bentley is the author of *The Playwright as Thinker* (1946), *Bernard Shaw* (1947), *In Search of Theatre* (1953), *The Dramatic Event* (1954, Beacon Paperback Edition, 1956), and *What Is Theatre?* (1956, Beacon Paperback Original).

A Century of HERO-WORSHIP

A study of the idea of heroism in Carlyle *and* Nietzsche, *with notes on* Wagner, Spengler, Stefan George, *and* D. H. Lawrence

by ERIC BENTLEY

Second Edition

BEACON PRESS *Beacon Hill* Boston

© 1944, 1957 by Eric Bentley. Second edition, revised and reset, published by the Beacon Press in 1957. First edition published in the United States by the J. B. Lippincott Company, 1944. Published in Great Britain as *The Cult of the Superman* by Robert Hale, Ltd., 1947. Printed in the United States of America. Library of Congress catalog card number: 57-9215.

For My Mother

Lives of great men oft remind us
  We should make our lives sublime.
                    —Henry Wadsworth Longfellow

Mein Sohn, ich hörte dich reden
  Von einem Heldengeschlecht
Wusste nicht, ahnte nicht, sah nicht
  Du warst ihr Folterknecht.
            —"Lied einer deutschen Mutter," Bertolt Brecht

The art of government is the organization of idolatry.
        —John Tanner, in Bernard Shaw's *Man and Superman*

Understand it well, this "of hero-worship" was the primary
creed . . . and will be the ultimate and final creed of mankind.
                              —Thomas Carlyle

Acknowledgments

I wish to acknowledge here, as I did in the first edition, the advice and assistance of Mr. William C. DeVane, Mr. Hermann J. Weigand, Mr. Edward N. Hooker, Miss Franziska de Graaff, Mr. Paul Radin, Mr. Clark Foreman, Mr. Jacques Barzun, Miss Tay Hohoff, and Mr. George Stevens; also of Dixon Wecter who today, alas, is no longer alive.

And, since reviewers cannot take for granted that their more caustic comments are welcome to the author under review, I should like, in this place, to thank two of the severer critics of *A Century of Hero-Worship* for helping me to change my mind on certain points. These critics are Mr. Sidney Hook and Mr. Richard Chase, who reviewed me in *The Nation* and *Partisan Review*, respectively.

Above all, on this occasion, I have Mr. Sol Stein to thank, for it was he who thought that the book should be reprinted.

New York, 1957   E. B.

Contents

xi

Foreword to the Second Edition

The outstanding defects of this book have their origin in the fact that I was unable to write it in the spirit of detached scholarship because I was trying to fight my way through the facts to their meaning. If I allow the book to be reprinted, it is because I believe that its merits have the same origin. And, in general, I am against any "official" type of criticism and history, preferring interpretations offered as one man's grapple with his theme and the world.

Although, in principle, the Beacon Paperbacks are complete and unabridged, I have myself chosen to delete not only a word here and a phrase there but one whole chapter. Fully to explain myself, I should have to write the story of seventeen years of my life—1940-1957. Short of writing such a story, which after all would be another book, the best I can do is to supply those who are interested with four different attempts made in this period to describe my subject and/or my attitude to it. Those who are not interested can skip to the first chapter.

1

Written chiefly in 1940, this book was first published in the United States (1944) with the following foreword:

Under the impact of war, revolution, and dictatorship, we are witnessing a revival of interest in heroes and hero-worship. On the one hand, books are appearing which call attention to the heroes of American tradition (*The Hero in America, American Heroes and Hero-Worship*), and on the other the role of the hero in history has been reinvestigated by so sharp an observer as Mr. Sidney Hook.[1]

[1] The book here alluded to—*The Hero in History*—is available in Beacon Paperbacks. (Note added in 1957.)

The present book has the rather different purpose of discussing the advocacy of hero-worship by modern writers who dislike democracy. It divides into five parts. The first two are devoted to Thomas Carlyle and Friedrich Nietzsche respectively. From a somewhat intimate study of the greatest English and the greatest German preacher of heroism, we turn in the third and fourth parts to a more general treatment of several similar artists; that is, artists who were confronted with similar problems and who met these problems in a substantially similar way. Richard Wagner is nowadays the most talked-of of æsthetic hero-worshipers, and to bring out both by contrast and parallelism the nature of Wagnerism, Part Three treats together Wagner and Bernard Shaw, the perfect Wagnerite; the chapter on Shaw is also an excursion in which the alternative to anti-democratic hero-worship is discussed in preparation for Part Five. Part Four consists of chapters on the most outstanding literary hero-worshipers of the twentieth century: Spengler, Stefan George and D. H. Lawrence. Part Five is at once a summing-up and an appraisal.

Of all five parts it may be said that, while the idea of hero-worship is paramount, rigid unity of structure and method has not been attempted; strict relevance has sometimes been sacrificed to the interest which a topic has in itself. The method, for example, has been more or less biographical according to the nature of the particular case. In the chapter on Stefan George will be found significant material never before available to the public; otherwise, biography has largely been confined to Parts One and Two.

In this book the word *heroism* does not mean just any sort of human goodness. It has reference to a philosophy of life that was intended by its champions to be to the centuries that lie ahead more than Catholicism ever was to the Middle Ages. The half-dozen minds examined in the following pages do not come together by accident. Each has one foot in the democratic and one in the fascist camp, and the story of their ambivalent heritage is as instructive as it is melancholy. We need not comb the literary record for "proto-Nazis." Nor need we adopt a patronizing attitude to these critics of democracy. For those who have no wish to prolong the nineteenth century into the twentieth and twenty-first, the criticisms of the old democracy offered by Carlyle,

Nietzsche, and the rest, will be valuable. Few of these writers were political scientists, but they speak with imagination and, because they are artists, their valuations are sometimes more relevant than those of the experts. To look into their minds is to look into the problem of mass civilization and minority culture. For instance: Has the artist been at home under democracy? In answering such a question one should think not only of celebrated critics of democracy such as those discussed in the following pages, but of all the homeless æsthetes and Bohemians driven to pessimism or revolt by the nineteenth-century system. Name the great writers of our time. Marcel Proust, Thomas Mann, James Joyce, Rainer Maria Rilke, W. B. Yeats, T. S. Eliot—their work implies dislike not only of what democracy actually is, but of what democracy is even in aspiration. So does the work of the less great: if the assumptions of Huxley's *Brave New World* and Jeffers' *The Tower Beyond Tragedy* are valid, then the whole liberal and democratic movement has been futile.

Democracy has not liked the artist, and the artist has not liked democracy, for culture in the narrow sense of the word has always been aristocratic, and the disappearance of aristocracy meant that the artist was left stranded. This isolation of the artist is unfortunate. Because the old regimes have offered no solution, the artist has hated the old regimes. But the new fascist regimes are worse. They are destroying culture altogether. Culture is left to us to look after, and in no branch of the national life is our unpreparedness greater. Now culture, as Matthew Arnold put it, is the study of perfection. A competent democracy will not only raise the general level of education; it will simultaneously maintain standards of excellence. This second task, to begin with at least, must be the task of a minority, and especially of the artists.

One need not apologize, then, for limiting a study of ideas to artists. We cannot always be preoccupied with journalists, even though their influence is in inverse proportion to their merit. Nor can we be preoccupied with the technical philosophers who have criticized democracy. The artist is important because his art is a storehouse of values, because he gives body and vitality to what else would remain inert and lifeless. In the end it may be true that poets are unacknowledged legislators. The poet is the stone that drops in the still pond of philosophy; professional philosophers are the spreading, concentric rings.

To study Carlyle, Nietzsche, Lawrence, Spengler, George, is to probe deep into nineteenth-century democracy, deep into the origins of fascism and Nazism, deep into the mind of the modern artist. Their insights are unusual; the difficulties they faced are common. They are ambiguous figures, all thesis and antithesis, but if, amid the shifting dialectic, one can reach a synthesis, the effort will not be vain. The view through the binoculars which they vouchsafe us will be focused and coordinated into one clear vision.

2

In 1945 I was asked to write something about Carlyle in *The American Scholar* on the 150th anniversary of his birth. I wrote as follows:

Carlyle's credit stands lower in 1945 than it has since the days when he was still failing to find a publisher for *Sartor Resartus*. His "good" influence lasted till—early in the twentieth century—it petered out in women's clubs and elementary college classes. His "evil" influence has also ended—for the present at any rate—with the death of Hitler and Mussolini, exactly 150 years after Carlyle's birth. Abandoned even by the universities, the last refuge of yesterday's favorites, Carlyle is now a nullity.

He will probably remain so. The life of his spirit might plausibly be dated 1795-1945. Few men live so long, and yet it is rather sad to think that one who has cut so large a figure in the world can in the end be committed to the most real of all deaths, oblivion. The titans of war and politics one is prepared to forget. Better so. But it is hard to let a titan of the spirit slip from sight. Is not literature immortal? It is commonly supposed to be so, and one cannot doubt that the imaginative element in a man's work is, in a sense, imperishable. But the fame of Carlyle was never literary. It was personal and moral. *Thomas Carlyle: How to Know Him* was the homely title of Mr. Bliss Perry's tribute. This is a debilitated late form of the Carlyle worship which in its heyday had been a moral passion. Today such a passion—even when diluted for the children or perverted for the fascists—is unthinkable. Carlyle is dead. To observe that he is still read in the graduate schools may, unhappily, be but a confirmation of this fact. When a writer is read only by those who are professionally obliged to read him it can scarcely be said that he is living force. However thorough and reverent an embalming may be, it seldom results in resurrection.

When the vast morgue of history has received another guest, an inquest is in order. What did the man die of? And what had he lived on? Looking back on Carlyle today we see in him much to annoy us and even more that leaves us cold. He was as much of a windbag as any of the liberals whom he mocked. He was not a great philosopher, nor can one regard what he did to English prose with much enthusiasm. If all his writings have their good moments, like Wagner's operas they have their bad halfhours. Why read his *French Revolution* or his *Frederick the Great*? As historiography they have been superseded; as literature they are affected, messy, and monotonous. A historian who writes at length must have a style that is endurable at length. Gibbon can be taken in long draughts like beer; Carlyle is a stiff whisky of an unreliable brand.

As for what Carlyle says, there is, no doubt, too much dangerous nonsense about it, and we are not today in a frame of mind to stand dangerous nonsense directed against the Negroes, the Jews, the French, or the common people. We are not in a frame of mind to listen to praise of Bismarck, Frederick the Great, and the Germans—whom Carlyle called "the First Nation of the Universe." Nor is Carlyle much more convincing, it may be felt, in the gentler mood of *Past and Present*. The remedies he there prescribes—such as silence, prayer, obedience, and emigration —sound more like a program for the disbanded Gestapo than for the United Nations. . . . In these days when it is comforting to find authors whom one may be excused for not reading, Carlyle will be among the first on our index. He is morally dangerous, æsthetically boring or repellent, and personally a neurotic whose neuroses are too evident and too simple to interest a public glutted with the most refined insanities. Why, it might be asked, if we condemn Ezra Pound and Charles Maurras and Knut Hamsun living, ought we to praise Carlyle dead?

Germany has offended. But there is another Germany. Carlyle has offended. But there is another Carlyle. There is the Carlyle whom Friedrich Engels praised and translated,[2] the Carlyle to

[2] Mr. Sidney Hook, reviewing the present book, observes that "some of Carlyle's language" found its way into *The Communist Manifesto* (*The Nation*, October 7, 1944). (Note added in 1957.)

whom Dickens dedicated *Hard Times* and Ruskin *Munera Pulveris,* the Carlyle who in America stirred the very different hearts of Emerson and Whitman, the Carlyle who in England was still able at the end of the century to spur on the young Havelock Ellis and the younger Patrick Geddes. There is the Carlyle who, for all his provinciality, made his presence felt in Paris, Madrid, Rome, and Berlin for at least half a century (excluding the use of Carlyle by the Nazis and the Fascists). This was a man who said things that needed to be said, though nobody was saying them. Here was a man who clung tenaciously to truths that were being denied or forgotten. Here was a man whose life was one long tempestuous voyage through the dangerous currents of a revolutionary age. Here was a man who questioned not only the respectable ideas of the time, as every critic is expected to do as part of his regular routine, but also the most "advanced" ideas of the time. This takes courage.

The world, then as now, had many doctors. Then as now there were the advocates of "normalcy," dominated by the fear of a red menace from abroad. Then as now there were the starry-eyed radicals who saw a democratic future arising from education and the ballot-box and beautiful shared experiences. Carlyle began by repudiating the *status quo.* After some traffic with idealistic socialism, he repudiated that also. Thereafter his task was to work out a scheme of things that would be as "realistic" as reaction and as noble as radicalism. Is not this still our task? Carlyle, it has to be admitted, did not altogether succeed in his attempt. He was sometimes content to parade his "realism"—as, say, Lawrence Dennis or James Burnham do today—and let the nobility slide. Carlyle did not have the answers. He had only the questions.

"He who asks the questions," says Oscar Wilde, another forgotten genius, "is never the one who answers them." This is not to lessen the importance of questioning. It takes the genius of a Carlyle or a Wilde to ask the right question at the right time with the right emphasis. Our tendency to prefer the genius with the answers is due to our superstitious reverence for dogma. Where today are the dogmas, the right answers, of the past? Some of them, no doubt, may be working well and according to plan. More are forgotten or in abeyance or in violent dispute. Our greatest teachers are not those who gave us doctrines or systems of metaphysics. They are the interrogators and the protesters and conundrum makers—from Confucius to Jesus, and from Voltaire to Nietzsche—whom we, with our respect for dogma, reward by crucifixion or—which in the long run is less flattering —by slander. The word for such a teacher is Paradoxical, Not Profound, or Confused. Carlyle belongs here.

Such teachers are notoriously Inconsistent. Like Whitman they contradict themselves and they don't care. Admittedly this is very naughty of them. What we need to remark, however, is the cause of their contradictoriness. It is their empiricism, their closeness to experience, their preoccupation with what actually happens. Doubtless a thinker is not entitled to be contradictory merely because he knows that nature and experience are so. One need not make a positive merit of our teachers' contradictions. Yet one must understand them not as logical flaws, but as sometimes legitimate products of an ironic and poetic rather than a logical awareness.

"I have solved the riddle of Truth," says Wilde. "A Truth in art is that whose contradictory is also true." A fantastic statement, enough to make any philosopher's blood boil. The philosopher— as such—has no sense of humor, therefore no sense of irony, therefore no sense of life. Carlyle was no philosopher. His closeness to concrete fact was not that of Bacon. It was that of Blake. He is to be judged by his struggles, his *obiter dicta*, his insights and hunches, and not by his metaphysic (which is chiefly half-understood jargon from Kant and Fichte). Carlyle appealed to many different people. What they found in him was the same thing: closeness to experience. Carlyle objected to poverty and to exploitation for the same reason: they limit experience. Through them man ceases to be an organic experiencer. He becomes a machine. What appealed to Engels in Carlyle was the passionate accuracy of his descriptions of the poor. What appealed to Ruskin was the passionate accuracy of his descriptions of the rich. In the face of the generalizing, sterilizing, mechanizing liberalism of the Benthamites, Carlyle spoke out for the human element, and became the inspirer of Dickens. When the first Labor Members of Parliament were asked about their teachers, most of them named John Ruskin, who would never have been a social thinker at all but for Carlyle, and who arrived at few social conclusions that were not already his master's. The first great Labor leader in Parliament, Keir Hardie, regarded Carlyle as an ally.

3

The first British edition (1947) was prefaced by some comments arising from the American reviews:

This book . . . was, I think, very kindly treated by the reviewers and by the public. Nevertheless, I had the impression that, while many praised, few agreed. Though I spoke more frankly and, therefore, more harshly of the shortcomings of Carlyle, Nietzsche, and the rest than some other critics have done, I claimed that there is a large positive element in them and that, specifically, the doctrine of hero-worship should not lightly be dismissed as Hitlerism. Moreover, I felt that while the errors of these thinkers are evident, at least to people brought up under relatively democratic conditions, their positive contribution needed a good deal of explaining. The discussion of my book in America confirms me in this view.

The great question is whether democracy is *in every respect* anti-aristocratic. Undoubtedly the democratic tradition has been a long struggle against the yet older aristocratic tradition. The question is whether the older tradition has to be totally scrapped. Undoubtedly, also, there are democratic thinkers who are completely anti-aristocratic and who can therefore claim to be more completely democratic than anyone else. I refer to the anarchists. If anarchy alone is pure democracy then the rest of us clearly are impure democrats. So soon as we have government at all, some would say, so soon as government is merely representative and not inclusive of the whole populace, others would add, democracy is impure or nonexistent. So soon, therefore, as we reject anarchy or the governmental democracy of very small areas, we commit ourselves to government by leaders, and finding the best leaders becomes a prime task, as we all acknowledge at every election.

I do not disagree with those who say that democracy means bringing more and more people into political life, and vesting more and more power in them. Respect for the average citizen is so fundamental a necessity that I all along took it for granted. Nor do I believe in elites as usually defined. T. S. Eliot's "To-

wards a Definition of Culture" is a defense of elites. Those who
have been born and bred in the relatively aristocratic society
which Eliot has adopted will have fewer illusions about its nature. The hereditary elites of the old tradition are as unconvinc-
ing as the eugenically-bred elites of which Nietzsche and Shaw
and Wells have dreamed. The idea of a separate caste of men believed to be deeply if not biologically different from others may
have all kinds of things to be said for it. But etymology, logic, and
history prevent us from calling it democratic.

If believers in leadership have often been prepared to give up
democracy, believers in democracy have been unsatisfactory in
their dealings with the problem of leadership. In actual affairs
—in the army or in schools—much is said about leadership, but
most often it is all taken to be claptrap, which it may very well
be. Where, then, are we to look for serious ideas about democratic
leadership? Not to official pronouncements of educators who wish
their boys "some day to be manager of that concern." Not, I
think, to our neo-Thomists, whose conception of democracy is
equivocal. My belief is that at this point we might do worse than
learn from such men as Carlyle and Nietzsche.

There is a second possibility, if Carlyle and Nietzsche are dead
and beyond recall. Our democratic tradition, if we are prepared
to go back beyond 1930, contains much advice on the subject.
Some of it is what they now call "Stalinist"—which includes
things that Ruskin and Shaw wrote before Stalin was heard of.
Since, however, Ruskin and Shaw are writers whom people
condemn but do not read, let me mention a name held higher in
esteem: that of William James. James's essay "The Social Value
of the College Bred" [3] puts forward the very aristocratic idea of
democracy which I have done no more than confirm. There are
aristocratic democrats more politically minded than James—such
as John Stuart Mill, who was inclined to favor giving more
votes to the educated than to the uneducated. Within the ranks
of professional politicians there is one of the founders of democracy, Thomas Jefferson, who wrote to Adams in 1813: "For I
agree . . . that there is a natural aristocracy among men. The
grounds of this are virtue and talents. . . . The natural aristoc-

---

[3] In *Memories and Studies*. But see also the section "Hero-Worship Justified" in the essay "The Importance of Individuals" from *The Will to Believe*.
(Note added in 1957.)

racy I consider as the most precious gift of nature, for the instruction, the trusts, and government of society. . . ."

There are superior people. Sometimes they are "universal geniuses," superior in many directions, like Jefferson himself. More often they are superior only in certain isolable respects. Such superiority is denied only by those, one would imagine, who encourage the common man to believe himself a better scientist than Einstein. To acknowledge it is not to question the concrete meaning which the democratic idea of equality, as long ago defined by Locke, can have—such as equality before the law. Superior people are not a caste. They are not another brand of bread; they are the leaven in the loaf. When we hear of superior people we too often think of popes, pundits, and tyrants, who are seldom superior people by any intelligent criterion. Or we think of scientists and professors, as William Morris did when he too glibly remarked: "Fancy a Carlylean aristocracy of talent; the country under the benevolent rule of Senior Wranglers and LL.D.'s!" Carlyle has certainly no respect for wranglers, senior or junior. These are not fairly chosen examples of superior people. We had much better think of Lincoln or Lenin. Like Jesus, these two more recent revolutionaries make it clear to us that the superior man may possess the common touch (which, perhaps, is as uncommon as common sense).

One of my American critics, Mr. Kenneth Burke, insisted [4] that my modified hero-worship is only the careerism which I had set out to condemn—the over-stimulated ambition of Samuel Smiles's *Self Help*. I had used the phrase: "Help the best men to the front," which sounds rotarian. But surely Mr. Burke should have known that there are other fronts besides shop fronts and that there are other kinds of success besides money-making. Mr. Burke writes: "Is it not precisely the inducement to individual ambition that has led to the pushing, elbowing, and scramble characteristic of democracy, even inciting men to strive after improvement of their social status?" Mr. Burke must be a bit of a rotarian himself. Personally I would not take so rotarian a view of the "careers" which are to be opened to talent. Why are "pushing, elbowing, and scramble" thought peculiarly characteristic of democracy? They were common enough in the eighteenth century. They are the very stuff of fascist society. . . . Another

[4] In *The Kenyon Review*, Winter, 1945.

critic associates "careers open to talent" with the inventor of the phrase, Napoleon, and with a modern exploiter of it, Hitler. But Napoleon and Hitler had many excellent slogans (what could be better than the Nazi slogan Bread and Freedom?) by which they meant a few wicked things. We want the excellence without the wickedness.

"Careers open to talent," when they come into their own, will not mean careers open to careerists. They will mean that the millions of talents now crushed and frustrated by poverty, war, fear, and obscurantism will be permitted and assisted to flower. Talents are needed (*pace* Mr. Burke) outside politics and business. They are needed in the arts and sciences. They are needed everywhere. William James said: "Our democratic problem thus is stateable in ultra-simple terms: Who are the kind of men from whom our majorities shall take their cue?" Carlyle said: "All that Democracy ever meant lies there: the attainment of a truer and truer Aristocracy or Government of the Best." This is not, of course, *all* that democracy ever meant. If I may quote myself: "Aristocracy is one of the goals of democracy."

It is not the only goal. As usual, Carlyle was partly wrong, and irritatingly wrong. What we are less willing to admit is that he was partly right, and much more irritatingly right, since he threatens some of our most treasured illusions about human nature and "the common man."

4

I want to call attention (it is now 1957) to the quotation marks around "Stalinist" in the above; to the linking of Lenin, Lincoln, and Jesus Christ; and to the bracketing, on another page of my first edition, of Lenin, William James, and Bernard Shaw. The chapter omitted from this new edition is about Shaw and, as I now read the book, this chapter seems to me to have spoiled the whole presentation. And I know how it happened. In the first, unpublished draft, finished in 1940 (there is a copy in the Yale University Library if anyone wishes to check up on me), Shaw was simply one of my awful examples of authoritarianism, and he seemed all the more a villain because the whole of that draft was written from the standpoint of out-and-out pacifism. In the following year, two things happened to me: I read André Malraux's *L'espoir* (without of course guessing that its author was already on the trail of quite other opinions) and I met Bertolt Brecht. It would be untrue to say that I became a Communist or even a fellow traveler. Nothing I have written comes any closer to Communism than the first edition of *A Century of Hero Worship* (1944), and *The New Masses* did not set its stamp of approval even on this. They did like it, though, up to a point, and unmistakably intimated that its author could readily either go forward to Communism or backward to the opposite. A more rigorously Stalinist reviewer in *Tomorrow* was less concerned to beckon to me; he knew that, if Marx-Lenin-Stalinism was fundamentally right, my whole approach was fundamentally wrong. By the time my next book came to be reviewed by the Communists (in *Mainstream*), it was made very clear that I had not gone "forward." [5]

But it is amazing what support the Communists have been able to command from writers who are neither members of the Party nor consistent adherents of its policies. In the middle forties, my political position was approximately that of many European liberals in the middle fifties: in effect, I was for the popular front —as if it still existed, as if it would go on existing indefinitely! During the period of the alliance with Russia (1941-45), I had slipped into assuming (rather than decided to believe) that liberalism and Communism could and would work together. Attempts to disrupt the partnership almost seemed a willful refusal to accept the world's one chance of peace; and so the roughest words I have ever used in print were about Arthur Koestler.

Lest I seem to be concealing anything, I will print here the three most offensive parts of the omitted chapter:

i. The world-struggle of the twentieth century might be re-

---

[5] The reviewers were Isidore Schneider, *The New Masses*, February 27, 1945, Harry Slochower, *Tomorrow*, April 1945, and Arnaud D'Usseau, *Mainstream*, Winter 1947. To do him justice, Mr. Schneider noticed something that was spotted by no other reviewer: "It seems to me that Mr. Bentley is fighting, in the pages of his own book, an unconcluded battle of his own. He is tormented by what he conceives as the conflicting claims of the individual and the collective."

garded as not two- but three-sided. The three sides are: first, the old order of what is called capitalism or plutocracy or "bourgeois democracy"; second, the new order of fascism or Nazism; third, the new order of Communism, Stalinism, or heroic socialism.

ii.   [Shaw's] praise of Hitler and Mussolini was on two counts only: their domestic efficiency and their proletarian origin. Stalin has both these attributes and many others pleasing to Shaw. He has been brilliantly successful in practice alike in domestic and foreign affairs. His success is Cæsarian in that the chief job has been bringing order out of chaos, turning decadence to discipline, removing rivals, securing the boundaries of empire, and resisting the foreign barbarian. Cæsarian temperament combines with socialist theory in recognizing the economic basis of society. Stalin succeeds without heroics and without oratory. . . .

iii.   Russia is neither a liberal's Utopia nor a fascist state. The Russian government is friendly to many liberal causes such as peace, racial equality, prosperity; it is hostile to fascism, exploitation, racism. The fools who expected Russia to be dreamlike have lost their dream; the international journalists who preferred America still prefer America; the liberals who hate situations with which only repressive measures can deal continue to be affronted.

If only Marxist philosophy could be liberalized, and if only the Russians were liberal intellectuals, the Soviet Union might please its liberal critics. If Russia had been more easygoing and pacifistic she would now be—a German colony. In the liberal rejection of Russia one can see Shelley's nihilistic attack on all government:

> The man
> Of virtuous soul commands not, nor obeys;
> Power, like a desolating pestilence,
> Pollutes whate'er it touches; and obedience,
> Bane of all genius, virtue, freedom, truth,
> Makes slaves of men and of the human frame
> A mechanized automaton.

One would suppose that Shelley had read Gide on Russia.

To some liberals, Shaw's praise of Stalin is akin to his praise of Mussolini, and in so far as Shaw prefers government frankly

understood as the exercise of power, this is so. But Shaw does
not believe that communism and fascism are the same. In communism there is hope; fascism, where it is not conservative, is
regressive.

Not all of this was, from the "left-wing" standpoint, entirely
sound. The word *Stalinism*, for example, was strictly taboo in
those circles, and a well-known "left-winger" refused to write
a blurb for my book unless I deleted the above remarks about
Stalin removing his rivals and securing the boundaries of his
empire. The three exhibits show that I had put my Nietzsche
studies to paradoxical use—in a tough-minded, not to say cynical,
defense of communistic power politics. Shaw was no longer an
authoritarian among authoritarians. On the contrary, he was the
solution to the whole problem, in that he combined the good
points of democracy with the good points of authoritarianism,
while being miraculously immune from the faults of both. He
was even (in my eyes) something better than a Communist:
he was someone who approved of Stalin for non-Communist
reasons, reasons that my Heroic Vitalists (Nietzsche and the
rest) had taught me to set store by.

Through what further observations, further studies, and further
sufferings, I became aware of the assumptions I was making,
I need not speak here at length. And luckily the theory of the
Shavian synthesis is no integral part of the book. On the contrary, it was an afterthought, and I never did succeed in finding
even an appropriate place for it in the sequence of chapters,
let alone in making it seem to belong with the rest of my thinking in the book. There is no clearer proof of its arbitrariness than
the ease with which it could be extracted. The loss was pure
gain. Whatever I had to say about heroes and hero-worship was
left intact. I have tried to make it stand out the more clearly by
cutting away a certain amount of verbiage with which it was,
in places, overgrown.

That the word *fascism* was used loosely throughout will surprise no reader of this Foreword. It is now used, I hope, only
with reference to the theory and practice of Mussolini and

Hitler. The term *anti-fascist* was, historically, even more important. Since being against Hitler and Mussolini was about the only "proof" of being anti-totalitarian that Stalinists could give, they tricked the liberal movement into assuming that "Are you an anti-fascist?" was a key question, indeed *the* key question: for it united Communists and liberals. The word *totalitarian* was as taboo as the word *Stalinist* because it encouraged dangerous thoughts, indeed *the* dangerous thought: that the Soviet Union was just as fair game for a critic as Hitlerism or the American attitude to Negroes.

The term *anti-fascist* does not appear in the book now. So soon as I became aware what assumptions I had drifted into, and what dangers I had let myself become blind to, I was able to see the confusions of the first edition.

I was one of those who, though critical of much in the Stalin regime, often felt closer to its ardent admirers than to its ardent enemies. This may have been partly the accident of acquaintanceship: one may be the personal friend of a Koestler or one may be the personal friend of a Brecht. But, even at that, how much notice did I take of those of Brecht's works which most clearly showed what the score was? I set aside *Die Massnahme* ("The Measures Taken") as one of the indiscretions of his youth. He, for his part, reissued it in 1956.

This short play might well be entitled The Quintessence of Leninism. Nowhere has the Leninist morality (of sheer opportunism) been so candidly advocated, nor the Leninist method (of underground conspiracy) been more openly preached. And, unlike Christians, Leninists practice what they preach: they encourage cheating, and whoever sleeps in their camp wakes up one morning to find himself robbed.

Though inclined to concede the misdeeds of Soviet Russia since 1924, I had come to make the unexamined assumption that Lenin was free from blame. I suppose now that I was particularly vulnerable to Leninism not only because of the stress it places on leadership but also because of its animus against all idealism. The modern intellectual tends toward a nihilism that is, in part at least, disgust with democracy; Leninism offers itself as the answer to a nihilist's prayer. Such seems to have been its appeal to Brecht himself, and I, too, felt the fatal attraction till certain personal experiences, along with world events and further study of Lenin's theory and practice, led me in the other direction. I have done my best to understand the cases of Alan Nunn May, Elizabeth Bentley, Alger Hiss, Whittaker Chambers, and the Rosenbergs. These cases fill in the mere outline afforded by *Die Massnahme* with abundant concrete detail. As for the hero-worship[6] occasionally provided by "heroic socialism," it should be judged simply by Lenin's criterion: as an instrument of the Party's struggle. Brecht puts it this way in the notes to *Die Massnahme:* "As for several ethical ideas like justice, freedom, humanity, etc., what Lenin said about morality holds: 'We derive our morality from the interests of the proletarian class struggle.'"

In this book I am concerned with a hero-worship which, though it is subject to exploitation at the hands of a Hitler or a Stalin, and though it sprang from motives whose impurity I have not glossed over, has also a positive meaning and a positive value. I hope I have been able to make this fact clearer than it was in the first edition.

E. B.

New York, 1957

[6] "I approached Stalin's portrait, took it off the wall, placed it on the table and, resting my head on my hands, I gazed and meditated. What should I do? The Leader's face, as always so serene, his eyes so clear-sighted, they penetrate into the distance. It seems that his penetrating look pierces my little room and goes out to embrace the entire globe. I do not know how I would appear to anyone looking at me at this moment. But with my every fiber, every nerve, every drop of blood I feel that at this moment nothing exists in this entire world but this dear and beloved face. What should I do? "The Soviet government handles the enemies of the people with a firm hand. . . .

"These are thy words, Comrade Stalin, I believe them sacredly. Now I know how to act." From *Pergale* (Victory), magazine, organ of the Soviet Writers of the Lithuanian SSR, No. 4, April 1950, p. 52. Quoted by C. Milosz in *The Captive Mind.*

Part One. Thomas Carlyle

*"And what's the use of a man if he cannot take
two sides of an argument?"*

—THOMAS CARLYLE

Chronology

1795   Born at Ecclefechan, Annandale, Scotland.

1806-9   At Annan Academy.

1809   Began four-year residence at Edinburgh University in preparation for the ministry.

1814   Took post as teacher at Annan Academy.

1816   Took post as teacher at Kircaldy Academy. Friendship with Edward Irving begins.

1818   Lost all remaining belief in Christianity on reading Gibbon.

1818-20   In love with Margaret Gordon. Studied law at Edinburgh.

1821   Fell in love with Jane Welsh.

1822   Spiritual crisis. Became tutor to sons of Charles Buller.

1824   Visited London and Paris.

1826   Marriage.

1828   Failing to secure academic post, decided on literary career.

1828-34   Lived chiefly at Craigenputtock Farm.

1834   Went to 5 Cheyne Row, Chelsea.

1836   First edition of *Sartor Resartus* (written some years earlier).

1840   Lectures on *Heroes*.

1843-50   Set his political hopes on Sir Robert Peel.

1843   *Past and Present*.

1845   *Cromwell*.

1850   *Latter-Day Pamphlets*. Death of Peel.

1852   First visit to Germany.

1858   Second visit to Germany.

1865   *Frederick* finished.

1866   Death of Jane Welsh Carlyle.

1874   Accepted Order of Merit from Bismarck; refused British title.

1881   Death.

*"He had himself become the type of critic who, by scolding
the bourgeoisie, makes good with it and becomes one of
its idols."*—EDMUND WILSON on *Bernard Shaw*

1

Thomas Carlyle was born in 1795 and bred among rude Scots
peasant-folk in the village of Ecclefechan near the English border.
He held a privileged but not a comfortable position in the family.
The eldest son of his mother, he was younger than the son of his
father's first wife. Thomas' mother was consequently a jealous
woman and Thomas grew up with a feeling of apartness and
superiority, a feeling which increased as he grew more and more
studious and as he prepared himself for the life of a minister:
being the eldest son of his parents he was pledged to learning and
to the Kirk. He earned a reputation as a Tearful Tom who never
took his sorrows lightly. His sorrows at school were not decreased
by his mother's strict injunction neither to start a fight nor to
offer resistance to aggressors. From his father, Thomas picked
up a pithy, rough dialect; from his mother, an earnest Calvinism;
from both, habits of industry. In Carlyle's locality and Carlyle's
time, the family was more effectually integrated than latterly, and
in the cottage at Ecclefechan Carlyle was a witness of good
though severe government for the first—and perhaps the last—
time. Wherever his intellect might lead him he could never
forget the benevolent despotism of his parents, nor their piety,
their poverty and their provincialism.

Reading the accounts of Carlyle as a student at Edinburgh
University, we recognize the Carlyle of tradition. The young
man was humorous, alike in the modern and in the Elizabethan
sense of the word. Friends compared his fantastic style to that

19

of one of his favorite writers, Laurence Sterne. His disposition they likened to Dean Swift. Carlyle was aloof, earnest, discontented and, above all, ambitious. "Heaven knows," he wrote in 1814, "that ever since I have been able to form a wish, the wish of being known has been the foremost." This frank avowal is followed by an appeal to Fortune to confer great offices upon the great and upon Carlyle the laurel of literary fame. Such remarks show what the once celebrated Dr. Chalmers, a great Scots preacher, meant when he declared (1820) that Carlyle was "a lover of earnestness more than a lover of truth." The ambitious man prefers preaching to philosophy, advocacy to analysis, action to objectivity. Carlyle from the first was the antipodes of Spinoza.

The gloom that was Carlyle's Calvinist heritage deepened through the formative years of early manhood. He endured poverty, ill-health, pain, and failure in love. Literary fame lingered. Only four years after the open expression of ambition which I have cited, Carlyle was pretending that his aspirations had been abandoned. "They were little else but dreams. To gain renown is what I do not hope, and hardly care for, in the present state of my feelings." But Carlyle's resolve to retire to his studies was a resolve to *reculer pour mieux sauter*. A few lines below this last remark, he writes that none but chosen souls can rise "to any height above the level of the swinish herd." He who believes in the Elect seldom believes that he is not elected.

During his teens and twenties Carlyle made the discovery that neither Annandale nor Edinburgh was the intellectual boundary of the world. New planets swam into his ken, planets whose existence the astrology of Ecclefechan had denied or ignored. He read voraciously. In the pages of Byron he tasted forbidden fruit. Visions of grandeur, visions of villainy, arose before his eyes, and from the histories of David Hume and Edward Gibbon he learned that villainy was not confined to the ideal world.

Carlyle was impressed but frightened and embarrassed by the new domain upon which he had entered. As if bequeathed an estate by a rich and unforeseen benefactor, he stood fascinated and goggle-eyed but diffident. The etiquette, the *mores* of Ecclefechan were not equal to the occasion, and Carlyle suffered all the agonies of the poor relation.

These agonies were lasting and various. They extended from embarrassment at eighteenth-century skepticism to embarrassment at high-society manners in London. Carlyle never made himself a part either of the cultured world or of the "social" world. He remained alone with his visions of Byronic grandeur. He showed his superiority to socialites and intellectuals alike by his Byronic acceptance of evil.

No doubt many have the impression that Edinburgh University was inefficient and unenlightened in Carlyle's day. But this is to take Carlyle at his word. In fact Scotland maintained the highest academic standards, and Carlyle's general condemnation is an extension of his particular dislike of the national tradition in Scots culture. A generation before Carlyle, Hume, and Robertson had identified Scotland with advanced thought of the positivistic type. Dugald Stewart, another champion of the Enlightenment, retired, leaving a disciple in the person of one Dr. Thomas Brown only two years before Carlyle arrived in Edinburgh. Carlyle hated Edinburgh, not because like Milton or Gibbon he found himself more educated than his preceptors, but because he was used to homeliness and the professors were urbane, because he was used to strong passions and they were controlled, because he was used to religious ardor and they were men of chill intellect, because he relied upon conscience and intuition and they upon reason, because he had been taught his place and they preached emancipation, because he believed in judgment and damnation and they—long before Charles Darwin —in the "progress of the species."

Carlyle knew he had to break with the Ecclefechan way of life, but he preserved as much of it as was possible in the circumstances. He did not shake off the parental yoke with the fierce joy of Samuel Butler's Ernest Pontifex or with the uncompromising finality of an Edmund Gosse. He was born too early for that, and the mechanism of his rebelliousness was different. When he was bullied by his schoolfellows at Annan Grammar School, Carlyle responded to assaults with sullenness rather than open rebellion. His response to intellectual assaults was similar, as we see from the days when he turned in bewildered, sullen disgust from Dr. Thomas Brown and his "association philosophy." From the start Carlyle's revolution was ambiguous. He turned from the old yet he hated the new. He detested the "ins" and loathed the "outs." In this he is the prototype of one species of modern intellectual, the kind that can see through the existing system but will not form an alliance with its enemies.

One reason for this was that he never lost his emotional attachment to the *ancien régime*. When Carlyle was twenty-four his mother took alarm at a letter in which he praised the great *philosophe* D'Alembert: "Beware, my dear son, of such thoughts. . . . Do make religion your great study, Tom." No man who has loved his mother as Carlyle did may cut the invisible navel cord of maternal attachment. Carlyle outgrew Christianity but he could never bear to hear Christian teaching criticized by others. When in later life he heard of Huxley's dictum, "In the beginning was hydrogen," all the mother in him rebelled and he said: "Any man who spoke thus in my presence I would request to be silent —No more of that stuff to me!"

Nevertheless the years 1814 to 1822 were years of turmoil for Thomas Carlyle. He left his pre-ministerial studies and took a job as a teacher at his old school, Annan Academy. Two years later he was invited to replace one Edward Irving, who was too fond of corporal punishment, at the Kircaldy school; Irving rather surprisingly came to give Carlyle kindly advice, and a significant friendship began. Two years later Carlyle fell in love with a very attractive girl named Margaret Gordon, whose family thought her too good for the impecunious student. In order to earn his way into the Gordon family, Carlyle left teaching and decided to study for a legal career, but when Mrs. Gordon packed her daughter off to London in 1820 he dropped the plan. He had now given up three professions—preaching, teaching, and the law—and was in despair. Must he rest content with the meager returns for articles in the Edinburgh Encyclopædia? Or could he become a successful professional writer?

In 1821 Irving introduced Carlyle to a young Scotswoman

whom he had almost married himself: Jane Welsh. Carlyle at once fell in love with her, but she did not immediately return his love, and his despondency, aggravated by dyspepsia, increased. In the next year there occurred a spiritual crisis which is comprehensible only when the state of Carlyle's mind in preceding years has been examined. One cannot take quite literally his own dramatized account of the crisis in *Sartor Resartus*. Like many converts to militancy Carlyle exaggerated later the degree of his earlier unbelief. There is little or no serious evidence that he ever really was an atheist or that he had ever much in common with the *philosophes*. He did study the historical evidences of Christianity and, finding them inadequate, gave up his ministerial career; he could not help being swayed by the suave rhetoric of David Hume; and when he read Gibbon—lent him by the religious fanatic, Irving—the last vestige of his faith disappeared. But all this is negative. Carlyle certainly felt that the eighteenth-century attack on religion was formidable, but he was far from accepting the tenets of the new liberalism or even any sort of positivist attitude. The collapse of Christianity haunted and tortured him into a phase not of science but of Byronic despair, Byronic anger, and perhaps Byronic exaggeration. Of the chapters in *Sartor Resartus* which describe Carlyle's spiritual progress, the most revealing is *The Sorrows of Teufelsdröckh*, in which Carlyle cites Byron and compares his unregenerate self to the guilt-haunted Cain and the Wandering Jew. Was not apostasy as bad as killing your brother or insulting Jesus? One day, as Carlyle was strolling down Leith Walk, Edinburgh, he was "born again" with the suddenness in conversion of John Wesley or St. Paul. Conversion to what? The articles of Carlyle's faith were long in evolving. What came to Carlyle on Leith Walk was not a creed, but an Everlasting Yea. Carlyle said Yes to life because he had found the virtue which hero-worshipers exalt above all others: courage. From that day skepticism was consistently depreciated by Carlyle.

Those who over-emphasize Carlyle's conversion follow the account given in *Sartor Resartus* with a literalness for which there is no warrant. For Teufelsdröckh the conversion was final, but Carlyle's own life consisted rather of conflicts than of decisive victories, and in 1823 he was still contemplating suicide. In 1831 he cried out: "How sad and stern is all life to me! Homeless! Homeless!" In the following year he lost, to his infinite sorrow, both his father and the man whom he had come to regard as his spiritual father, Goethe. Only for brief periods was the feeling of homelessness appeased through Carlyle's long life.

2

Margaret Gordon, Edward Irving, and Jane Welsh—these were, I think, the only deep attachments Carlyle ever experienced outside his own family. Goethe was to be a sort of god, but attachments to a deity are seldom very personal and never very comfortable; John Stuart Mill was to be a good friend for a time, Emerson an amiable visitor and correspondent; but the soul of Carlyle dwelt apart from all these. What of the three to whom he came closer? Margaret Gordon he saw seldom and that often under chaperonage, though she gave him a piece of advice that will interest those who search for the origin of Carlyle's hero-worship: "Remove," she wrote in her farewell letter, "the awful distance between you and ordinary men by kind and gentle manners; deal mildly with their inferiority." Irving probably came closer to Carlyle, but it is unlikely that his advice was half so good. He was everything that Carlyle might have been if he had been less sane, less complicated, less sensitive to the spirit of the age. He was a successful Scots preacher, at once highly ambitious and indecently devout, eloquent, clever, erratic, unbalanced, and altogether distasteful. It is greatly to Carlyle's credit that he escaped the clutches of this creature. Irving, however, had in 1822 procured him his job as tutor to the children of the wealthy Charles Buller. And Irving introduced him to Jane Welsh.

It is by a strange quirk of fate that Jane Welsh has become an historic figure with some fifty index-cards to her name in the larger libraries. She was indeed a spirited and intelligent woman, a woman of un-Victorian phrase and un-Victorian aplomb, a woman who puffed at her husband's pipes, dined alone in restaurants, rode on the tops of buses, walked unaccompanied in the streets and said, "Idiot!" to the man who misinterpreted her boldness; a woman who managed to live forty years with an enormously difficult husband. But that is all. In her larger ambitions she failed entirely. Despite her literary intentions (she confessed later that she had married Carlyle out of ambition, which can only mean ambition to be connected with a writer) she wrote no book. Despite early intellectuality she subsided into acquiescent housewifery. If she is famous, it can only be said that she climbed to fame on her husband's shoulders and that she owes much to the present obsession with biography which finds every minor Victorian a fascinating subject of detailed study.

Not long after Carlyle's death the Carlyles became a byword for marital incompatibility, an archetype for the cliché conception of Genius at Home. Later Carlyle's brother, and also his most thorough biographer, David Alec Wilson, objected and pointed out that the main sources of the earlier view were James Anthony Froude, an historian whose inaccuracy in other fields had been demonstrated, and one Geraldine Jewsbury, a fussy and effusive friend of Jane's whom they considered neurotic, or at least unreliable. The only other person who claimed to have special first-hand information was Frank Harris, a literary adventurer whose autobiography is perhaps the most scurrilous book ever written by a serious man of letters about himself, and whose mendacity is an evident and proven fact. Following this line of observation, the tendency of late years has been to pooh-pooh the Froude tradition and to maintain that Carlyle's was, all things considered, a rather satisfactory marriage. This is going too far. That Froude was an inaccurate historian is not to say that he would invent whole episodes in the life of his friend. A recent investigator with no axe to grind has vindicated Froude to a great extent.[1] Another has shown that Geraldine Jewsbury cannot be dismissed as an unreliable witness.[2] Even

[1] *Froude and Carlyle*, Waldo H. Dunn. London, 1930.
[2] *Geraldine Jewsbury*, Susan Howe. London, 1935.

Frank Harris' evidence, though always to be viewed with skepticism, could nevertheless be true; one tends to forget that Harris' reputation as a critic was high among such men as Bernard Shaw and Oscar Wilde. Upon the whole, then, one is not entitled to reject the Froude-Jewsbury-Harris version, the less so since all that the opposite party has alleged is (a) that it is irrelevant and (b) that it is obscene. If it were irrelevant they should not have bothered to take issue with it; if it is obscene one cannot conclude that it must therefore be untrue.

Froude's view—confirmed, as we now know, by Jane Carlyle's physician—was that Thomas Carlyle was sexually impotent. According to Geraldine Jewsbury he was seen on the day after his wedding tearing up the plants of his Edinburgh garden in uncontrollable fury. Subsequently, it appears, he was not very sensitive to the embarrassments and disadvantages of Jane's position as wife of an impotent husband. It seems that she secretly longed for children and slowly pined away. That all this has little significance for the non-biographical critic of Carlyle's works is obvious enough; that it has considerable significance for the critic of Carlyle's personality is equally evident. Carlyle's marriage was a strange one. During the courtship Jane declared that she loved him but was not in love with him, and she seems to have valued him chiefly as a tutor and potential great man. Consequently Carlyle was complaisant and embarrassed until the official engagement legitimatized his status. Then a change took place. Whatever his sexual shortcomings, Carlyle made sure to establish himself as master. He lost interest in Jane's education and began to stress the male Victorian's view of marriage: Jane was to be mistress of a doll's house. That authoritarian politics combine with a low view of women, we in the twentieth century have seen, and if it be objected that Carlyle's marriage was typical of his age, one must reply that its typicality was aggravated by the husband's inability to fulfill his part of the contract and, furthermore, that the role of women in the lives of Mill, Browning, Ruskin, and other Victorian writers was not "typically Victorian."

In 1826 Carlyle was married. Within two years the high-

spirited girl who had declared she would not consent to live in
the old farm of Craigenputtock even with an angel was living
there willy-nilly with her by no means angelic husband; and
after six years of it her spirits were no longer so high. Her will
had been broken. Independence of judgment and hopes of a
literary career of her own were gradually abandoned—but not
without struggles and misgivings. For Jane was not a simple
person. She did not blame everything on her husband. She
knew that her own weakness was also to blame, and the bitterness of this knowledge became a further cause of friction. Though
the two Carlyles felt for each other a warm affection, there was
lacking both the physical union and the intellectual comradeship
without which marriage is a mockery.

3

Meanwhile, what had Carlyle achieved in the years of courtship and early married life? His rise to fame was gradual but
well-planned and steady. As ever, Carlyle alternated between
frank ambition and a pretense of total indifference to fame. Today he seeks an appointment at the highest institutions of learning; tomorrow he flees to Craigenputtock so as not to be corrupted
by the great world. Through all vicissitudes he wrote. Between
1819 and 1823 he wrote fifteen articles, all competent and impersonal. Soon longer articles of his, more personal and con-
troversial, were published by the best periodicals. As tutor
to the Buller boys, Carlyle visited London and Paris for the first
time. The effect they had on him is worth recording: they
shocked him by their worldliness much as Rome had shocked
Luther three hundred years earlier. In fine, the twenties were
Carlyle's period of apprenticeship. And the trade he learned
was the criticism of civilization, specifically English civilization.

When a Scot or an Irishman wishes to criticize England he
settles in London and is paid by an English publisher to do the
job. In 1834 Carlyle went to London for good. After initial
difficulty in selling *Sartor Resartus,* his first really individual
full-length work, Carlyle was able to find a public without trou-

ble. His house, 5 Cheyne Row, Chelsea, was visited by all the celebrities of London. He was famous at last.

It was in the years 1837-40 that Carlyle became a literary lion. Though his reputation was assured by the publication of *The French Revolution* in 1837, Carlyle was in need of money and allowed himself to be persuaded to lecture in public. He was as much aware as any that the chief attraction would be his queerness, his Annandale accent and unsophisticated manner. He chose as his subject in 1837 the history of German literature. One of his reasons for studying German was, perhaps, that few in his day were acquainted with the language and he felt the need of originality. In classical and polite learning, Carlyle could never have competed with the group that was already regnant in the literary world. But to translate the new German writers was— among other things—a piece of strategy in the campaign for fame. If the translations themselves were unpopular, he would strew his original works with quotations and allusions. It is not surprising then that the first course of lectures consisted of an eccentric account of German literature.

The stage was cleverly set, for Carlyle had chosen his new friends carefully. In April, 1837, Richard Monckton Milnes received a letter from a friend of Carlyle's named James Spedding announcing Carlyle's lectures. Subscribers were needed and the fashionable Milnes had been chosen to get them. Spedding states the case jokingly: "Some name of decided piety is, I believe, rather wanted. Learning, taste, and nobility are represented by Hallam, Rogers, and Lord Lansdowne. H. Taylor has provided a large proportion of family, wit and beauty, and I have assisted them to a little Apostlehood. We want your name to represent the great body of Tories, Roman Catholics, High Churchmen, metaphysicians, poets, and Savage Landor." It was arranged that the lectures should be given at Almack's, a fashionable club. On the day of the first lecture, coaches thronged the surrounding streets. The best people in London paid their guinea to hear the new genius, before going on in the evening to see Macready as Strafford in Robert Browning's new play. At this period, it should be recalled, Carlyle was not the bewildered and bleary-eyed figure of the Whistler portrait, but strikingly brisk, virile, and even handsome.

From this time on, Carlyle had a role to fill. He was the tiger-cub of the rich. He had to be violent enough to amuse them without endangering his own position. Since the Victorians liked nothing better than being reproved by their Great Men, Carlyle had scope for his indignation; though very few took him seriously. Only a few days before his death, he confessed to Froude: "They call me a great man now, but not one believes what I have told them." They called Carlyle great from 1837 on, and Carlyle welcomed the belated acclamations. Henceforward, his life consisted of public fame and private heartburning. Privately, he remained "gey ill to live with," an erratic and a deficient husband. Publicly, he was the ladies' man. A majority of the audience at his lectures consisted of women. The blue-stocking Harriet Martineau was a disciple. A Quakeress named Caroline Fox who attended some of the 1840 lectures records her delight in Carlyle's physical beauty and grandeur. Lady Harriet Baring, later Lady Ashburton (the wife of a banker who helped to give Carlyle a better impression of capitalism), became so close a friend of Carlyle's that Jane was for a time apprehensive. Under the pressure of fussy disciples Carlyle often wrote platitudes and poeticisms whose inevitable destination was the spinster's mantelpiece. His works abound in Beautiful Thoughts for the Hour. But, happily, Carlyle could not annihilate the mind which had been growing for forty years before he met peeresses. He made his bow to the rich, but privately he boggled. Carlyle was an introvert who could never, even for the sake of fame, become a socialite. He would retire to his study and his Byronic musings and leave Jane to entertain the guests.

How, then, was the soil prepared for the philosophy of heroism by 1840, the year of the lectures *On Heroes*? Circumstances helped to turn Carlyle, first, against the old Christian dispensation and, second, against the new democratic liberalism. Indeed, he turned against the second in order to have his revenge on the philosophers who had turned him against the first. Carlyle was a lonely man but not a submissive one. As a child he did not resist the bullies openly: he harbored resentment against a hostile world. He could not conform and he would not rebel. Or rather he would not join hands with other rebels against the old society and its values. He hated the philosophers for their cleverness for he knew they had robbed him of his primal innocence. He hated Byron for giving him the knowledge of evil. He hated the rich for their fanciness and the poor for their stupidity (except at those terrible moments when he envied the power of the rich and pitied the helplessness of the poor). He felt that the world as he discovered it in Edinburgh, London, and Paris was corrupt and decadent. Lonely and apart he would watch the decadence. But first he would become famous and respected among those upon whom he called down fire from heaven.

If it was a shrewd observation that, had Jesus Christ come to earth in the nineteenth century, Monckton Milnes would have fêted him at the London Clubs, one should not be surprised that Carlyle allowed himself the pleasures that Jesus Christ was not expected to resist. He was the provincial genius become the darling of the drawing-rooms. An American lady, Margaret Fuller, visiting Carlyle in 1846, found him like Siegfried and laughed him off. Her account reveals some of the forces which made Carlyle a philosopher of heroism. "All Carlyle's talk that evening," she says, "was a defense of mere force, success the test of right. If people would not behave well, put collars round their necks. Find a hero and let them be slaves. It was very Titanic and anti-celestial. . . ." Carlyle wished to shock the ladies and to impress them with his Titanism. He did not realize that the ladies loved being shocked but were unwilling to notice that their tiger-cub was growing up. It is easier for us than for his contemporaries to understand what Carlyle most wanted to convey.

4

The facts of Carlyle's personal growth do not of course fully explain or explain away his theory of heroes and hero-worship.

By this time we have lost patience with the psychoanalytical method of criticism which says: Shelley wrote that because of his Œdipus complex, or: Carlyle worshiped heroes because of his indigestion. We have lost patience also with that anti-Victorian debunking which would lead us to say: Carlyle was neurotic and his neurosis made him a fascist; for though all fascists may be neurotics, not all neurotics are fascists, nor are all neurotics Thomas Carlyles. For all that, we must not ignore the fact that biography is just as essential a part of cultural history as economics or philosophy. One cannot prove an opinion unsound merely by showing that its champions are neurotic; but one can show why a particular person's experience called for a certain view of life; one can show how an idea grew in the individual, who is after all the chief concrete reality in the social organism; and one can show this with a more intimate exactitude than is possible to the historian of epochs and trends.

The life of Carlyle does not tell us what is universally true or false about hero-worship, but even if we believed in fixed universal truths, we would still need to know what sort of personal meaning and validity a view might have in practice. The life of Carlyle does not fully account for the recrudescence of hero-worship in modern civilization but it does reveal how one of the great champions of the idea, one of its widest disseminators, came to think as he did. If one regards the thinker as the chief dynamic of history, then the experience of one thinker is of first-rank importance; if on the contrary one regards the thinker as a mere chip on the wave of history, his experience is still important, since, determinists tell us, through him realities are consciously comprehended. A chip is tangible; a wave elusive. More important still, the historian is not concerned with "pure" ideas but with ideas in the complex of social reality. Since, however, one cannot unerringly point to ideas and demonstrate their relation to the totality of social phenomena, is it not safer, before venturing generalizations about epochs, to examine ideas in the context of a single life? Where are ideas operative if not in men?

Thomas Carlyle, who with others resuscitated the idea of hero-worship in the modern world, was born in a district where border warfare had made hard blows and rough justice traditional. From his family Carlyle took a harsh and narrow religion which preached the doctrine of an elect and which gave him an obsession with ethics and a desire to surpass other men which he never lost. The status of the family in Scotland and the peculiar position of Carlyle in his particular family helped, as I have shown, both to show despotism in a favorable light and to make of Carlyle a man apart, lonely, with a sense of spiritual calling and superiority. The cry "homeless! homeless!" rings through his whole life, for he gradually left his family behind, then his class, then his country, finally becoming a sort of exile from the whole epoch, a Jeremiah. Everything around him seemed mean and worthless. Machinery and the bourgeoisie were destroying real manhood. Himself frustrated professionally and economically, his body frustrated in its digestive and probably in its sexual functions, Carlyle had visions of a human splendor which neither he nor the new age had realized. If there was something satanic about the visions, that was natural to one who had rid himself of puritan religion with so much ado; if there was something dictatorial about his hero, that was to be expected from one who lost three fathers in succession—God, James Carlyle, and Goethe. One cannot fail to note that the delusions of grandeur without which there is no hero-worship were systematized by Carlyle in the years following the death of his two earthly fathers, years in which Carlyle won his first victory—that over the spirit of Jane Welsh Carlyle.

On top of all this came Carlyle's second victory, his victory over the reading public and (which was much the same thing) the polite world. This conquest made of him a Jeremiah with a difference. He became a self-conscious Sage and Great Man. London society received him and compromised him; another Scots peasant, Ramsay MacDonald, might have learned from Carlyle's precedent. The position of the Victorian prophets— and it was Carlyle who started the prophetic tradition continued by Ruskin and Arnold—was anomalous. They sought popularity among the very people they affected to despise. Hence their frequent subterfuges and contradictions. And in Carlyle there was another source of trouble. The hero-worshiper is a man—to resort to jargon—with an inferiority complex. He is made to feel inferior and he knows he is superior. He is alternately arrogant and exaggeratedly modest. Consistency is not a Carlylean virtue. Indeed the whole Romantic Movement pointed back from the logical symmetries of rationalism to the contradictoriness of actual experience. This of course did not give the Romanticists the right to contradict *themselves* either consciously, like Whitman with his "Very well then, I contradict myself," or unconsciously, like Carlyle, but some of them did so all the same. How Carlyle contradicted himself we shall see in the sequel.

"We must renounce ideals."
—CARLYLE in *Frederick*, I, i, 3

"Knighton: *Where are these modern barbarians to come from?*
"Carlyle: *I don't know. History does not exactly repeat itself, but we want a superior race.*"

1

On Heroes, Hero-Worship, and the Heroic in History—such is the full title of the 1840 lectures—is an expression of Carlyle's mental confusion and one of his least convincing works. But certain important ideas may be extracted from it, and it is a significant record of a state of mind. The chief tenet of *Heroes* —that great men should rule and that others should revere them— is related by Carlyle to other important tenets such as the following:

(1) The world cannot be understood by the old creeds and philosophies. It can be understood by intuition and history.

(2) History, or evolution, is an organic growth (like the tree Igdrasil in Norse mythology), arranging itself in epochs and repeating itself in cycles.

(3) Society also is organic. The organism (subsumed under such heads as History and Society) which grows is Life itself.

(4) Yet organisms fail. Periodically, there is catastrophe followed by a fresh start; Carlyle appeals to the *Götterdämmerung* and Phœnix myths. Evolution is a saltatory. Individuals and societies experience rebirth.

(5) The core of a man's feeling (unless he accept death and cease to be a man) must be affirmation of the life-process. In

34

this cruel process, courage will be more valuable than love. The human ideal will not be the saint but the nobleman.

(6) The hero (i.e. man of courage and nobility) is "sincere" and does his "duty," i.e. he acts intuitively, without the interference of mechanical philosophies or restrictive codes. He co-operates with "the real tendency of the world" and so becomes an instrument of history and progress. Through the recognition of necessity, he becomes free.

(7) The philosophy of heroism is partly pragmatic. The hero recognizes facts squarely and acts boldly. He therefore prefers intuition to reflection, faith to philosophy, ardor to detachment, reverence to urbanity, temerity to caution, speed to the suspension of judgment.

(8) The hero's function is dual. First, he is a pattern for others to imitate, in himself a justification of life. Second, he is creator, and through him history moves forwards and not backwards: history is the biography of Great Men. (When Carlyle says, as he sometimes does, that history is the biography of *all* men, he has in mind his belief—discarded later in the interests of consistency—that all men have elements of greatness in them.) The hero is life *in all its potentialities*: hence he is poet, prelate, king, or god, according to circumstances.

In short: Carlyle's hero-worship does not begin or end with his admiration of great men. It is part of a philosophy which at some points is simply German historicism deriving from Herder and at others approaches the vitalism of Bergson and the pragmatism of James. The philosophy as a whole, as we shall see, is close to Nietzsche and perhaps even closer to the exponent of historical Nietzscheanism, Oswald Spengler. The symbol of the *Götterdämmerung* representing the decline of our world anticipates Wagner; the symbol of the Phœnix was frequently used in relation to social rebirth by D. H. Lawrence. But before enlarging further on the historical currency of Carlyle's views let us look more closely at his version of the hero.

2

Since a sound Carlyle scholar, B. H. Lehman, has already enumerated all Carlyle's uses of the word *hero* from his article on Nelson in Brewster's Encyclopædia (1820-23) to *Heroes and Hero-Worship*, I shall simply refer the curious to his book.[1] For my purposes here, let it suffice that the doctrine of Heroism is stated several times before 1840. Instances are the praise of "the old practice of Hero-worship" in the 1832 essay on Goethe, and the fuller statements in *Sartor Resartus*. Here is an extract from Carlyle's essay on Walter Scott: "Understand it well, this 'of hero-worship' was the primary creed and has intrinsically been the secondary and tertiary, and will be the ultimate and final creed of mankind; indestructible, changing in shape but in essence unchangeable; whereon politics, religions, loyalties and all highest human interests have been and can be built, as on a rock that will endure while man endures."

The heroes of this period are the chief authors whom Carlyle had to review—Goethe, Dr. Johnson, and Robert Burns. Goethe was for a time Carlyle's ideal man. "This man," he said, "if we will consider of it is appointed to be ruler of the world." Goethe was important in the usual two ways. First, he justified life by revealing what man can be. He is of all time. Second, he was a landmark in history, a promoter of good, a "world-changer and spiritual revolutionist," an instrument of progress. All good things, says Carlyle, must pass this second test. In his admiration of intellectual heroes, Carlyle is close to our New History which replaces kings and generals by philosophers, scientists, and artists. There is another modern hero second to Goethe only: Napoleon. Napoleon is a window through which we see the hidden ways of nature. He too is great because he broke in pieces the mockeries of the eighteenth century. Napoleon and Goethe are, according to Carlyle, the only great men within living memory.

In the essay on "Goethe's Works" a distinction is drawn which Carlyle, had he ever thoroughly systematized his theory of leader-

[1] *Carlyle's Theory of the Hero.* Durham, N. C., 1928.

ship, might have put to further use. This is the distinction between the Great and the Noted Man. (The more systematic Emerson made use of it in *Representative Men.* Emerson's *talented* is Carlyle's *noted.* Sidney Hook presents a modified version in his *eventful* and *event-making* men.[2]) The Great Man puts his stamp on the age in which he lives, the Noted Man is "the emblem and summary of the Ideal which the age has fashioned for itself." The example Carlyle gives of Noted Men is Beau Brummell. And since he denies greatness to all contemporaries except Goethe and Napoleon one concludes that all the Romantic poets of the epoch are Noted Men. But there is no purpose in a further investigation of the problem since it is confused by Carlyle's inclusion of Burns and Rousseau among his heroes and by his statement that everyone can be heroic. Is a hero not necessarily great? Imprecision is a characteristic of Carlyle's terminology.

Carlyle denies greatness to Scott. But a kind of distinction is imputed to the German scholar Gottlieb Heyne, to James Boswell, and, later, to Carlyle's disciple, John Sterling: that is, the distinction of the hero-worshiper rather than the distinction of the hero. Of the two sorts of men praised in *Sartor Resartus* (III, 4)—the craftsman and the original thinker—these three seem to be examples of the former type: the faithful workman. The faculty of hero-worship is itself a form of heroism. Gottlieb Heyne was faithful to the exact fact in labors that reached the limit of his capacity. As for Boswell, Carlyle seems to have been more communicative in the lectures of 1840 than in the written version that we read today. Caroline Fox took a note of his saying: "Before others had discovered anything sublime, Boswell had done it and embraced his (Johnson's) knees, when his bosom was denied him." The doctrine of hero-worship explains how Carlyle came to differ so widely from Macaulay in appraisal of Boswell. Macaulay admired Johnson but despised Boswell for his prostration before the demigod. Quiet industry wedded to unflinching loyalty is, however, the Carlylean prescription for every man who cannot be a master. Hence Carlyle's

[2] See *The Hero in History.* Beacon Paperbacks. (Note added in 1957.)

gratitude (which appears excessive to those who do not see how the hero-doctrine works *a contrario*) to his loyal retainer, John Sterling.

Recognizing the hero among one's contemporaries is a high vocation, says Carlyle. But searching through his works and the biographies, one does not find that Carlyle often announces the discovery of living greatness. He has least difficulty in dismissing the highest reputations. Of the gentle Elia, he said: "A more pitiful, rickety, gasping, staggering, stammering Tom Fool I do not know." The pious Keble was a little ape, John Henry Newman had the intellect of a good-sized rabbit, Lord Macaulay was irremediably commonplace, Wordsworth small and dilute, Coleridge weak and ineffective, Whistler absurd. . . . Such was Carlyle's jealousy that he despised Dickens living and praised him dead. He admired Erasmus Darwin more than Charles. He had little that is good to say of contemporary literature. While French literature was "sad, sordid, semi-delirious, and in good part, *infernal* stuff," Mill's *Autobiography* (to cite a monument of sobriety) was "the autobiography of a steam-engine," and Mill's essay *On Liberty* "the greatest nonsense I have ever read." Gladstone was contemptible, and Disraeli "a cursed old Jew not worth his weight in bacon." The phraseology of anti-Semitism which, perhaps, Carlyle inherited from Burke, he employed to stigmatize Heinrich Heine as an unworthy successor to Goethe and Schiller: "a dirty, blaspheming Jew." The despondency of his late years drew from Carlyle the comment that of all the important people he had met, whether literary or political, perhaps none was really great or worth remembering. Carlyle went beyond other Victorian prophets in refusing the age all title to greatness and heroism. He made exceptions of only two men: Sir Robert Peel and Otto von Bismarck.

It has been plausibly maintained that Carlyle's chief ambition was to be a man of action when the day came, and that from his early years he regarded his own literary works as mere *disjecta membra*. However this may be, when the fates drove Carlyle into a literary career he concocted the theory that all literature consisted of the *disjecta membra* of men who could have been leaders had circumstances favored: a hero is a hero at all points and, potentially, in all directions. Set on his feet by literary success before 1840, Carlyle turned his thoughts definitely towards political achievement.

It was at this time that Sir Robert Peel, Prime Minister of England 1841-46, and founder of the new Conservatism, became his hero. Carlyle wove his ideals of government into his *Cromwell*, where his idealism and his realism were most nearly wedded. A copy was sent to Sir Robert and gratefully acknowledged. In 1848 Lady Ashburton arranged that Carlyle should sit next to Sir Robert at a dinner at Bath House. Then in 1850 came the *Latter-Day Pamphlets*, and, while they were yet appearing in monthly numbers, Carlyle received an invitation to dine with Peel. The dinner passed off successfully, and the pair met again soon afterwards. But a few days after this last meeting, Sir Robert Peel died of heart failure. Carlyle received a blow that was more than personal bereavement. Sir Robert was the only hero in Britain. "Except him," Carlyle lamented, "there was nobody I had the smallest hope in." All desire to enter public life now faded, and the gloomy stoicism of Ecclefechan—"Work, and despair not"—resumed its sway. The obligation to perform the job at hand was for Carlyle, as for his Frederick the Great, all the law and all the prophets.

Carlyle, then, certainly had some desire—one cannot be sure how strong it was—to be a great man of action. His sourness is to some extent explained by his failure to become one. The fervor of his hero-worship is the creation of his personal failure, the exaggerated respect of an ambitious bookworm for the man of action. Carlyle was too magnanimous, or too self-indulgent, to despise the dictator. He hated the type of bookworm who, out of petty jealousy, pretends that men of action are, of their nature, inferior to bookworms.

Oliver Cromwell, William Pitt, Robert Peel—this is the genealogy of English heroism in two hundred years; each less decisively great than his predecessor. Peel was the only Englishman who came close to greatness in the nineteenth century. To the other great man of the age—Bismarck—we shall return.

3

Since Carlyle repudiated metaphysics and exalted history, it will be well to know exactly what account of human history he had in the back of his mind when he was writing his detailed accounts of the French Revolution, Oliver Cromwell, and Frederick the Great. We can know this by studying the lectures of 1838. (The best edition is based on the manuscript of one Anstey, who took notes at the lectures. Anstey's title reads: *Lectures on the History of Literature or the Successive Periods of European Culture* (Bombay, 1892). The New York edition of the same year is the one chiefly in use in America. At least it appears in bibliographies. Though the book is one of the most valuable vehicles of Carlyle's opinions, it is not yet read even by those who write books on Carlyle as an historian.)

Carlyle's view of the Hero is adjusted to his view of history. His view of history is somewhat as follows. History is our proper study because it is the study of facts, because it is the study of man, and because it is the study of both facts and man *in the flux of becoming*. History as "philosophy teaching by examples" is impossible since we must start with the facts and later arrive at principles; we do not, with Bolingbroke, start with principles and draw our examples from history. History is the starting point of all knowledge.

Carlyle concludes, with the kind of logic that characterizes his individualist adversaries, that history consists of the biographies of all individuals. But this view is not insisted upon. In the first place, it gives place, occasionally, to the statement that history is the collected biographies of great men. In the second, it is in conflict with the celebrated collectivism of Carlyle, that is, his belief that groups of men (such as nations) constitute organisms which live according to a plant-like pattern of growth and decay. This idea is stated in the chapter "Organic Filaments" in *Sartor Resartus* and belongs with the theory that history consists of alternating periods of affirmation and negation. Sometimes, the metaphor of articulation is used. A Faith struggles to find a voice; then, it becomes articulate in an institution such as a Church; thirdly, its big manly voice turns again towards childish treble and a new Faith is required. History is flux, conflict and recurrence.

This conception of conflict is ultimately based upon a dualistic metaphysic. It is often manifested in a dualistic ethic. History flows onward and recurs, forming a ring of necessity within which the human will operates. Carlyle may use the language of conventional religion and morality to describe this necessity—it becomes the Moral Law, Duty, or God's Will—but it is clear from his respect for brute fact and his view that all force is moral, that *God, Duty,* and *Morality* are by-products of history or fact, and not vice versa. History is the taproot. When a man turns from Christianity to create a religion out of the historical process, he finds it difficult to account on the purely historical level for the dæmonic and the celestial, for the black and the white. Determined not to make out that all was gray, as the Benthamites did, Carlyle contrived to mix the elements of good and evil anew. "I find," said John Sterling, "his fundamental position is the good of evil: the idleness of trying to jump off one's shadow." How difficult this attempted synthesis proved we shall see when we examine *Frederick the Great.* For the present, let us consider the picture of human history which Carlyle had in mind as he wrote.

The tripartite scheme, Ancient, Mediæval, and Modern, was already in Carlyle's day the Procrustean bed into which historical learning had to be fitted. Within these bounds, the body and soul of European culture are conceived to live and move.

The age of Homer (to summarize the 1838 lectures) is the first great age recognized by Carlyle; and Odysseus, "a much enduring man," is the first hero to satisfy him. It might be expected that Plato would be one of his heroes, as he later was one of Emerson's Representative Men, but Carlyle, anticipating Nietzsche, has no liking for him or for Socrates. An age of faith and action is followed by an age of philosophy and talk (the nineteenth century is always in Carlyle's thoughts) and "Socrates was the emblem of the decline of the Greeks" (p. 31). His writings are made up of "a number of very wire-drawn notions about virtue" (p. 32). The healthiest periods, Carlyle holds, are not the periods of great art or thought, but those of action.

The Romans are more to his taste than the Greeks, who remind him, in their vehemency, their sharpness, and their puerility, of the French. The Romans were men of action, for true greatness is unconscious and silent. They did their duty and got the upper hand. They knew that liberty consists in following the best guidance for conduct whether at one's own behest or under compulsion. Virgil, like Plato, represents the advent of effeminacy and the decline of a culture. Carlyle cites the appellation *pius Æneas* as evidence of the insipidity of Virgil. (Had he known that *pius* means "dutiful" or "filial," he might have had to change his view.)

Upon the heels of Roman unbelief follows the greatest of all epochs of belief: the Catholic age of faith. As usual, Carlyle avoids discussing the tenets of the faith ("it is not our part to touch on sacred things," p. 57), because for him these are mere offshoots of the historical fact. That Carlyle should suppose his reticence to be a result of the sacredness of his belief is, since he was not a believer, a curious instance of rationalization. The cries of *"Wer darf Ihn nennen?"* are the more vehement because they are the means by which he concealed himself from himself. The great human facts of the Middle Ages, as given by Carlyle, are: first, the loyalty of men to their superiors; and second, the institution by which the loyalty is canalized, the Church. Carlyle passed on to Oswald Spengler the trick of explaining an antithesis by citing two opposed personalities. Spengler more than once cites the meeting of Jesus with Pilate to show the difference between Truth and Fact. Carlyle finds the greatness of mediævalism in the abasement of the Emperor before Pope Hildebrand (who, like Carlyle, was lowly born) at Canossa. This was a victory of the Spirit of Europe over the Body of Europe. For the rest, Carlyle's treatment of the Middle Ages is even sketchier than his treatment of the ancient world. It was, he says, an age of gold because it was an age of action. Peter the Hermit is singled out for his heroism. Mediæval literature is said to be a late product (according to the pattern). Chaucer is ignored. Chivalry is found to have penetrated warfare and this is one way in which the Middle Ages marks an advance on the ancients.

Carlyle turns next to the evolution of the national state, and there is a lecture on each of the chief European nations and its character. His judgments are sweeping. The French are always vapid and the Germans deep. "Trial by jury is essentially German" (p. 113). King Alfred was the founder of the British Constitution (p. 136). Shakespeare is the epitome of the great Elizabethan Age (p. 138). There follows a routine account of the eighteenth century and the French Revolution, and a plea for a Worship of Sorrow.

A somewhat broader view of modern history is taken in the essay on "Jesuitism" in *Latter-Day Pamphlets,* where Carlyle demarcates the boundaries of affirmation and negation in recent times. The Reformation was (as in *Heroes*) the next step after Catholicism in the march of progress. After this Carlyle's philosophy of progress is not so easy to apply; progress is set back by the advent of Jesuitism. Thesis and antithesis in the eighteenth-century dialectical conflict are the forces of revolution and the forces of Jesuitism. The nineteenth century needs a system that combines the freedom from theology of the revolutionaries with the discipline and obedience of the Jesuits.

A sense of the wickedness of the eighteenth century dominates Carlyle and prevents him from clarifying his historical theories. Valid and crucial as is his attack on the mechanistic *philosophes,* there is too much of the Scotch peasant in Carlyle's hatred of French civilization. As a puritan he dreaded gaiety, as a poor man he envied the lavish, as a man "between two worlds, one dead, the other powerless to be born" he hated the French for their clarity of mind. So the Revolution is considered the judgment of an angry and vindictive God upon a frivolous people. Ecclefechan determined also his view of Oliver Cromwell and the rebellion. Narrowly confined to morals and psychology, Carlyle's histories ignored both theology and economics. There is no serious discussion of differences in religious doctrine, nor does Carlyle ever seem to realize that Hampden, for example, became famous for his refusal to pay a tax. His approval of Oliver is a hero-worshiper's approval of a dictatorial character, a powerful instrument of destiny, and it is also the glee of a puritan over a righteous breaker of idols. Since 1660 England had been ruled by the godless, that is, by those who found no purpose in life, hence the black situation in the nineteenth century. That Charles II was brought up in France was in itself bad enough. That he was a wit, a roué, and a Catholic, finished him.

Sir Robert Walpole is for Carlyle the type of the ensuing age of shame. Walpole "adjusted the conflicting Parliamentary Chaos into counterpoise," but he gained for England no hand's-breadth from the Night-Realm. The parliamentarian is the antithesis of the hero. Hearing this, we in the twentieth century know what to expect next. When Carlyle declares that Walpole ignored the Laws of Nature, he explains what he means: Walpole neglected the army and navy.

The appeal to the laws of nature is consonant with the historicism which gradually came to dominate most of Carlyle's serious thinking. This was the world that was "powerless to be born." But the dead world of Ecclefechan constantly intrudes, sometimes with contradiction, sometimes with mere forms of words that can be translated into pragmatic terms. For all his antagonism to the word *progress*, Carlyle believed progress to be a fundamental law; yet his Calvinism died so hard that he is famous for his gloominess, and Nietzsche thought him a pessimist. Where France was concerned, Carlyle could never surmount the puritan's distrust and the boor's hatred. In 1870 he called France "vapouring, vainglorious, gesticulating, quarrelsome, restless, and oversensitive."

Casting his mind over the broad course of human history, Carlyle discerned a progress which he thought would continue in the future. But when he came to look at recent events, two prejudices warped his judgment: a national prejudice against France and the prejudice of a young intellectual against his immediate forebears. Carlyle hated the eighteenth century for being lighthearted, as Lytton Strachey hated the nineteenth for being thickheaded. The philosopher of progress often finds that progress has been suspended for his own lifetime.

Nevertheless Carlyle had hopes. There were still forces of order in the world, though ousted from their proper position. In England, Carlyle was not always sure where the hope for order lay. But he was sure that no ballot could discover the hero, and as a realist he transferred his attention from the parliamentary talkers to the men who turn the wheels of the new civilization: the industrialists. He cites with approval the work of a benevolent Quaker employer. He hopes at times that Captains of Industry will be a new aristocracy. Late in life, he believes that the hereditary aristocracy, whose names set his mouth agape and whose wives lionized him, cannot be so bad. "Aristocracy by title, by fortune and position, who can doubt but there are still precious possibilities among the chosen of that class?"

Many of Carlyle's remedies—such as silence, prayer, work, obedience, and emigration—are fantastic panaceas. But there was one very material object of his confidence: the Prussian army. We shall discover how Carlyle came to this conclusion by glancing at his three great historical works.

4

The three works on which Carlyle bestowed the better part of his literary life are *The French Revolution* (1837), *Oliver Cromwell's Letters and Speeches* (1845), and *The History of Friedrich II of Prussia called Frederick the Great* (1865). The first occupied him for some six years, the second for five, and the third for thirteen. So great was the labor that to the reader of Carlyle's life the other works seem no more than incidents in a long story.

The French Revolution exemplifies the dicta of Novalis that "all history is an evangel" and that "history is one great anecdote. An anecdote is an historical element, an historical molecule or epigram." To this day it remains readable, queer, extravagant, full of talent, a racy Scots humor, and a feeling for melodrama.

There is no true hero in *The French Revolution*. Danton and Mirabeau are giants, but not Carlylean heroes comparable in stature to Cromwell or in complexity to Frederick. Carlyle's attitude had not changed a score of years later when, in the Proem to *Frederick*, he spoke of the men of the French Revolution as "terrific Drawcansir figures . . . and even a certain heroism, stage-heroism, in them." It is true that, a page earlier, Carlyle makes a drama out of the meeting of Mirabeau and Frederick by calling it the meeting of "the last of the old Gods and the first of the modern Titans," but he proceeds to show that even Napoleon, though he used up more gunpowder, was less great than Frederick. Napoleon's wars were founded upon "Drawcansir rodomontade and grandiose Dick-Turpinism," Frederick's upon veracity, courage, and insight (pp. 7-8). The revolutionary leaders, then, are not Great nor, exactly, Noted. They are heroes of melodrama. The heroes of *The French Revolution* are larger than average, which is Aristotle's first requirement of a tragic hero, but they are not greatly *superior*. If this is what Carlyle believed, his presentation is oddly appropriate, for the style of the book, effective up to a point, is, finally, a little forced and phony. (The prose of *The French Revolution* glows scarlet as under the artificial impulsion of the bellows; *Frederick* crackles loudly as if the fuel were heaped on the fire by a recklessly veteran hand.)

Neither *The French Revolution* nor *Cromwell* tells us much about the Hero that has not already been mentioned in this book. The former exemplifies the idea cited by Carlyle, in his stern Goethean epigraph:

Diesem Ambos vergleich' ich das Land, den Hammer dem Herrscher; Und dem Volke das Blech, das in der Mitte sich krümmt.[3]

The book is the chief expression of Carlyle's apocalyptic vision which elsewhere we glimpse through crannies. The French Revolution is itself an apocalypse in which a world is in conflagration:

---
[3] "I compare the land to this anvil, the hammer to the ruler; and the tin which writhes in the midst to the people."

Wehe dem armen Blech, wenn nur willkürliche Schläge
Ungewiss treffen, und nie fertig der Kessel erscheint! [4]

The warning is solemn, though there is a danger that those
who go to Carlyle for poetic style will miss the prosaic truth he
is trying to communicate, namely, that the French Revolution
is a "celestial-infernal event," proving that the world is a
celestial-infernal kind of place, and that any attempt to ignore
the angelic-dæmonic nature of man will bring in its revenges.
The dæmon will avenge himself upon the angel. There is a fine
irony in the Christian language of Carlyle's neo-paganism.

Cromwell carries us back to an earlier age when heroism could
grow to full flower. Here was an ideal against which a Sir
Robert Peel, sighing after the days that have been, could measure
his own lesser heroism. In the seventeenth century the conflict
between religion and practical politics did not seem impossible
to resolve. Carlyle found Cromwell the easiest to praise of all
his heroes. His writings on Cromwell are more tranquil and less
interesting than *Frederick* because in Cromwell he found no
problem and no immediacy. His Cromwell studies were escapist
antiquarianism, a flight from the urgent problems of modern
destiny, which were Carlyle's major concern and in the face
of which he showed his greatest imagination and insight.

5

Soon after the death of Peel, Carlyle embarked upon a more
hazardous enterprise, an attempt at a deeper understanding of
the contemporary scene. The spontaneous combustion of the
French Revolution had been portrayed in his earlier work. It
had now become clear that the French Revolution inaugurated
an era of anarchy which might last two centuries or ten. "Millennium of Anarchies;—abridge it, spend your heart's blood upon
abridging it, ye Heroic Wise that are to come!" [5] In 1856 he

---

[4] "Alas for the poor tin if only haphazard blows strike uncertainly and the
kettle is never ready!"

[5] *Frederick*, XXI, i: a passage cited at length by Richard Wagner in the
Introduction to *Die Kunst und die Revolution*.

gave democracy another fifty years. Here is a portion of Carlyle's analysis that seems less ridiculous today than it did in his own time. Carlyle's belief in this theory was firm and not at all capricious. It lies at the root of his slight confidence in the staying-power of democracy. He cast about for something that would outlast democracy: and found it in Prussia. The Heroic-Wise of the future—though it might be a hundred years hence—must follow in the tracks of Frederick the Great. This is Carlyle's final social analysis and his final theory of leadership.

Carlyle found the composition of *Frederick the Great* wearing, and his own utterances sometimes lend countenance to the view that he had chosen his hero ill, that he had tried, as his wife put it, to make a silk purse out of a sow's ear. By an accident, according to this view, Carlyle happened to choose a hero who did not really suit his purpose.

But this view leaves too much unexplained. Carlyle was reading Preuss's standard work on Frederick in 1844. In 1851 he undertook a course of serious reading on Frederick without definitely committing himself to a biography. We are bound, therefore, to believe that he embarked upon the task with a full understanding of its nature. Again, it is true that he considered writing the lives of other heroes, but who were they? According to John Nichol, one of his earlier biographers, they were William the Conqueror, Simon de Montfort, the Cid, and the Vikings: one and all soldiers and hard, practical men. Carlyle, it can hardly be denied, was pondering in these years the nature of political practice in an investigation of his view that success is its own justification. The man of the fifties was not the idealist of the twenties. The spiritual problem of Carlyle's youth was to find courage and justify positive thought and action. The problem of his middle age was to prove that action which has lasting results, though it appear brutal or dishonest, really is justified and can bear the detailed scrutiny of the courageous historian. Carlyle's second problem, then, was to test the efficacy of his early philosophy of courage and action by confronting it with the harsh facts of history.

Frederick the Great is long, because Carlyle wished to see history as a solid, to see every man in the flesh and to see every incident in movement, to discern every human implication of the complex process of conflict and victory. Immersion in detail was not for Carlyle an eccentricity or a scholarly addiction but a necessity of his mental struggle towards the solution of the chief problem of all his thinking: the problem of morals and history, values and evolution. That Carlyle was constantly beset by doubt is clear; that he occasionally found the problem too much for him is probable. At such moments he longed to repudiate Frederick and declare him a villain. But the importunate longing was suppressed and the battle of *Frederick*, though it left Carlyle exhausted, was fought to a finish. Afterwards he fought no more spiritual battles, but lived out an old age in which the two sides of his nature, still in contradiction though no longer in conflict, continued to express themselves with all the mellowness and tameness of senility.

Such is the story we gleam from Carlyle's biographers, reluctant as they may be to draw conclusions. Let me now trace the genesis of *Frederick*.

On the fourteenth of November, 1851, Carlyle wrote to Lady Ashburton, saying that though he would prefer a hero of his own country, his interest in Frederick was growing. "Frederick," he wrote, "the more I know of him, pleases me the better; a Man and King whose love of reality was instinctive and supreme. . . . I find him the last of all our 'Kings'; and with some prophecy in him too of being the *first* of our coming Kings: the details poor Preuss (my dull Historian) gives me of his faithful incredible indefatigable toil in 'governing' Prussia and making it great and free (free of the Devil, I mean) are worthy of perpetual remembrance." In 1851, then, as his knowledge of Frederick became more expert, Carlyle's admiration increased. Frederick is the first and last of monarchs. He sums up the history of past kings. He inaugurates a new line. Frederick and Prussia are the hope of modern Europe because they are great, and their greatness depends on toil and upon a belief that freedom means compelling men to do right. The right, it becomes obvious later, is the successful and inevitable. Carlyle has swung from the quietism and pessimism of his youth to the opposite extreme of success-worship. From the determinism of a naïve Christianity he has turned to the determinism of a narrow historicism.

As his reading proceeded, two thoughts were borne in upon Carlyle: that a life of Frederick was necessary, yet that it would mean a tremendous struggle with himself. "I foresee," he tells Lady Ashburton, "I shall have a furious wrestle with that subject, if it ever come to anything." This on the eleventh of January, 1854. Two years later Carlyle was the more determined that the work must go through. It is clearly not true that a distaste for Frederick grew in direct ratio with Carlyle's knowledge. On April 3, 1856, Carlyle told Lady Ashburton how the prospect of universal suffrage disgusted him. "Amid such phenomena," he wrote, "someone must write a life of Frederick."

Such is the spirit in which the work was undertaken. The chief obstacle to its speedy completion, aside from its magnitude, was Carlyle's age, his feeling that he might be too old for such an endeavor. "I am twenty years too old for writing *Frederick*," he told Allingham (*Diary*, 23rd June, 1860), "but must go on." A soundproof study had been built on top of the house in Cheyne Row and there Carlyle sat, surrounded by his documents and by portraits of the King, determined that he would finish *Frederick* or that *Frederick* would finish him.

The difficulties which forced Carlyle to complain were not difficulties of scholarship such as Dryasdust might overcome, but the personal problems which we have found in Carlyle's life and work. In point of fact, Carlyle exaggerated the difficulties of research in a very natural rationalization of his struggles. Only one professional historian, Norwood Young, seems to have paid much serious attention to Carlyle's histories, and he informs us that Carlyle exaggerated to an almost incredible extent the amount of labor required for his historical works. For instance: to get credit for more research than he had done, says Mr. Young, Carlyle told readers of *Cromwell* that the King's Pamphlets (or Thomason Tracts) were not catalogued when in fact they were. *Frederick* was written largely from materials assembled in the Cheyne Row study.

Carlyle, it is true, visited Germany twice, and his journal for the second visit has now been published. But all that the story of these two visits discloses is that Carlyle was much less concerned with other people's writings on Frederick (which he refused to look at) than with the atmosphere of the places where Frederick's battles were fought and won. An important writer, Varnhagen von Ense, has recorded the meeting of Carlyle and the German poet Ludwig Tieck in 1852. Carlyle was obsessed with his own Frederick problem and assumed that all other topics were trivial beside this one. When Tieck, whose reputation in German letters was at that time second only to Goethe's, tried to discuss Coleridge, Carlyle emitted a loud contemptuous laugh. Because Carlyle refused to debate what Tieck considered his "crazy view" (*verrückte Ansicht*) of Frederick, Tieck very naturally concluded that Carlyle was not scholar enough to write about Frederick at all. Norwood Young shares Tieck's opinion. As a scholar and historian, he sees nothing in *Frederick* but proliferation of detail, factual error, and approval of wickedness.

There is abundant evidence of Carlyle's moods and thoughts in his later years quite apart from the text of *Frederick*. The arteries had hardened, and while as friend and husband Carlyle became more affectionate and mild, his general opinions found more and more a harsh and dogmatic expression. The spirituality alike of Ecclefechan and the German mystics disappears, and religious phraseology is more and more obviously a mere manner of speaking. The gentle old man seemed to take a masochistic pleasure in the callousness of his attitudes to Negroes and the unemployed; though, when faced with the immediate prospect of cruelty and violence, Carlyle was usually revolted, and as to foreign policy, he was fairly consistently (1854-56, 1861-65, 1870, 1878) an isolationist, because he thought the slaughter purposeless. While he advocated shooting idlers, he was charitable towards even the "undeserving poor" when he met them in the street. He hated cruelty to animals. Yet the growing harshness of his political pronouncements cannot be overlooked. Christian compassion was often more than matched by Machiavellian realism. It is as if, when he could relax his personal ambitions and could become personally much more amiable, Carlyle must publicly overweight the Machiavellian side of the scale. Compensation was a mental device frequent with him.

The revolutionary year of 1848 (not to repeat the story of Peel and the *Latter-Day Pamphlets*) had jolted Carlyle into attitudes which he would otherwise have acquired more slowly. The year inaugurated the final period of Carlyle's working life, which was characterized by the harsh "realism" which marked the middle decades of the century. In these years was made Carlyle's last and most bitter attempt to solve his central spiritual problem. If the attempt failed it was nevertheless a manly effort. The wear and tear were so great as to leave him for the last fifteen years of his life (1866-81) the mere husk of a man.

The events of 1848 and hero-worship of Peel had fired Carlyle to write his most violent political tracts, the *Latter-Day Pamphlets*, in which leaders were exhorted to drill their peoples into subordination with the whip and the treadmill. Out of this mood, which was a lasting one, grew *Frederick*. That *Frederick*, completed in 1865, had not disabused Carlyle of his National Socialism is shown in *Shooting Niagara* (1866) and his letter to *The Times* (1870). It is shown by his passionate defense in 1866 of Edward John Eyre, justly charged, it would seem, with tyrannical and brutal conduct as Governor of Jamaica and condemned by John Stuart Mill, Herbert Spencer, and T. H. Huxley. The verdict of the only scholar who has thoroughly investigated the matter is that Eyre was a liar, a blockhead, and a despot, and that Carlyle could have no reason for his attitude but approval of tyranny and belief in the inferiority of the colored races.[6]

Bismarck he certainly believed to be the greatest of his contemporaries and the continuator of Frederick's great work. He rejoiced at the Prussian achievements of 1864-70 and was praising Bismarck as late as 1877. Alexander Carlyle, who always tried to paint his uncle in the most respectable colors, maintains that

[6] *The Myth of Governor Eyre*, Lord Olivier. London, 1933. Especially Chapters II and XX.

Thomas lived to acknowledge the error of his ways and indeed it seems that he occasionally felt wistful over Bismarck, as was natural if my interpretation of his character is correct. But in 1874 Carlyle refused a British peerage and accepted a Prussian Order of Merit, and when in the following year Bismarck sent birthday greetings, Carlyle replied: "Allow me to say that no honour could have been done me which I should have valued more highly." *Frederick* itself proves that Alexander did not understand.

6

It is not easy to be on intimate terms with this problematical monster of a book. It is huge, ill-tempered, and forbidding. If it is humorous, the humor too obviously partakes of the cruelty which Bergson found in laughter. Carlyle treats Frederick William's crazy brutality with frightening *bonhomie*. He nonchalantly describes how a whore sits by the corpse of a soldier cutting off his gold-braid, how her hand is shot off and how another whore immediately steps into her place and keeps on cutting. Yet, for all the crochets and humors, for all the machine-gun style, the book can be interpreted, and that without the consultation of anything outside its own pages.

Frederick is an investigation with some irony (that is at once Carlyle's self-defense and the way he suggests the two-sidedness of the main problem) of power-politics in the modern world. Carlyle approves of power-politics, though so keen is his insight into the chicanery of diplomacy and the murder of war that Keir Hardie, the first Labor M.P. and a pacifist, chiefly respected the book for its exposure of these evils. Carlyle's irony, however, does not imply repudiation of the cruel processes he pitilessly reveals, but their acceptance by a divided mind. Hence it is insulting Carlyle to maintain either that he adopted "the faith of all sensible people" (D. A. Wilson's phrase) and turned in distaste from the cruel struggle for worldly power, or that he wholeheartedly devoted himself to a nineteenth-century totalitarianism. He felt the positive appeal of both sides more strongly than other men, and if his awareness of the weaknesses of liberalism was so strong that he appealed in reluctant despair to illiberalism, his case may have all the more interest today.

The greatest force making for order, and therefore for the good life in the modern world, was, Carlyle increasingly felt, Germany, and, within Germany, Prussia and, within Prussia, the Prussian Army and, at the head of the Prussian Army, the Prussian Ruler. Recent publicists have familiarized us with the distinction between the spirit of the Prussian Army and the pacifistic spirit of the rest of Germany. Carlyle made the same distinction and unhesitatingly gave his vote to the Prussian Army. Prussia, he said, was the hope of Germany, because elsewhere there was nothing but noise and radicalism. To quote an authoritative report of Carlyle's conversation: "The King, he thought, was right if, as he believed, he meant to have no one but himself meddling in the affairs of the army, for that was and ever had been in Prussia the reliable, honourable body, which had done everything for Prussia."

If Carlyle was willing to grant so much in conversation, he was willing to grant more in print, and Frederick's ruthless invasion of Silesia is portrayed as: "The First Nation of the Universe rashly hurling its fine-throated hunting-pack, or Army, of the Oriflamme, into Austria—see what a sort of badgers and gloomily indignant bears it has awakened there!"

Frederick is the story of the rise of a military caste in which, according to the author, lay the chief hope of the nineteenth century. Carlyle had not always been preoccupied with military history, but that he should be increasingly so was in the logic of his thought. Before 1837, battles do not seem to have occupied him much. In *The French Revolution* they take their place among other historical determinants. In *Cromwell* they illustrate the workings of the historical process which is called *divine*— i.e., immune from criticism and deserving of respect. In *Frederick*, the battles are the chief concern of all chief personages except the Mephistopheles of the piece, Voltaire.

Some have been puzzled by the inordinate length of the tale of Frederick's ancestors, which might, they think, have been compressed into a single chapter. Carlyle devoted three books to it because the history of the Hohenzollerns and the rise of the Prussian military caste was with him paramount. It is the subject of the whole work, Frederick being the exemplary leader. In this sense, it is true that the role of the hero in Carlyle is smaller than some have supposed. The hero, Carlyle insists, is incomprehensible apart from his context.

The history of the Hohenzollerns is not a mere list of heroes and heroisms, though heroism is the central fact in history. It is "the history of a State, or Social Vitality, growing from small to great; steadily growing henceforth under guidance: and the contrast between guidance and no guidance, or misguidance, in such matters is again impressively illustrated there" (III, ii). The Hohenzollerns helped history to unfold, they willingly enacted the inevitable, so this fatalistic story goes; their freedom was the recognition of necessity.

This notion is expressed by Carlyle in the metaphor of Destiny —always a dubious concept—or by an appeal to equally questionable Laws of the Universe. Frederick's claims to Silesia must be valid because "allowed by the Destinies," and the Hohenzollerns prospered "by conforming to the Laws of the Universe; instead of trying by pettifogging to evade and profitably contradict them. . . . Resist the Devil, good reader, and he will flee from you!" (III, ii). The Devil is evidently a hangover from the Ecclefechan days, and his Hell Carlyle by this time regarded as a mere device to frighten men into virtue. In *Frederick* the Devil is a metaphor meaning "what is contrary to the good" and therefore what is contrary to the historically destined.

For Carlyle the one thing humanly necessary was sincerity, the frank confrontation of the actual; and, therefore, the greatest evil was to respect the non-actual, the fictitious, the Sham. The Sham is known by its weakness and eventual failure. It seems implied that the Carlylean Hero is he who recognizes what is Sham ahead of time, who does not need to wait for the historical proof, who sees at once the facts in themselves as they really are. The first of Hohenzollern heroes was Henry the Fowler, whom Carlyle thought to be "essentially the first sovereign of united Germany." The nature of the Carlylean analysis of early

Prussian history may be gauged from Carlyle's characterization of Henry: "The Father of whatever good has since been in Germany; he subdued his Dukes . . ." (II, i). The second of the Hohenstaufens and "greatest of all the Kaisers of that or any other house" was Frederick Barbarossa, who, holding in his hands the reins of the world, was the friend of nobility and the scourge of anarchy, a terror to evil-doers and a benefactor of well-doers. (Nietzsche's favorite Hohenstaufen was the Emperor Frederick II, whom he classed with Alcibiades and Julius Cæsar as the antidote to weakness in an age of dissolution. Apart from Barbarossa, Carlyle's enthusiasm was given to the Hohenzollerns.)

So much for the general lessons of *Frederick*. The rock to which these lessons cling is Frederick himself, the final Carlylean hero. In this portrait, the historian, the evolutionist, and the Machiavellian in Carlyle eclipse the metaphysician and the mystic. The resistance which Carlyle had to overcome to achieve this finds expression in the crabbed style, the humor, the mannerisms: all these are signs of embarrassment, the kind of embarrassment Carlyle might have felt had his mother found him flattering the bullies she had taught him passively to resist.

In the first chapter of the first book of *Frederick*, the King is described as "to the last, a questionable hero," not a parlor hero or a monastery hero, but a hero involved in the equivocations, the compromises, and the dirt of actual life. Since life is dirty, the hero must acknowledge the fact, acknowledgment of fact being the hero's *sine qua non*. He must inevitably be immersed in the dirt upon which he operates. Wrongdoing springs only from a failure to acknowledge the tragic nature of history, the inexorability of facts. The man who is undefiled by pitch (Carlyle is careful not to state the matter thus) must be in the wrong, for he has not been willing to sin and compromise. He has not seized reality by its filthy hand.

Carlyle had now completely discarded Christianity; he had thrown a bomb also into the heavenly city of the eighteenth-century philosophers. He taught that Frederick of Prussia was the greatest man of the eighteenth century, a miracle in a century of falsehood, because Frederick recognized sad facts, because he was no hypocrite or phantasm but had been proved by the outcome to be a Reality. The philosophers knew that the hopes of man were bright, his aspiration infinite, his intentions broad, and his desires unrestricted, but Frederick thought little of desire divorced from calculated expectation. Carlyle himself had learned to put away the immortal longings that swayed his youthful heart. As a mature man, he had no belief in the immortality of the soul. He tried to rest content with the sad facts of history and so he came to interest himself in Frederick, not in the ideals of the young Prince Frederick who wrote the *Anti-Machiavel* but in the achievements of the soldier, in "the man himself and what of strength he had to wrestle with the mud-elements, and what victory he got for his own benefit and mine" (I, i, iii).

It would be hard to emphasize this aspect of Frederick more than Carlyle himself did. He emphasizes it not only in the relation of the monarch's exploits, but in the preliminary sketch (I, i) and in the account of Frederick's early years (IV, xiii). In fact, one of the reasons why Carlyle dwells so long upon Frederick William is that the old martinet educated his son to believe that the end of life is violent action in the framework of historical necessity (IV, xiii). If the young Frederick did not grow in favor with God and man, he acquired an unequaled sense of the limitations of human potentiality. Such a sense is of course highly desirable. Yet who is the political philosopher whose ethics stem from a belief that the limitations of human potentiality are fixed and unalterable and that therefore the absolute soldier-prince is the master of reality? It is Machiavelli.

In his early essay *On History Again,* Carlyle had described history as the true epic poem and universal divine scripture. The doctrine is significantly modified in *Frederick.* "All history," Sauerteig is made to say (I, i, iii), "is an imprisoned Epic, nay an imprisoned Psalm or Prophecy." The word *imprisoned* sets the tone for the volumes that follow. History remains the true gospel, superseding metaphysics—so much is sound pragmatism. But Carlyle, now in line with the more mechanistic naturalism of the middle century, sees history governed by laws of its own nature, so that the future is wholly determined by the past. Real novelty is thus denied, the imprisoned epic is as arid as the telephone directory. Carlyle draws the correct conclusion: "We must renounce ideals. We must sadly take up with the mournfullest barren realities." In maturing his conception of the hero, Carlyle has made him so realistic that he is no longer heroic.

Such is the conclusion of a lifetime of spiritual conflict, a lifetime's journey from Ecclefechan, a lifetime's journey alike from the old religion and the new bourgeois liberalism.

CHAPTER III

Heroic Vitalism

"One is tempted to ask Carlyle: 'Are you yourself really justifying the action, or are you taking refuge from a decision in a cloud of words that would have one meaning for your mother and another for yourself?' "

—SIR HERBERT GRIERSON.

1

Carlyle's histories are a criticism of life. If Gibbon is the historian of an age of reason, Carlyle is the historian of an age of individual enterprise, an age of violently contending states, which he hopes will be the precursor of an age of heroism. Carlyle did not need a "source" such as his editors love to discover in Fichte or Shelley for his philosophy of heroism. Such ideas were an expression of contemporary reality. William Blake, for one, had already spat out the ethic of perfectibility and had, in an age of urbanity, rediscovered the dæmon of the Unconscious. He had even declared, as a young man, that the energy which St. Paul called sin was good and that the abyss which men called hell could be married to the peak which men called heaven. Blake said that Milton was of the devil's party without knowing it, and Shelley created a myth out of anti-theism, by loosing Prometheus from his chains. One of the few beliefs which the romanticists had in common was that the artist is both solitary and superior, a hero apart from the herd. On the continent of Europe no poet had more influence than Lord Byron, hero and hero-worshiper, rebel and satanist, athlete and cripple. An introvert pretending to be a rake-hell, a hypochondriac obsessed with the thought that the tree of knowledge was not that of life, a cynic who pretended to prefer the Rienzis to the Christs (as Nietzsche pretended to prefer Cesare Borgia or Cagliostro to Parsifal), Byron is the bad conscience of the nineteenth century. Every part of his experience is relevant. The sexual rebellion of romanticism, for instance, finds in him a terrible example. The sex antagonism which the modern age (Nietzsche, Strindberg, Shaw, Freud) stresses has its complement in a feeling that the lover should be as nearly as possible a projection of the self. Not unconnected with the resurgence of endogamy in our time, this feeling is more directly related with the incest-motive which is found in Shelley's *The Cenci* and Wagner's *Die Walküre*. The fact that Nietzsche's best friend— and worst enemy—was his sister pales beside the possibility that Byron actually committed incest.

Had I to choose two men as illustrations of Carlyle's starting point, they would be Byron and the German historian Herder. For if a new picture of the individual and a new view of good and evil are essential to Carlyle's philosophy, so is the new historical and evolutionary appetite. Herder, the father of historicism, with his clearly expressed evolutionary outlook and his cyclical interpretation of history, is the best single symbol of the new historical mind. Like most philosophers of history before Buckle and Marx, and like Nietzsche after them, Carlyle was above all a psychologist, though a psychologist prepared to accept the new concept of a group mind and the new concept of the Spirit of the Age.

A contemporary of Byron's, Carlyle felt the appeal of the romantic dead and the noble ruin. He admired grandeur more than utility and defiance more than defense. This admiration is a symptom of the Carlylean attempt to infuse æsthetic standards into history and politics. The infusion is done by sleight of hand, for Carlyle was heir to Herder and, faced with the charge of æstheticism, could demonstrate the depth of his understanding of history and brute fact.

Carlyle's philosophy of history is a reinterpretation of the Romantic love of the heroic past in the light of the new evolutionism. Into the word *hero* new meaning and new life are infused. Starting from Walter Scott's schoolboy (or schoolgirl?) love of the *preux chevalier,* Carlyle ends in *Frederick* with a "realistic" conception of greatness. Yet, as all his successors were

to do later, Carlyle clings to the æsthetic attitude to the hero—
which is one of sheer wonder unmitigated by sociological con-
siderations—and he continues in a succession of sentimental
regressive fantasies, to wish himself back at St. Edmundsbury
being bossed around by Abbot Samson, or at Marston Moor keep-
ing his powder dry with Oliver. Hero-worship (in Nietzsche,
too, who was infatuated with the histories of his friend Burckhardt) partakes of nineteenth-century antiquarianism (cult of the
Middle Ages, cult of the Renaissance) which is a projection on
to the page of history, now one of the chief outlets for personal
fantasy, of the escapist yearning:

> *O wüsst' ich doch den Weg zurück,*
> *Den lieben Weg zum Kinderland!*
> *O warum sucht' ich nach dem Glück*
> *Und liess der Mutter Hand?* [1]

Cultured Europe was awakened from her dream of peaceful
perfectibility and perpetual encyclopædism by the Romantic
Movement—and by Napoleon. Goethe's *Faust*, the profoundest
expression of Romanticism, left rational man where the Fifth
Symphony left Mozart; and in the Ninth Symphony Richard
Wagner was to find his inspiration and point of departure. But
it was Napoleon who composed the tune that all Europe had to
sing. It was Napoleon who smashed the old instruments and
started a new rhythm. Instead of the eighteenth-century reality
of effete feudalism and the eighteenth-century dream of a society
of the free and equal, he offered himself as a Great Man, somber,
swift in action, and bad. Napoleon was overthrown, but it was
not overlooked that the offer might be repeated by others.

The genius of Carlyle did not consist in his "sageness" or his
"poetic" style: it consisted in the way in which, like a sponge,
he sucked in so much of the current of the age. He and Byron
are the only figures of European reputation among contemporary
English writers. Because these two men were more deeply
immersed in their own time they are today more relevant to ours.

[1] "Oh, if I knew the way back, the dear way to the land of children! Oh,
why did I seek happiness and leave my mother's hand?" (Klaus Groth).

Carlyle was no magician. It was because he saw deep into contemporary life that his prophecies of the future were so well founded. Many Englishmen thought Carlyle a genius with no insight into nineteenth-century politics, a poet but an eccentric. Abroad, Carlyle was not without honor. Emile Montégut, a French disciple, wrote in the *Revue des deux Mondes* (1850): *"Le culte des héros n'est pas autre chose que le résumé de toutes les doctrines contemporaines sur les grands hommes, résumé entrepris pour démolir ces doctrines et les transformer en les ennoblissant."* Carlyle became one of the most influential writers of his age. Going back to him today what do we find?

2

We do not find the Carlyle of tradition. We find that we must stop thinking of Carlyle as a Victorian religionist with an oddly inexplicable fondness for power-politics. By this time he deserves to be taken more seriously. The textbook editors have made a mistake if they think *Heroes* is Christian, and their mistake deserves probing. I propose an interpretation that makes of Carlyle neither saint nor mentor, but which gives to his life-work not indeed a perfect unity yet a rough homogeneity, a unity of effort and tendency. Not all the apparent contradictions in Carlyle can be explained, but many of them can be accommodated by a little interpretation. To deny ourselves the right to interpret is to brand Carlyle a fickle fool.

One critic of Carlyle, and the acutest, has dared so to brand him. Friedrich Nietzsche, in his brilliant and ignored remarks on Carlyle, accepted him at his face value, without interpretation or excuse. Very reasonably Nietzsche dismissed Carlyle as a shallow muddle-head and the worst English writer he had ever attempted. Nietzsche defined *Carlylismus* as the need for an absolute affirmative, an everlasting Yea, which sprang from weakness and conflict.[2] Carlyle, on this view, never had the courage

[2] *Antichrist*, 54. The second edition of Nietzsche's *Werke* (ed. Gast and Horneffer, Leipzig, 1910-26, 20 vols.) has been used throughout. References are to Nietzsche's numbered sections except when otherwise stated.

to avow his skepticism, because his rude Scottish upbringing prevented him from perceiving the subtlety and complication of intellectual problems. Nietzsche said that Carlyle was always in search of a strong faith, confusing the desire for belief with the will to truth,[3] but that the vehemency of his manner, his spluttering anger, his chronic need of noise are evidence that he did not believe what he pretended, even to himslf, to believe. Carlyle overstressed religion in order to hide the shocking fact that he did not believe in religion, hard as he might try. Passionately dishonest with himself, Carlyle was an atheist, according to Nietzsche: an atheist who made it a point of honor not to be so.[4] When Carlyle transmuted his dyspepsia into a moral adulation of the Hero, the theory put on a religious dress.[5] This was the crowning hypocrisy. Beneath the gown of Sir Thopas the Curate lurks a wily worldling.

This verdict of Nietzsche's is the inevitable one for a keen critic who, unprejudiced by the Victorian tradition of Carlyle-worship, accepts what he reads in Carlyle *without interpretation.* Happily, Nietzsche was so acute that his very denunciations afford a starting point for interpreters. If we transpose the tune of his denunciation into the key of descriptive diagnosis we can agree that, if Carlyle was not hypocritical, since hypocrisy implies consciousness of duplicity, he did conceal truths from others and from himself, and the workings of his mind were tortuous and ambiguous. If he disbelieves, we may expect to find him over-compensating for his disbelief by fervid professions of faith.

In *Heroes and Hero-Worship* we encounter a conflict between Christianity and a secular outlook which respects the spectacular and the successful, such as the Hero. Of course, the fact that Carlyle professed religion and at the same time preached the sword does not of itself prove that his life was a conflict between a religious and a secular outlook. Many religions have themselves preached the sword. Oliver Cromwell and Joan of Arc found no

---

[3] *Der Wille zur Macht,* 455.
[4] *Götzendämmerung,* Streifzüge, 12.
[5] *Ibid.,* 44.

problem here; the Scots of Annandale combined puritanism with brutality. But Carlyle was not Joan or Oliver, nor was he in harmony with his own forefathers. He entered upon the perilous quest that is a life of speculation. He was forced to feel, though he never entirely realized it, that "our thoughts are ours, their ends none of our own." His intellect led him into realms of experience that Ecclefechan and Annan had ill prepared him for. Soon he poured the new wine of historical imagination into the old Calvinist bottles and the result was not satisfying. Even if Carlyle never brought this duality into full consciousness, its workings in his subsequent life are none the less intricate and interesting.

The best minds in the nineteenth century came to have a very radical notion of what Christianity means. One's first thought is of Tolstoy, but it was Carlyle himself who said: Christianity "is against war altogether, teaching men even not to resist violence." [6] At the same time the bitter struggle for existence that Hobbes and Darwin agreed to be man's history was more and more in men's thoughts. Must one make the choice between Jesus and Hobbes? Carlyle seems to have felt so. He poses too clear-cut an antithesis and spends many years oscillating between the extremes.

What Carlyle increasingly felt to be the great reality was, as we have seen, *das ewige Werden,* the ceaselss flux of becoming, the relentless unfolding of history. It was forgotten for a long time that Carlyle was primarily a historian, not a metaphysician, and that he exalted history above all other studies, asserting even that history embraces all other studies. History was not only the sole sure source of information but the sole fount of wisdom. Moreover, generalizations about Society can have little value unless they are reached inductively from the study of individuals. History, says Carlyle, is the sum total of biographies.

These arguments, though rudimentary, remind the modern reader of a more advanced Evolutionism. *Evolutionary* may seem a strong word to apply to one who continued to scoff at

[6] 1838 Lectures, p. 96.

"the progress of the species"[7] (even though in the end he seemed to accept Darwinism[8]). *Progressive* might be a more accurate description of Carlyle's belief, had the term not the most inappropriate political implications and were not Carlyle's emphasis much less on progress than on process. He did believe in progress, however, though without much consistency. He argued, for instance, that the intensity and sincerity of belief, not the tenets of belief, were the criterion by which to judge a people and an epoch; yet he regarded Paganism, Catholicism, and Protestantism as a progressive succession towards some sort of truth which presumably was not to be measured by intensity of feeling. Carlyle accepted "the development hypothesis" without exactly agreeing with the philosophers of Progress, who made improvement too swift and easy, or with the evolutionary biologists, who made advance too slow and too material.

Evolutionism is not limited to the biological theories of Darwin. Those men are Evolutionists for whom the hypothesis of Development is the basis of their beliefs, for whom history takes precedence of metaphysics, and for whom becoming takes precedence of being. Carlyle's reverence for the flux of becoming and his argument for starting from the given facts of personal experience are alike prelusive of Bergson.

3

Let us look more closely at Carlyle's Evolutionism. Carlyle strikes at the root of religion by questioning the finality of any formulation of truth. Truth, he says, citing Schiller, *immer wird, nie ist*—never *is*, but is always in process of becoming. The statement is elaborated quite explicitly, as follows: "As Phlogiston is displaced by Oxygen, and the Epicycles of Ptolemy by the Ellipses of Kepler; so does Paganism give place to Catholicism, Tyranny to Monarchy, Feudalism to Representative Gov-

[7] E.g. *Frederick*, Bk. I, Ch. I, iii. The Centenary edition of Carlyle's Works (ed. H. D. Traill, London, 1899-1923, 30 vols.) has been used throughout.

[8] *Autobiography of Moncure D. Conway*, 2 vols. Boston, 1904. Vol. I, p. 403.

ernment—where also the process does not stop." [9] In his 1838 lectures, Carlyle speaks of "the impossibility of any creed being perpetual." In *The French Revolution,* he is equally lucid: "All things are in a state of revolution, strictly speaking, in change from moment to moment in the Time-World of ours. In fact, there is nothing else but revolution and mutation, the former merely speedier change."

"In this Time-World of ours": the implication here might be presumed to be Platonic, a better Eternal World being assumed, fixed and immutable. Yet this Platonic implication is not easy to reconcile with a Truth that never *is* but is always *being created.* The contradiction is complete and will, I hope, be more fully understood before the end of this book. Another red herring with which Carlyle misleads the reader is the hint of teleology that he occasionally drops, incompatible as teleology must be with relativism. "The human soul," he says in the 1838 lectures, "in fact develops itself into all sorts of opinions, doctrines, which go on nearer and nearer to the truth."

On the whole it is fair to say that for Carlyle, as for Bergson, evolution (or history) is purposive without being teleological. How then does one have an object for worship? Bergson is more consistent in rejecting the idea of fixity altogether. Carlyle says that a "vital force" [10] which is one and indivisible informs all mankind, and he invests this life-process with an aura of sanctity, which inevitably has shocked those Christians who have ears to hear. Frederick Denison Maurice, for instance, being a good Christian, was scandalized at the "wild pantheistic rant" of Carlyle's lecture on Mahomet, and wished that Carlyle could be brought to believe in Christ's Incarnation and Resurrection. For Carlyle not only honored the flux of history; he worshiped the one fixed point in the flux, the hero. Man is to be justified, so Nietzsche also was to formulate the matter, not by a goal but by his highest examples.

[9] "Characteristics."
[10] *Heroes,* p. 106.

4

How is it established that the hero is, in Carlyle's phrase, "the rock among all rushings-down whatsoever"? Actually, no very strong argument is offered by Carlyle. His faith in the hero is intuitive. Eighteenth-century philosophy had called in doubt the old eschatology, and the religion of humanity was superseding the religion of theology. Those who were dissatisfied with average humanity, however, had perforce to believe in superior humanity or believe in nothing. Now belief in the most effective agents of history dovetails easily—too easily—with belief in history as the key to all problems. History is the new theology, the hero is the new God. Or, as Carlyle puts it in *Sartor Resartus* ("The Centre of Indifference"): history is the divine book of revelation, the hero is the inspired text. By nature both worldly and religious, Carlyle tries to reconcile the two elements in his nature through a philosophy of heroism. He postulates the hero because, in the first place, the hero is human, fleshly, successful, the highest product of the evolutionary process, and because, in the second place, men may transfer to the hero the feelings they had associated with God. The hero is an instrument of progress and a justification of life. His achievements are substantial, the hope he holds out is unbounded. Through him body and spirit, time and eternity, policy and religion, are reconciled, Carlyle thinks, in a new *Weltanschauung*.

A word about the physical and temporal side of the hero. Criticism of Carlyle has often been so source-ridden that the Carlylean hero has been equated with the Fichtean leader—who is simply a receptacle for the Divine Idea. Johann Gottlieb Fichte, the philosophic spokesman of anti-Napoleonic German nationalism, had been taken up with philosophic idealism and Christian theology, but Carlyle, on the other hand might, with Walt Whitman, have called himself a personalist, a believer in the individual—the specifically human. Fichte starts with the Divine Idea and exemplifies it in a hero; Carlyle starts with a

hero and clothes him with emotive language, which is often
flavored with Fichtean idealism.

It has been correctly observed that Carlyle is at his best as an
artist when depicting a man's appearance and that he had a
portrait-painter's interest in physical idiosyncrasy, in the light
of the eye, the wart on the cheek, the tilt of the head. Yet this
observation does not come well from those who believe that
Carlyle is a great artist with nothing to say, for the same aptitude
that made Carlyle a portrait-artist made him a lover of man
with a personalist philosophy, i.e., a faith that men are more
than eating-machines or thinking-machines, that they are the
creative source of all good and that the highest delight is delight
in men. Carlyle loves the flesh and blood of a man more than
any Idea. Because he is a vitalist and a personalist, he is most
at home with individuals and with dramatic narrative. Carlyle's
nostalgic re-creations of the past give the impression that he
would like to be merged with the process of nature. He makes
himself a part of the past, a comrade of Cromwell's, a courtier
of Frederick's. He concerns himself only with that portion of
history that is still "frondent" and growing in contemporary
culture. He feels himself to be a twig on the tree Igdrasil.

Thus Carlyle passes from the secular to the religious: the
hero is flesh and blood, therefore he is part of the mystic stream
of becoming. Freely as Carlyle borrowed phraseology from the
new German philosophy, from Fichte, Novalis, and Schelling,
freely as he bandied the name of Immanuel Kant (always a name
to conjure with), his grasp of metaphysics was never firm, nor
his interest vivid. Recent researches on the influence of German
philosophy on Carlyle have proved nothing if not that he was a
mere expropriator in this territory.[11] He acknowledged no sort
of responsibility to the owners of the goods he had expropriated.
He used German thought to suggest erudition, to create a foreign
and "romantic" atmosphere, to hide his heresies from himself.
Kantians have differed among themselves, but it is not easy to
see how a Kantian could believe that "all force is moral" [12]

[11] See *Carlyle and German Thought*, C. F. Harrold. New Haven, 1934.
[12] *Heroes*, p. 39.

or that slavery is a necessary social institution. Carlyle clinched the matter when he said of German metaphysics in 1838: "I got nothing out of them." [13]

5

To maintain that Carlyle did not believe this world to be a mere copy of an ideal world, a symbol of a higher reality, a shadow and a fiction beside the substance and the fact of God, is on the face of it to give Carlyle the lie, since he asserted his faith in this idealism over and again. And after a fashion he believed what he said: at least he was always striving after the sincerity which he envied in his heroes. But he found the conflict between the old religion and the new evolutionism inescapable. The two outlooks might at some points be reconciled, but not at all. On the one side, so it seemed to Carlyle, the great oversimplifier, there were power, success, hardness, on the other meekness, crucifixion, and love. To some extent Carlyle succeeded in transferring his religious feelings to his new religion of power. A rough sort of armistice would be patched up between his religious sentiments and his secular sentiments. But there is also much that is contradictory, much that is blurred and imprecise, in Carlyle's writing. He was attempting the impossible task of concealing and resolving the conflict at the same time. Let us see how he went to work.

There is a passage in his *Notebooks* where Carlyle sets forth his view of the writer's vocation in the religious terms he inherited from his parents: "Every man that writes is writing a new Bible or a new Apocrypha; to last for a week or for a thousand years: he that convinces a man and sets him working is the worker of a miracle." These sentences do not imply Christianity or even a belief in the supernatural. They are the expression, by one reared in Christianity and supernaturalism, of approval for writing which is a stimulus to action. Those who doubt this should look closely at Carlyle's comment on these lines of his own. In parenthesis he adds: "Strange lan-

[13] 1838 Lectures, p. 189.

guage this: but it is as in the immigration of the Northmen,
or any other great world-revolution, two languages must get
jumbled together and old words get new meanings; all things
for a time being confused enough." In this sentence, Carlyle,
not so dimly as might be expected, apprehends the revolution
that is going on in the world around and in the microcosm of his
own mind, a revolution in which the new historical or evolutionary
outlook is supplanting Christianity. This conflict was partly unconscious and therefore prolific of contradictions in Carlyle's
opinions. He liked to call anything "Christianity" of which he
approved. He spent many years defending the Prussian army and
state for their power and ruthlessness, and at the age of eighty
he said: "Germany is in a state of theological transition. Dogma
is yielding to fact. The Christian Church is changing; but the
grand truths of Christianity are unalterable. In the hands of
Bismarck, the chiefest statesman of the age, Germany's progress
is as certain as the rising of tomorrow's sun. Nothing is to be
feared." [14]

Now at the period when Carlyle thus assented to the grand
truths of Christianity, it is known that he regarded Jesus Christ
as purely human,[15] that he professed no belief in personal immortality,[16] that he scouted the idea of hell,[17] and that he did
not believe in turning the other cheek but rather in:

> *The good old rule, the simple plan,*
> *That he should keep who has the power,*
> *And he should take who can.*

Am I extravagant in assuming that "the grand truths of Christianity" means "such beliefs as are so important to me that I
wish them to be surrounded with an aura of sanctity"?

These subterfuges, if not wholly conscious, made Carlyle so
uncomfortable that on one occasion when a harmless clergyman

[14] *Carlyle,* D. A. Wilson. London, 1923-39, Vol. VI, p. 367.
[15] *Inner Life,* J. B. Crozier. London, 1908. Vol. II, p. 388.
[16] *A Diary,* William Allingham. London, 1907, p. 203: "Death and the
Future. We know nothing—must leave all that alone."
[17] *New Fragments,* John Tyndall. London, 1892, p. 377.

told him that he agreed with his religious opinions, Carlyle turned on him with an angry: "Who told you what my religious opinions are?" His cries of *"Wer darf Ihn nennen?"* and his requests for silence are understandable tricks.

The transcendental vocabulary of Carlyle serves two chief purposes. First, it helps him to conceal his heterodoxy from himself and as a result is the cause of some confusion of ideas. Second, it enables him to state some eminently tenable beliefs poetically, which are now capable of restatement in pragmatic terms. Of the first kind, examples have already been given. The second sort includes most of Carlyle's pronouncements on the sanctity or supernaturalness of such things as the hero, or man in general, or society, or history. What he attacks is, after all, what many later thinkers were to attack: *mechanistic* science. What he defends is what Bergson and the so-called "irrationalists" of the late nineteenth century were to defend: intuition as against logic in the mind, life and organism as against machinery in the external world. This is what he means when he protests that moderns are driving God out of the universe, and when he declares that man is a spirit and a mystery. Sometimes his language is plain: "The healthy Understanding we should say, is not the logical, argumentative, but the Intuitive."

As to the rock among all uncertainties, that, as we have seen, is the Hero. He is described—not surprisingly—in religious language, and that Carlyle was trying to make a religion out of the creative processes of history, and history interpreted "realistically," is decisively shown in his frank acceptance of power and wrongdoing. Carlyle's hero wears a halo, but his name is Machiavelli. It is natural that Carlyle should at first be most at home with men like Cromwell who combined worldly prowess with spiritual faith, but increasingly, we have seen, Carlyle's heroes were of another kidney: Governor Eyre, Bismarck, and Frederick the Great. As early as 1843, he wrote an essay stating that he could not help loving Dr. Francia, the efficient and merciless dictator of Paraguay. A Hero, to rephrase the matter, is both a revelation and an influence. As revelation (of "God," if you wish) he vindicates history and is an exemplar. As influence, he contributes to history and furthers progress.

When Carlyle says that spirit determines matter, he means that in the end the hero's personality gains the mastery over necessity, or, recognizing very exactly the boundaries of necessity, becomes itself a free agent. That is why, as early as 1838, Carlyle calls hero-worship not merely the primary, secondary, and tertiary creed of mankind, but the ultimate and final creed. Politics and all human interests, *including religion,* are built on it.

Carlyle was dedicated to—prostrate before, if you will—the historical fact. What he hated was a non-human and non-historical approach, whether Christian as in Paley or hedonist as in Bentham. This approach he denounced as Materialism, Mechanism, or Sham. Like later critics of nineteenth-century materialism, Carlyle called attention from philosophy to history, from metaphysics to evolution, from mechanism to organism, from statics to dynamics, from the dead to the living. Not possessing the vocabulary of modern social psychology to describe habit and custom, he followed Burke in employing transcendental rhetoric for this purpose, a rhetoric which he stole from German metaphysicians whom he never understood. If he had a serious theology that went beyond mere routine invocations and mere forms of words, it was pantheistic. "Why do I not name thee God?" asks Teufelsdröckh of Nature in a highly serious passage. The only argument for the existence of God, Carlyle once said, is that what happens in this world is obviously what should happen.[18] The remark starts from history and infers a sort of presiding—or perhaps, pervading—deity. All these beliefs may seem innocuous enough, and in tune with American democracy, yet when a child of Ecclefechan is so skeptical about heavenly authority, it is not surprising that in his bereavement he worships earthly authority and earthly heroes.

[18] Allingham, *op. cit.,* p. 268.

6

For Carlyle's outlook I propose the name Heroic Vitalism, a term that is meant to embrace both a political theory, Aristocratic Radicalism, and a metaphysic which, inverting Carlyle's expression "Natural Supernaturalism," we might call Supernatural Naturalism. Now that we have arrived at an understanding or at least an interpretation of what Carlyle was really after and how his religious professions are connected with his Machiavellianism, we are in a position to restate his world view. First, Supernatural Naturalism.

Near the beginning of the first lecture on heroes appears the following quotation from the German Romanticist Novalis: "There is but one Temple in the Universe and that is the Body of Man. Nothing is holier than that high form. Bending before men is a reverence done to this Revelation in the Flesh. We touch Heaven when we lay our hand on a human body." Carlyle's comment is: "We are the miracle of miracles—the great inscrutable mystery of God." Novalis came in very handy. The religious language helps Carlyle to conceal (as usual) the revolutionary nature of his inference which is: "Forget the conjuring tricks of Jesus. Mankind himself is the greatest possible miracle and in his life is to be found the only divinity we can know." Carlyle—Nietzsche struck home—was an atheist who made it a point of honor not to be so.

All things are miraculous; had Carlyle read Blake's *Auguries of Innocence,* he would not have regarded himself as the discoverer of this truth. Yet the sacramental attitude to the natural was of peculiar use to Carlyle, as it was to Bergson and Nietzsche later. Abandoning the Platonic idea and its modern equivalent, the Kantian *noumenon,* they transferred the feelings of religion to the worship of this world. This is clearly an advance on the neutral-toned nihilism of the earlier naturalistic philosophies. But, as usual, Carlyle and Nietzsche saw only corybantic paganism as the alternative to Christianity. If the cruel struggle for existence is a necessity and a good, they conclude, the morals which condemn cruelty are neither necessary nor good.

Carlyle never pursues these lines of thought far. He struggles in the direction I have charted. It was left to Nietzsche to complete the journey. But if Carlyle's Supernatural Naturalism did not evolve into a belief that everything is the Will-to-Power, it did evolve to a belief that everything but heroism is a flux and a conflict. "There is nothing else but revolution or mutation," we learn in *The French Revolution*. The same book, for all its apparent transcendentalism, affords a picture of the universe as a "Complex of Forces" which rise and decline: "All embodiments of Force that work in this miraculous Complex of Forces, named Universe—go on *growing*, through their natural phases and developments, each according to its kind" (Part I, Book VII, Ch. 1). In this sentence we have the three essential features of Supernatural Naturalism. First, the "supernatural," "divine," "miraculous" element. Second, the element of brute force; the process is cruel, inexorable, or dæmonic. Third, the whole universe runs on harsh biological principles, which are called the Laws of Nature, the Laws of the Universe, or even (*Frederick*, XIII, 1) the Laws of Heaven. These Laws Carlyle comes to rely on more and more. On one page in *Frederick* (Vol. IV, p. 191) they are invoked four times.

Aristocratic Radicalism is the political theory that springs from this metaphysic. The naturalism that was coming to supersede Christianity in the eighteenth century was not Carlyle's Supernatural Naturalism, but—as he saw it—a leveler's naturalism by which every valley was exalted and every mountain and hill laid low. The native docility of man was the psychological tenet that suited the social statics of incipient utilitarianism. Aristocratic Radicalism differs from the philosophic radicalism of 1800 in that its view of history is dynamic and its view of man is dæmonic. According to Carlyle the process of decay, which follows flowering, is not usually peaceful. Here the plant image retreats before the image of fire. A new epoch is born like a phœnix from the ashes of the old.[19] *The French Revolution* is an articulation of this belief.

The pattern of Heaven and Hell is engraved on the mind of the Aristocratic Radical. Where the liberal sees a level plain he sees mountains and valleys; where the liberal sees human docility, he sees a divine soul or a dæmon. The conflict of opposites which Carlyle believed to be the historical process is manifest in the nature of man. "In wondrous Dualism, then as now, lived nations of breathing men; alternating in all ways between Light and Dark; between joy and sorrow, between rest and toil. . . ." Such is Carlyle's characterization of the twelfth century in *Past and Present*. It is a naïve and dangerous dualism which cancels the utility of Carlyle's incipient pragmatism. Certainly a psychology with a hell in it is apt to be more realistic than the pleasure-and-pain psychology of the eighteenth century, but when the heaven-hell pattern pervades a man's thought it makes him an extremist, a man of insanely ruthless reasoning, ignorant of the great civilizing principle of the golden mean.

7

The anthropology and psychology upon which Carlyle's politics, like all Aristocratic Radicalism, are based, are clear enough. The anthropology is that of Hobbes—life in a state of nature is nasty, brutish, and short—which the scientific anthropology of the nineteenth century did little to destroy. According to this anthropology, restated in *Past and Present,* "Venerable Justice herself began by Wild-Justice; all law is as a tamed furrowfield, slowly worked out, and rendered arable, from the waste jungle of Club-Law." [20] Not all modern anthropologists could endorse this view of human origin. Many have indeed repudiated it and all its Hobbesian implications. They have shown that early

---

[19] *Sartor Resartus*, III, 5 (The Phœnix). For phœnix image, see also *Heroes*, Lecture 1; 1838 Lectures, p. 185. Compare D. H. Lawrence.
[20] *Past and Present*, II, 1.

food-gathering tribes were largely peaceful and sociable.[21] But Aristocratic Radicals of all periods believe that man is a beast of prey until he is restrained by constituted authority.

Carlyle's psychology is by now the most prevalent one. He believed in the primacy of the "Unconscious," [22] a term which he must be among the first to use. This belief produced his theory of knowledge, in which intuition is too naïvely exalted above reason, and his theory of motive and action. With Freud he believed that there is in man's mind a fund of crude, directive energy, which is thwarted at peril. In the French Revolution, the mental volcano which Freud calls the Id erupted into convulsive action. Carlyle imagined the Id as a band of Furies. The Parisian mob runs forth "with dances, triumph-songs, as of the Furies" (Part I, Bk. V, Ch. 9). The day when Paris makes conquest of its king is called "Eumenides Sunday" (I, v. 8). "For they lie always, those subterranean Eumenides (fabulous and yet so true) in the dullest existence of man;—and can dance, brandishing their dusky torches, shaking their serpent-hair" (I, v. 4). In this manner Carlyle applies the psychology of the unconscious to whole societies.

The social outlook that emanates from such views is venerable enough. Since the universe is built on Darwinistic biological principles, since society is like a human body, the one thing necessary is the maintenance of proper function: the feet must run, the arms must carry, the head must direct. If this natural Order (one is bound to encounter the word in any study of Aristocratic Radicalism) is upset, physic is needed and, sometimes, surgery. Up to this point the philosophy of Carlyle might be regarded as the classical aristocratic philosophy of European culture. It is the philosophy not only of Aristotle and Augustine but of most responsible and influential thinkers until modern times. In the Orient it is a part of the Hindu religion. The Confucian Mencius implied it when he said: "Without the gentlemen there would be no one to rule the common people,

---

[21] See especially The Growth of Civilization, W. J. Perry. London, 1928.
[22] Misc., III ("Characteristics"), p. 10: "The Involuntary Unconscious."

and without the common people there would be no one to feed the gentlemen."

Aristocratic Radicals since Carlyle, however, believe not only that there is a natural, organic order but that, because of the dæmonic character of man, the natural order is occasionally upset. If the gates are not to be opened to chaos, therefore, it is doubly necessary always to preach Order, Hierarchy, and Obedience. Above all it is necessary that those at the peak of the hierarchy, upon whom the rest depend, should be respected, perhaps even beyond their merely personal worth. This does not, for Carlyle, mean that the leader's office is to be respected apart from the leader—a doctrine he explicitly denied (*Frederick*, XXI, viii)—but that the leader should be, in anthropological language, a *mana* personality, above criticism and dispute. The hero, in a word, should be worshiped or at least revered— a doctrine which is repeatedly stated in Shakespeare in conjunction with a mediæval cosmology and without modern evolutionary preconceptions. But Carlyle was groping towards a utilitarian justification for doctrines that were defended metaphysically by Aristotle and Augustine. In this respect the thought of this great "revolutionary" is highly conservative and indeed regressive. The word *groping*, indeed, is probably the most accurate description of Carlyle's mental processes, and not wholly a discreditable one. It is the fantastic mixture of foresight and atavism, revolutionism and conservatism, that makes Carlyle a fascinating, if eccentric, thinker. His starting point is the present: the world of bourgeois liberalism. He looks back with envy to the ordered hierarchies of more classical societies and to the burning faith of times that knew not Reform. On the other hand he looks forward through generations of conflict to an age when poverty and idleness will have been abolished and when the mechanistic view of life shall be superseded by a belief in vital energy and practical will. The paradox of Carlyle's vision of the present is that it is all past and future.

8

The old God was dead. Carlyle was not the first to see this, but with other great Romanticists he was among the first to see that God's death was a negative fact, in itself nothing to rejoice at, and that, if God's death were not to be pure loss, new values would have to be found in place of the old. The new bourgeois liberalism was not a new system of values—Carlyle is in part right—but only a complex of ideas instrumental to the overthrow of the old regime. To regard these ideas as ideals would be sheer nihilism.

So Carlyle set out on the spiritual journey which has now been traced in some detail. His case against the eighteenth century is as exaggerated as Lytton Strachey's case against the nineteenth, and his failure to see merits in Victorian liberalism and its useful, if limited, historical function is responsible for the unrealism of his own politics. The radical who is utterly impatient with all the practical radicalism of the moment usually becomes a reactionary, and Carlyle is no exception. Any humane ideal in the nineteenth century must have its starting point in the growing humanism of the previous age, and the best ideas of Carlyle do have their source there. The idea, for instance, that man is primarily a feeling and acting being, deeply rooted in Western tradition, had been re-established by one of Carlyle's bogeymen, Jean Jacques Rousseau. The Carlylean idea that the mere aggregation of votes was no infallible way to social justice follows directly from Rousseau's famous distinction between the general will and the will of all.

The Romantic Movement, by which I mean the whole abandonment of classical traditions which took place between 1750 and 1850, was an attempt to recognize a new society that was then being born and to recognize the new truths created by the new society. In this process rationalism itself played a part but, as I have insisted, a negative one. Rousseau's anti-rationalism played a larger part by broadening man's conception of man; Kant, Fichte, Coleridge, and Goethe pointed to the centrality of moral problems; Carlyle brought all these ideas to Britain where no practical alternative had been offered to sheer Metternichean conservatism except the utiltarianism of Jeremy Bentham and his countless followers. For all its usefulness, utilitarianism had two serious limitations: it took a rigidly middle-class view of politics; and it inherited eighteenth-century psychology. Carlyle had a distinct contribution to make in both provinces.

In politics he showed that contemporary liberalism relied excessively on mechanical devices and external adjustments, and that the freedom which it offered the people was more theoretic than real, since the economy of freedom—laissez faire—condemned the workers to unrelieved suffering. Carlyle's peasant upbringing and his hatred of industrialism made him look for a solution beyond the liberalism of a class which had merely substituted its own tyranny for that of the landed aristocracy. As early as 1830 Carlyle's writings had attracted the attention of the Saint-Simonians, a group of socialists who sought a new society through cooperation, and Carlyle translated Saint-Simon's *Le nouveau christianisme* which they sent him. This anti-bourgeois Carlyle is the Carlyle who did much to inspire Friedrich Engels' *Condition of the Working Classes in England in 1844*.

To the left of the practical Benthamites who were busy effecting the transition from aristocracy to plutocracy were more idealistic and theoretic radicals of the same tradition who sought to make out of eighteenth-century liberalism a new world view. At its extreme this radicalism is anarchism, the *reductio ad absurdum* of laissez faire. Carlyle saw very clearly the danger that the theoretic type of radicalism would hold for the intelligentsia, and the objections he stated were also taken over by Marx and Engels: that politics are a struggle for power and that therefore the seizure of power is as necessary to a just as to an unjust regime. In his demonstration that cash was now the only nexus between man and man; in his belief that freedom requires the recognition of necessity; in his historical, often dialectical, interpretation of social phenomena—in all these Carlyle has passed beyond Benthamites, Anarchists, and Utopian Socialists to Marxism.

In one respect, the Marxists advanced scarcely a step beyond the *philosophes*, and this is in their psychology. For them human nature was very much a known entity and therefore results could be predicted in the human sphere with the same precision and with the same intellectual instruments as in the mechanical sphere. For Carlyle, however, as for modern psychology, human nature entailed much more than calculable self-interest, much more for both good and evil. With one hand he reaches back to the Pauline conception of man as sinner; with the other he reaches forward to modern depth-psychology.

What is one to make of the foresight of Carlyle, erratic as it was? I have suggested that in various ways he anticipates the thinkers who superseded the *philosophes* and the Benthamites, such thinkers as Marx and Engels, Nietzsche and Bergson, Freud and Jung and—above all—William James. Assuming commonly held views of the nineteenth century, this fact might seem to have only picturesque significance, since James is not commonly accorded special historical significance. If, however, we follow A. N. Whitehead in his belief that William James's pragmatism was just as great a revolution in thought as Francis Bacon's experimentalism, Carlyle's pioneering work takes on greater meaning, for he hammered out on the anvil of his own experience many Jamesian positions, including the central ones: the pragmatic view of truth, the depth-psychology, the high respect for the superior individual. His life was one long fight against contemporary orthodoxies. To mechanistic Benthamism he opposed his own social dynamics, to Coleridgean idealism his own pragmatism, to the chill impersonality of both his own personalism.

So much is to Carlyle's credit but no more. His readers know in what a bizarre fashion his originality is offset by verbiage, ill nature, crudeness, fantasy, and diabolism. His pragmatist attitude to history becomes worship of that very Success which William James was to call the bitch goddess; personalism becomes the superstitious dogma of hero-worship. Success worship and hero-worship are, from the standpoint of democratic pragmatism, much worse than exaggerations of truths. They are dangerous errors based on the belief, very frankly professed by Carlyle, that all power is "moral" and that tyranny is wholesome. How did Carlyle fall a victim to ideas so arbitrary, so unpragmatic, so subversive of civilized values? Part of the explanation is that Carlyle was groping after ideas which he did not clearly see, but this is no full explanation of so positive a view so positively reiterated. A more searching analysis would stress, as I have tried to do, the revenge which Carlyle took on the liberal educators of his youth, his total, uncritical rejection of that eighteeenth-century humanism which was the beginning of modern democratic thinking. Angry with the tradition of culture, Christian and modern, Carlyle flies in the face of civilization itself, pragmatism becomes Machiavellianism, respect for the individual becomes irrational abasement before tyrants. If, therefore, one side of Carlyle prefigures the best in democratic thought, another side prefigures the highbrow illiberalism of the twentieth century, the illiberalism of Knut Hamsun, Léon Daudet, Lawrence Dennis, and the professors of Hitler's Germany.

Part Two. Friedrich Nietzsche

"I know both sides because I am both sides"
—FRIEDRICH NIETZSCHE

Chronology

1844 Born in the village of Roecken, near Leipzig.

1849 Death of Nietzsche's father.

1850 Family settles in Naumburg (also in Saxony).

1856-64 Attends Schulpforta.

1864-65 At Bonn University.

1865-68 At Leipzig University.

1867 Period of military service.

1869-79 Professor of Greek at Basel.

1869-72 Friendship with the Wagners.

1870-88 Period of all Nietzsche's published works.

1870-75 Was housemate of Franz Overbeck at Basel.

1876 First Bayreuth Festival. Nietzsche breaks with Wagner.

1881 Nietzsche's first important mystical experience at Silva-plana.

1882 In love with Lou Salome.

1883 Second important mystical experience at Portofino. Death of Wagner.

1883-85 *Thus Spake Zarathustra.*

1885-90 His sister in Paraguay.

1888-89 Mental breakdown.

1889-1900 Insanity.

1900 Death at Weimar.

CHAPTER IV. A Biographical Sketch

"In the Theages Plato says: 'Every one of us would like if
possible to be master of all men and above all to be God.'
This attitude must return."—The Will to Power, 958

"In the end I would very much rather be a Basel professor
than God."—NIETZSCHE to Jacob Burckhardt,
6 January, 1889

1

Many have written the story of Friedrich Nietzsche's life. But
apart from the autobiography which Nietzsche himself prepared
for the public, all biographical material has been in the hands
either of Nietzsche's sister, Elisabeth Foerster-Nietzsche, or of
Professor C. A. Bernoulli. Frau Foerster was able to draw
directly upon memories of her brother back to his early childhood, and in her Weimar archives she began collecting letters
and notebooks long before her brother's death. At Basel, Professor Bernoulli had access to the correspondence of Franz Overbeck, Nietzsche's intimate friend and colleague.

Elisabeth started publishing biographical matter in 1900,
Bernoulli in 1904, and as late as 1931 controversy was still in
progress between Basel and Weimar. Basel held that Nietzsche
had serious love affairs, that he had been in love with Cosima
Wagner, that his friendship for Overbeck was the mainspring of
his later life, and that he hated his sister. Weimar minimized
both the love affairs and the friendship for Overbeck. Frau
Foerster set the stamp of hagiography upon the life of Nietzsche.
E. F. Podach's Nietzsches Zusammenbruch (1930), which was
favorable to Basel, was angrily answered by Weimar in Paul
Cohn's Um Nietzsches Untergang. Podach brought forward
medical documents which hinted that Nietzsche was syphilitic.
Cohn fretted and fumed.

But 1930 was the year of Cosima Wagner's death, and five years later Frau Foerster followed her to the grave. With Lou Salome, who lived till 1937, they were the last survivors from the drama of Nietzsche's life. Today, therefore, the truth about Nietzsche should not be so bedeviled with the jealousies of factions.

In this biographical sketch, we shall be concerned with the life of Nietzsche only in so far as it was a quest for a higher humanity. United with Nietzsche's desire to create an aristocracy are two complementary impulses: an unfeigned envy of the *real politiker* and a yearning for the infinite. A subsequent chapter will cope with the ideas which sprouted from these impulses. Here and now, the circumstances in Nietzsche's life will be noted that kindled his aspirations towards a higher humanity, his admiration for the strong politician, and his craving to be one with the sun and the mountains, himself transfigured into superman.

2

The origins of Friedrich Nietzsche, who was born in the village of Roecken, near Leipzig, in 1844, are significant. This archenemy of Christianity came of a line of clergymen on both his mother's and his father's side. This great champion of aristocracy and the superman came of a family that was small-bourgeois in fact and in outlook. As a child, Friedrich gave no indication that he was not in the family tradition. He was, for one thing, extremely, abnormally religious. "At twelve years of age," he wrote later, "I saw God in all his glory." As clearly as Kierkegaard's or Dostoevski's, Nietzsche's was a religious mind, and not merely in his younger days. *Gottergebenheit* (surrender to God) was his own description of his mental attitude. All through his life he continues to surrender; but the God he surrendered to was not always the same one.

The tight little Lutheran home gave Nietzsche many lasting traits, including a contempt for common humanity, admiration for discipline, a habit of hero-worship, and a haughty, anachronistic sense of honor. His mother and grandmother taught him to admire Napoleon, and their outlook was a combination, common in their class, of religious fervor, social snobbery, and cheap Prussianism. As a child young Friedrich possessed a porcelain King Squirrel who reviewed the toy troops in the manner of the Prussian monarch after whom Friedrich Wilhelm Nietzsche had been named. When in Nietzsche's tenth year the Crimean War broke out, he acquired an intense interest in the art of war.

The atmosphere of the Nietzsche home was pseudo-aristocratic and therefore stuffy. Pastor Nietzsche died in 1849, the family moved to Naumburg, and the young Nietzsche had to settle down with female relatives of the starchiest kind—his grandmother Nietzsche, her two daughters Augusta and Rosalie, his mother, and his sister Elisabeth. If Nietzsche was proud, he learned to be so from his austere housemates. "We Nietzsches scorn to lie," said one of his aunts; and it seemed that they all said things like that. On the other hand, if Nietzsche was rebellious, it was in the first instance the oppressive piety of Naumburg against which he rebelled. He belonged to the class which subsequently proved the most susceptible of all classes to Hitler worship. When the hour struck in 1933 the surviving Nietzsches and Oehlers (his mother's family), including his sister, did in fact accept Hitler as the superman! Undoubtedly Friedrich Nietzsche was the least nazistic member of the family; undoubtedly he struggled against Naumburg. Yet there is surely some connection between his excessive penchant for grandeur and that of his class. Incidentally, like the jealous peasant, Thomas Carlyle, Nietzsche claimed aristocratic ancestry upon very scanty evidence.[1]

He never lost the somewhat starchy self-righteousness, the readiness to take offense, the conspicuous chastity not altogether intended, the vehement haughtiness spasmodically asserted, the

[1] *Ecce Homo,* "Warum ich so weise bin," 3. See *Journal of British Archæological Association,* Vol. IX (1853), for an article by Carlyle himself entitled "Short Notices as to the early History of the Family of Carlyle, which the Conqueror found in England, and a branch of which was ennobled in Scotland."

pitiable isolation of the spinster. His extreme piety as a child won him the name, in the school at Naumburg, of the Little Minister. His missionary zeal drew wonder even from his sister, a prig of the first water. On one occasion he could not bear to hear of the courage of Mucius Scævola, who did not flinch when his hand was burnt off, without seizing a box of matches and firing them against his own hand.[2]

Yet in truth Nietzsche's physical courage had its roots in the habit of brooding upon ethics which life in a fatherless home full of officious women had encouraged. He was no athlete—he had not the knack of sports. His virtue erupted in irrational and explosive outbursts. With his impulsive emulation of Mucius Scævola, one might compare his sudden proposal of a duel to a companion with whom he did not pretend to have any quarrel. The naïvete is frank, bold, engaging, but also a trifle wanton. Nietzsche was a bookish lad and had not always a sense of prosaic fact. Agile, sensitive, and abounding in energy, he tended to overleap the ordinary. As he put it in *Thus Spake Zarathustra*: "I don't find it easy to believe that little people are necessary." Nietzsche was like Hamlet: his brooding did not remove him from the realm of action, but it so far crippled him that his actions were sudden, violent, and unreasoned. His intimates consisted, like Hamlet's, of women with whom he failed, men with whom he quarreled, or self-disregarding disciples (the musician Peter Gast was his Horatio) whom he patronized.

3

Nietzsche's adolescence was spent at Pforta school. It was here that he burnt his hand—appropriately, for was not Pforta the Rugby of Germany which Fichte himself had attended? Here boys were not merely filled with learning, but disciplined—one might almost say drilled—for manhood. Nietzsche, as one might have guessed, did not easily make friends, but in 1861

---

[2] *Cf.* Rousseau in his *Confessions:* "One day at table, while relating the fortitude of Scævola, they were terrified at seeing me start from my seat and hold my hand over a hot chafing-dish, to represent more forcibly the action of that determined Roman."

he received a Shakespeare for Christmas and we gather from subsequent comments that what chiefly impressed Nietzsche was Shakespeare's creation of men of granite, his delight in sheer strength.

Byron also spoke to Nietzsche's adolescence—not the Byron of the satires, but the Byron of Satanism. Nietzsche found replicas of the gloomy chasms of Byron in his own soul as Carlyle had in his. In his last years, he acknowledged a profound relation between himself and *Manfred*, Byron's somber and meretricious drama which so deeply affected Goethe, Carlyle, Schumann, Strindberg, and many others. He was ready for this exegesis of diabolical ethics at the age of thirteen. As a child Nietzsche admired strong men, in accordance with the views of his relatives. As a youth, he admired them because he was restive. In his twentieth year, he chose to write essays—his most considerable effort to date—on Ermanarich the Ostrogoth and Theognis of Megara. In heroic poetry, Ermanarich was the type of a ferocious, greedy, and treacherous tyrant; he had the beautiful Swanhild trodden to death by horses and his son hanged; he killed his nephews and, in the end, himself. Theognis was a poet of the sixth century, B.C. He exalted the military virtues; decried the democrats; advocated loyalty to friends, revenge upon enemies. Julian the Apostate recognized him as a glorious pagan. He supplied Nietzsche with the idea that an aristocracy should be scientifically bred, like horses.

When at the age of twenty Nietzsche left Pforta for Bonn University, he had acquired an interesting set of opinions and attitudes. He had been taught to admire strong politicians and to think of himself as an aristocrat whose great virtues are fearlessness and willingness to assume leadership. He had also acquired the habit of self-absorption. At the age of fourteen he had written an autobiography. This work and the short *Vita* which he had to present at Pforta six years later are enough to show how closely, how anxiously, Nietzsche took stock of his own behavior. He meditated on human excellence, on the masters of reality who had molded affairs after their heart's desire. Proudly he felt his superiority to the mass of mankind. Were little people really necessary? For himself he knew there was one central, experienced reality: a great longing that could never be appeased, a longing for the kingdom, the power, and the glory.

This longing drew Nietzsche onwards and upwards, but as we learn from *Thus Spake Zarathustra*, much in his temperament and his constitution drew him in a contrary direction. Visions of Manfred, Coriolanus, and Napoleon rose alluringly before the inner eye, yet the more he strove to be like them, the more he resembled their antitype, Parsifal. Despite his struggles to be bold and bad, Nietzsche remained singularly innocent and loving. His efforts at wickedness fell flat. In a frenzy of self-assertion he got drunk while still a schoolboy at Pforta. Remorse tortured him afterwards. When, during his first months at Bonn, Nietzsche made a desperate attempt at fast living, he reminds us of Tolstoy's Pierre, a dreamer of dreamers, who enjoyed his youthful truancies—including the hilarious escapade with the bear—before returning to his dreams.

4

From 1864 to 1868 Nietzsche was a student, first at Bonn, then at Leipzig. He was now a man, acutely aware of the loneliness of the human situation. During the whole of his childhood and youth, his sister tells us, he yearned for the paternal friend he had so bitterly missed through the premature death of his father. With maturity he, like Carlyle, suffered the loss of his heavenly father. Having read David Strauss's *Life of Jesus*, he discarded Christianity (though in time he resented Strauss's influence, exactly as Carlyle resented the influence of Gibbon and Hume). An earnest search for a new faith and a new father began. However much Nietzsche, at a later stage, ridiculed the idea of truth, as an undergraduate he was wholly devoted to it. If consolation is what is needed, he advised, then be religious; but let those who aim at truth abandon complacency. Moderns, knowing their Freud, are in a position to understand what the loss of his father had meant to Nietzsche. It meant, on the one hand, that he was always on the lookout for a father-substitute and, on the other, that his love for his sister and his mother was excessive and troublesome. Once again, we find Nietzsche being drawn in opposite directions: towards an heroic and paternal ideal and towards a loving and maternal ideal.

His religious conflict—which moderns may find more puzzling —is similar. Every reader of Carlyle, Ibsen, Strindberg and the rest knows how much loss of faith meant to men of the nineteenth century. It was as much a matter of torment as the loss of a lover. Nietzsche lost his God. He was left with numerous sentiments, some attaching themselves to his masculine and heroic ideal, others to the feminine and charitable. This duality in Nietzsche's character recalls Carlyle, and in due course comparisons will be made. At present we are to note that as the conflict grew to a first crisis, at the outset of manhood, Nietzsche was immersed in a new philosophy of life that met, for a time, many of his needs. This was the philosophy of Schopenhauer.

There is reason to mention the influence of Schopenhauer in a biographical sketch rather than in a discussion of Nietzsche's final philosophy. The impact of some few authors upon Nietzsche was not such as may readily be comprehended under the academic term "literary influences," for it was an impact as powerful and direct as that of thwarted passion or mystical union with nature. The two great influences of this kind were Heraclitus, the pre-Socratic great-grandfather of Heroic Vitalism, and Arthur Schopenhauer.

One day Nietzsche picked up at a bookstore a little-known book of metaphysics: *The World as Will and Idea*. He hurried home, ran to his room, threw himself into the corner of the sofa with his prize, and opened his heart to the genius of Schopenhauer. Nietzsche found in it a vision of human life that he could never forget. "In this book," he wrote, "I saw a mirror in which I espied the whole world, life, and my own mind depicted in frightful grandeur. In this volume the full celestial eye of art gazed at me; here I saw illness and recovery, banishment and refuge, hell and heaven." Between these polar opposites, Nietzsche oscillated for the rest of his life.

No commentator on Nietzsche has failed to note his "derivation" from Schopenhauer. The story is somewhat as follows: As a moral philosopher, Nietzsche came late in a chain of development. Already in the eighteenth century Hume had shown that morality had no absolute sanction. Kant replied to Hume. It was true, Kant argued, that reason as generally understood could not vindicate a Christian morality, but there was a second kind of reason, Practical Reason, which could and regularly did dictate Christian morals to every unperverted man. Practical Reason is, on customary standards, a non-rational faculty, a kind of moral intuition. In the formulation of this concept Kant stands at the head of the line of modern thinkers who have reminded rationalists that man is primarily an active, feeling creature, not a thinking machine. Some of these thinkers have taken this to be sufficient excuse for rabid attacks on reason. Among idealists Fichte best shows us the meaning of popularized Kantian philosophy as a psychological and social force. In *Die Bestimmung des Menschen,* for example, a lengthy chapter on Faith upholds knowledge arrived at without reason, knowledge automatically prompted by the will to believe and directed towards "moral" action.

Now what Schopenhauer did was to reinterpret the non-rational impulse which tells man how to act. Since for him there was no beneficent God, the inner voice was not a message from heaven, a higher and more practical reason, but only the whispering of will, that is, instinct. Man is a donkey lured on by the carrot of blind will which informs all things. Schopenhauer's philosophy, with its elaborate assumption of so many Kantian premises, such as the hypothesis of a world more real than that apprehended by the senses and the dichotomy of will and idea, is the most ironical comment on idealistic philosophy that was ever penned.

Such is the ancestry of Nietzsche's philosophy as it has often been rehearsed. But there is another aspect to the story that should be stressed in any study of heroism. With Rousseau and the Romantics, Fichte emphasizes the undeniable fact that man must act and that therefore action is primary and philosophy secondary. This was the source of the attraction to Fichte which so unphilosophical a man as Carlyle experienced; Carlyle's conclusion is that training for action is the most important educational pursuit and that the man of action is the greatest man. The conclusion considerably narrows the meaning of *action*, yet Fichte is the first in a line of modern philosophers whose writings are chiefly instructions as to how to become a great man; we have seen how far Carlyle carried this attitude. Schopenhauer himself ought to be known as one of the great philosophers of leadership, for though most of his major work is given over to metaphysics, the root of his commentary on life is his own feeling of superiority to the herd and his own balked ambition. His pessimism is his revenge upon the public. The seminal part of his philosophy is his aspiration towards human excellence, an aspiration which preoccupied German writers from Goethe to Stefan George.

Schopenhauer recognized the excellence of the artist and the philosopher in the realm of ideas, and of the hero and the saint in the realm of will. It is evident that what attracted Nietzsche was not only the doctrine of will, but the Schopenhauerian attitude to men. Nietzsche, like Carlyle, desired to be opposed alike to the revolutionists and the authoritarians. Schopenhauer was to his purpose because the Schopenhauerian mind, while it struck at the basis of accepted teachings, was utterly illiberal. Where it was radical it was misanthropic, where it was conservative it was cynical. In his will, Schopenhauer left money not to the revolutionaries who made the revolution of 1848 but to the police who put them down. In his hierarchy of spirits, the artist and the philosopher are in the first rank; in the second is the *savant*, in the third the practical man, in the fourth the proletarian, in the fifth and last the savage.[3] Nietzsche's endeavor was not so much to elevate the practical man to the first rank as to merge Schopenhauer's first three ranks into one superhuman being. Nietzsche turned against Schopenhauer in later years as he turned against most of those who were the inspiration of his youth. The truth is that he never accepted all the chief tenets of Schopenhauer. The name of Schopenhauer was the flag under which he was proud, for a time, to advance.

[3] *Parerga*, Vereinzelte Gedanken, 333. *Sämtliche Werke*, ed. Deussen, München, 1913-33. Vol. V, p. 656 ff.

Were we to regard Schopenhauer and Nietzsche as, first and foremost, psychologists, we should find them agreeing more closely than they did as metaphysicians. We should discover not only a concept of unconscious activity and rationalization with implications as far-reaching as Freud's, but an interpretation of human nature that is close to Alfred Adler's. Schopenhauer said of man: "Where possible he will enjoy everything and hold everything. But when this is impossible, he will at least control everything. 'Everything for myself and nothing for others' is his motto. Egoism is colossal. It towers over the world." [4] Now though Nietzsche despised Schopenhauer for believing rather in a will-to-live than in a will-to-power, this passage from the *Anti-moralische Triebfedern* comes very close to the Nietzschean will-to-power. Nietzsche, as is well known, injected a Satanic toxin into the philosophy of his master, but his chief alteration of the Schopenhauerian will-to-power was to convert it from mere egoism to a cosmic force striving toward a higher species. The Nietzschean hero does not, like the Christian and the humanitarian, live for his fellows. He does not, like the Schopenhauerian, live for himself. He lives for his children.

But this is to anticipate. What must be established forthwith is the state of Nietzsche's mind when he discovered Schopenhauer in 1865. Already he was advancing from boyish ambition and hero-worship to a deeper understanding of the irrational human nature which his predecessors had rediscovered. Fichte had established the primacy of action and, in the light of historical and evolutionary thought, Nietzsche began to think that no living creature would have been preserved if the tendency to affirm had not been cultivated more assiduously than the tendency to suspend judgment, if men had not preferred to mistake and fabricate rather than wait, assent rather than deny, decide rather than be in the right. Schopenhauer had shown that dreams provided imaginal fulfillment of wishes. Nietzsche began to wonder if systems of thought, of morals and valuations, might not equally be a mere offshoot from a physiological stem. Might not metaphysics be a gigantic wish-fulfilling dream? Later in

[4] *Ibid.*, Vol. III, p. 667.

life, Nietzsche regarded consciousness itself as a more or less fantastic commentary on an unknown text. He did not even regard consciousness as a permanent human possession: it was an inessential attribute that might free us from a burden by disappearing. In his early Schopenhauerian days Nietzsche was urged towards thoughts such as these. His career is not a succession of *volte-faces* but has an astonishing continuity.

5

Nietzsche's discovery of Schopenhauer was a preparation for one of the most pregnant episodes in his career: his association with Richard and Cosima Wagner. When he first met Wagner at Leipzig in 1868, Nietzsche had already been delighted by *Tristan und Isolde,* which he had studied in Von Bülow's piano score, yet Wagner won his ascendancy over Nietzsche less by his music (from the first Nietzsche disliked *Tannhäuser, Lohengrin,* and *Die Walküre*) than by his personality. Nietzsche may of course have believed that he was captivated by Wagner's art, by the new music in which subject and object fade into nothingness and the listener is face to face with things in themselves, yet in truth his sister was nearer the mark in her belief that what held Nietzsche was Wagner's tremendous will-power and instinct of command. Wagner, Nietzsche thought for a time, was the highest of higher men and he held the key to a new epoch of art and a new epoch of life.

Fichte believed the irrational promptings of man's mind to be providential and good; Schopenhauer thought they were a part of the blind force of will and evil. Nietzsche combined Schopenhauer's diagnosis with Fichte's judgment of value: he found man's striving to be mere will-to-power but he thought it very good. Wagner was the first and only man personally known to Nietzsche who exemplified the will-to-power and who seemed, in his magnetic grandeur, to be a precursor of the superman.

Who was the Wagner whom Nietzsche knew? He was a composer of considerable years, European reputation, and boundless vanity. In 1864 he had been sent for by King Ludwig of Bavaria and installed at Munich as the leading musician of the country. Owing to his debts, his tricks, his adultery, and other complications, Wagner had to leave Munich two years later with his mistress, Cosima, the illegitimate daughter of Franz Liszt and wife of the conductor, Hans von Bülow. But he had not lost his reputation or his appeal. In the midst of the German crisis of 1866, when the very existence of Bavaria was at stake, King Ludwig ran off to Triebschen, near Lucerne, where Wagner was living, to bring the musician back to Munich. Wagner refused to come. He was on top of the world, but, for the time being, angry with the world. For the first time in his life he showed some inclination to settle down. The Triebschen years were the happiest and most stable of his life.

When Nietzsche first visited Triebschen in 1869, Cosima was eight months pregnant with Wagner's third child, and Wagner was at work on the last act of *Siegfried*. Especially after the birth of the child, his first son, Wagner was at his best before the young man, eloquent, magnetic, utterly self-confident. Many lively hours of animated conversation were spent, but each of the two men was under a misapprehension about the other. Wagner, famous and getting on towards sixty, with most of his composing behind him, regarded Nietzsche as another disciple, a propagandist for the idea of music drama. For Nietzsche, Wagner was by all means an inspiration but an inspiration to his own ends. "Wotan was to resign," one critic has it. "Wagner's music was only matins; Siegfried was heir to the throne; Nietzsche would bring the new image."

In 1871 Nietzsche published *The Birth of Tradegy*, in which he advertised Wagner by way of working out the thoroughly Nietzschean idea of a synthesis of Apollo and Dionysos. Misgivings assailed him. Wagner had tantrums, and Nietzsche blushed at the indignity of it. Could this be the greatness of which he had dreamed? Increasingly Nietzsche saw in Wagner the embodiment of the cultured Philistine for whom bigness was beauty and pomposity greatness, the Reich German who represented the vulgar splendor, crass materialism, and shallow optimism of middle-class Germany.

But Wagner was not alone in the Triebschen villa. Frau Cosima was one of the outstanding women of the age, no George Sand to be sure, but a secondary talent, one whose conscious mission it was to support, guide, even lead, a genius. Biographers differ as to her real nature, yet she was no Mona Lisa but a brisk, managing sort who possessed also in full measure the feminine x which critics describe in such words as Sphinx, Siren, and Dæmon. The uncanny power of Cosima's personality wrought upon the young and inexperienced professor of Greek. There is now little doubt that he loved her, and not with that purely spiritual love which alone his Lutheran sister was prepared to allow him. His love was timid, youthful, secret, and unrequited. It showed itself through the cracks, as repressed love will, in indirect ways, in the disguised mythic form, for instance, which Nietzsche's innermost thoughts not uncommonly assumed. He was in his fantasy the Dionysos who should steal Ariadne-Cosima from Theseus-Wagner. Or Wagner was old Wotan; Cosima, closer to Nietzsche's own age, the young Brünnhilde; Nietzsche himself the hero Siegfried. On the one hand Cosima was to Nietzsche a sinister figure, largely responsible for Wagner's turning to religion later in *Parsifal*; on the other she was the eternal mother and the eternal bride; she had indeed the fascinating ambiguity of Sphinx, Siren, and Dæmon.

In three short years Nietzsche's regular visits to the Wagners came to an end when in 1872 Richard and Cosima left for Bayreuth, where they were to establish their theatre and their shrine. But the Wagners, even more persistently than the ghost of Schopenhauer, pursued Nietzsche all his life long. When he was not under their standard he was doing battle against them. Men do not take the sad path to what is called maturity without continual backward glances at their youth: Nietzsche's nostalgic longing for Triebschen, that "happy isle," is as evident in his outbursts against Wagner as in his early enthusiasm. The first thirty years of Nietzsche's life were an attempt to live down the piety, chauvinism, and small-bourgeois stuffiness of Naumburg; the next twenty were an attempt to escape from his hero-worship of Wagner and his devotion to Cosima. Sometimes, indeed often, the hero-worship and the devotion conflicted and became identified with the great conflict of masculine and feminine that dominated Nietzsche's life. When he despaired of making the egregious Richard into a hero, he had the more solid and maternal Cosima to fall back on.

The climax of the Nietzsche-Wagner relationship had come in 1871 and 1872 when Nietzsche heard a concert of Wagner's own music at Mannheim and Beethoven's *Ninth Symphony* conducted by Wagner at Bayreuth; the catastrophe, preceded by many misgivings and premonitions, came in 1875 and 1876. In the former year Nietzsche infuriated the pathologically jealous maestro by bringing to Triebschen a copy of Brahms's *Triumph-lied,* and but for the intervention of Cosima would have been thrown out. A year later, sick and skeptical, he left Basel for the first Bayreuth Festival, where tragedy was to be reborn from the spirit of music before the eyes of the Kaiser of Germany, the Emperor of Brazil, the King of Bavaria, and a crowd of *Spiess-bürger.* There was much lionizing of the Meister, much philistine chatter and forgathering, much palaver and beer, and no tragedy at all. When a mechanic in his shirt sleeves appeared on the stage instead of Valhalla, which refused to rise, the thing seemed to Nietzsche symbolic of Wagnerism in general. He wept bitter tears and left the festival. Between him and Wagner there was henceforward an unbridgable gap.

Yet Wagner was the one great man Nietzsche ever knew; Cosima, with Lou Salome, the only remarkable woman. The strength of Nietzsche's attachment to Wagner emerges even from the most virulent philippics against him. The depth of Nietzsche's attachment to Cosima emerges even from the record of his insanity. When all the energy and restraint of conscious will had collapsed, he addressed a note of five words of Cosima, whom he had not seen for many years. It read: "Ariadne, ich liebe dich!—Dionysos." Taken to a clinic at Jena, Nietzsche said: "My wife Cosima Wagner brought me here." Had he really shaken off the Wagners as is commonly supposed? Did Saul of Tarsus forget the road to Damascus?

6

"Your brother and his friends," Wagner wrote to Nietzsche's sister, "belong to an absolutely new and wonderful order of men, in the possibility of whose existence I never believed before." Wagner's desire for a new order of manhood found an echo in Nietzsche's heart. Ever since, as a boy, he had belonged to literary clubs, the idea of a community of free spirits solving the great problems of existence grew in Nietzsche's mind. (It was not superseded until the fourth book of *Thus Spake Zarathustra* was written, and Nietzsche resigned himself to complete solitude.) From 1869 to 1879 he occupied a chair at the University of Basel. Naturally, therefore, a large amount of Nietzsche's thought in these years was given to higher education, to the idea of training an *élite* of leaders. He stated his opinion in *Schopenhauer as Educator* and in *The Future of our Educational Institutions.* An association called the Destroyers was proposed for men willing to sacrifice themselves to the discovery of truth. "The bad and the false should see the light of day!" The old edifices were to be destroyed and "we do not know whether it will ever be possible to build." Nietzsche intended to buy a "modern monastery" to house his free spirits. Though he revived this scheme at least once, it was never carried out.

Nietzsche was so embarrassed by his woman's heart that he made the most violent virile protest that has ever been heard. He had the training of an intellectual and sensed his own tendency to suspend judgment rather than affirm, to prefer being in the right to making a decision, to refrain from doing a good thing because he could not do a better. He had imbibed the best that had been thought and said for thousands of years and he felt, with Karl Marx, that the point is less to understand the world than to change it. All the wiseacres since Plato, he realized, had been prolific of blueprints for Utopia. "Until philosophers became kings," Plato had it, "cities would never have any rest": true, but both in the heart and in the head philosophers were unfitted for kingship. In the head was unavailing contemplation and in the heart was compassion. The philosophers had the right answers and their sympathy was Christian enough. But they were futile. Nietzsche felt hampered by intellectual hardness and emotional softness. His intellect was expert at frigid analysis. As to his emotions, they are recognizable enough from the day when he was called the Little Minister to the memorable day at the beginning of his breakdown when, in a flood of tears, Nietzsche flung his arms about the head of a horse under the lash. "I was not born to hate and be an enemy," wrote the archfoe of the whole epoch.

Nietzsche strove to develop his masculinity. In 1866 he had been an ardent supporter of Bismarck's Austrian war. Though in 1870 he was forbidden to fight for the fatherland, since by this time he had had to become a Swiss citizen in order to keep his post at Basel, Nietzsche was eventually allowed to serve as an ambulance-man. It is ironic to think that precisely when he wished to assert his pugnacious spirit in fighting he was permitted only to tend the wounded under the sign of the cross of Jesus. During the war there came to Nietzsche one of those apocalyptic experiences which form the nuclei around which his thought gathered. One day, when his heart was "well-nigh broken with pity," Nietzsche heard behind him the gallop of horses. As he turned, in awe and surprise, to watch the arresting spectacle of charging cavalry, he felt for the first time that "the strongest and highest will to life does not find expression in a miserable struggle for existence but in a will to war, a will to power, a will to overpower." The way this thought emerged is curious. Nietzsche's first reaction was of terror and compassion. Then instead of protesting at the absurdity of the event as a pacifist might or standing aghast and finding the poetry in the pity as Wilfred Owen did, Nietzsche carried his thoughts forward to the exigencies of action. His conclusion was: "What a good thing it is that Wotan lays a hard heart in the breasts of commanding generals, otherwise how could they bear the awful responsibility of sending thousands to death in order to raise their people and themselves to dominion." It is implied that whatever might be thought of pain and death, there is one necessary and overruling good: the will to dominion.

7

Nietzsche's early career had been respectable and successful —probably too much so. To the joy of his family he was given a professorial chair at the age of twenty-four because of the impression he had made on the Leipzig scholar, Friedrich Ritschl. Nor was his middle life, for all its strange episodes, without a solid and prosaic background. At Basel he made three significant contacts with older colleagues. The most celebrated of these was Jacob Burckhardt, author of *The Civilisation of the Renaissance in Italy*; to him Nietzsche owed his conception of Hellenism and especially of the neo-Hellenism of the Renaissance. The palæontologist Ruetimeyer led Nietzsche to reject Darwin in favor of a version of evolution that was not dependent on sheer chance or sheer mechanism. Above all, Nietzsche's housemate, Franz Overbeck, exerted a steadying influence on him and was probably the best friend he ever had. Overbeck was in most respects Nietzsche's opposite. An historian of the church, he kept his disbelief in Christianity a secret from the public; he was a mild and serene skeptic, the only man, perhaps, who could have persuaded Nietzsche to make his criticism of religion substantial, informed, and historical.

Such personal contacts and academic interests compose the sober warp of Nietzsche's life; the woof, however, was a succession of discomforts and disappointments. His troubles had begun in 1868 with a fall from a horse, which resulted in a broken rib and prolonged illness. His military service ended in his contracting dysentery and diphtheria because of his solicitude for his sick charges. In 1871 the publication of *The Birth of Tragedy* lost Nietzsche his chances of professional fame. Attacks on the book bred in Nietzsche the hatred of professors which occupies so large a place in his subsequent writings. (The chief enemies of professors are always other professors.) Nietzsche's professional failure, caused in the first place by the obscurantism of his colleagues and clinched by his continual sickness, effected a change in his hopes. He no longer looked for a higher humanity by means of educational institutions but rather from the independent intellectual. Nietzsche was disappointed in turn by many groups of men. The professors were only the first he despaired of.

The second and most devastating disappointment was over Wagner. "From his early youth," says Frau Foerster, "an ideal, a wonderful, secret, still-veiled ideal, had hovered before my brother. He looked for the ideal leader, one who might bring the type man to a higher stage of perfection. He has tried to mold Democritus, the pre-Socratics, and especially Heraclitus, into the form of his ideal leader. But it was above all in Schopenhauer and Wagner that these lofty aspirations had been centered." That Nietzsche never shared the idealist pessimism of Schopenhauer is evident from the writings of his so-called Schopenhauerian period in which he described pessimism as abhorrent ("Pessimism . . . which nature shuns as truly unnatural") and in which he vindicated a Heraclitean philosophy as he was always to do. But Nietzsche hoped to find in the opposition of Wagner and Schopenhauer to the age, in their aspirations after a new aristocracy, a rallying-point for his own efforts. "For I had had nobody," he laments in *The Case of Wagner*, "but Richard Wagner." Nietzsche's allegiance to Wagner was chiefly personal, not doctrinal, and no man could have lived up to the idea which Nietzsche, in his fervent hero-worship, had formed of his idol. Furthermore, the fact that Nietzsche more than once vainly imagined that his friends would follow the stages of his own development, sharing his fresh enthusiasms and his savage disillusionments, is a larger cause of his repeated disappointment and his final withdrawal from society.

"The lonely Nietzsche"—he had been a studious and solitary child, but the loneliness that followed the comradeship of student life and the early successful years of teaching was an adult, soul-torturing loneliness. In the years 1872-89 Nietzsche drew further and further apart from his fellows until in the end he had to create a mad world of his own to live in.

"What you need," was a doctor's advice to Nietzsche in 1876 "is a nice Italian sweetheart." Nietzsche proposed to a girl he hardly knew as impulsively and foolishly as he had challenged his friend to a duel. He was so much occupied with cosmic problems, according to his sister, that he had a bad memory for everyday occurrences. His mind had not a practical focus: and since he claimed to be so pragmatic, so much in love with action, this fact is significant. Nietzsche's sex life is a brief catalogue of *gaucheries*. He was always defeated and died dreaming of manly grandeur.

The results of Nietzsche's ailments have often been debated; his autobiography, *Ecce Homo*, is our warrant for attaching to sickness the highest importance in literary interpretation. Aside from a broken rib, fever, dysentery, and diphtheria, the decade of the seventies was not survived without continual and agonizing neuralgia. If Carlyle had a rat gnawing at his stomach, Nietzsche had one gnawing at his very brain. He was also nearsighted. Perhaps his progressive withdrawal from society was encouraged by myopia.

8

Nietzsche believed that physical sickness teaches mental health. Suffering is cathartic and convalescence a sort of mental pregnancy. He seems, like so many artists of the nineteenth century, to have manufactured abnormal mental states by the use of drugs. The calms of Nietzsche are the eerie calms of a dream world. His joys are the unearthly joys of the inebriated. They remind one of the periods of euphoria to which victims of tuberculosis are subject.

The feminine side of Nietzsche found its most ecstatic satisfaction in communion with nature. Among Nietzsche's mystical experiences the most celebrated came to him in Switzerland as he stood by the rock of Surlej on the lake of Silvaplana, August,

1881. Exactly what happened on that fateful occasion is not known. We do know that as a result of a visionary experience as decisive as Carlyle's on Leith Walk, Nietzsche conceived the idea of Eternal Recurrence and wrote in his notebook: "Six thousand feet beyond man and time." In such moments Carlyle and Nietzsche overcame their repugnance to human life and uttered an everlasting Yes. An intuition of eternity freed them from the stress of the psychological and historical outlook.

The doctrine of Eternal Recurrence has often, since the Pythagoreans, received serious treatment at the hands of philosophers. In the present context it is chiefly of interest, however, in that it reveals to what curious shifts Nietzsche's feminine nature was driven in its fight with his masculine ambitions. Long before Nietzsche tried to justify the doctrine by argument, he believed in Eternal Recurrence upon mere intuition, upon the promptings, that is, of his religious heart. Throughout the year 1881, as we learn from Nietzsche's letters to Peter Gast, Nietzsche was haunted by a fear that this year might be fatal to him, because all events recur and he had attained the age at which his father died. It is evident that Nietzsche's belief was no mere doctrine of cyclical epochs but a superstitious obsession, an illusion, which in the manner of a paranoiac he built into a system.

That Eternal Recurrence is to be interpreted biographically rather than philosophically is suggested also by a chapter in *Thus Spake Zarathustra*, where it is expounded and, perhaps, connected with the vision at Surlej and the memory of Nietzsche's father. Eleven months before his death, Pastor Nietzsche had met with a fall, and the scene, with a dog howling near by, had impressed itself on the memory of his son. Zarathustra's words, in the chapter—"The Vision and the Enigma"—where Eternal Recurrence is most graphically presented, are as follows: "Did I ever hear a dog howl like this? My memory ran back. Yes. When I was a child, in distant childhood. . . . But there lay a man! And there! The dog leaping, whining, its hair bristling . . . did I ever hear a dog cry for help like this?"

Some months before his death, Pastor Nietzsche stumbled.

Some months before the walk by Silvaplana, Nietzsche had foreseen a crisis. "It was at this age," he wrote to Peter Gast, "that Dante had his vision." The description of the crisis in "The Vision and the Enigma" we may take to be a description of the mystical experience. Nietzsche heard a laughter that was not human laughter and then a thirst gnawed at him, a longing never to be appeased. *"Eine Sehnsucht, die nimmer stille wird"*: cathartic suffering and voracious yearning bear Nietzsche beyond time to eternity. If he could not be superhuman by ruling men with an iron hand, he would be superhuman by escaping from men altogether. If he could not realize his virile dreams of power, he would yield himself like a woman in a trance of mystical joy. It is the paradox of Nietzsche's life that he used the strength he drew from his mystical experiences to further his strivings towards a philosophy of power.

9

It was in 1882 that Nietzsche heard that Malwida von Meysenbug, a rather dubious patroness of the arts who dreamed of founding a small community of the superior, had a new protégée, the daughter of a Russian general: her name was Lou Salome. When Nietzsche met her, an imbroglio ensued which biography has only recently cleared up.

The first version of the episode, that of Nietzsche's sister, was that the charming young Russian—she was twenty-one—set her cap at the chaste, retiring philosopher in whose life passion had no proper part. C. A. Bernoulli, a less *borné* observer, provided a second version: Nietzsche and Lou Salome would have got along well together had not Nietzsche's mind been poisoned against her by his jealous sister. Both these versions make of Nietzsche a purely passive figure, the victim of one scheming woman or the other. Not until both women were in their graves was a fuller version available in E. F. Podach's *Friedrich Nietzsche und Lou Salome*.

Lou Salome, whom we find later taking her friend Rainer Maria Rilke to hear Stefan George read his poems, and whom readers of the youngest generation may know only as the author of *Thanks to Freud* (1931), was in 1882 a callow, clever, earnest, and unusual girl. She had been befriended by a member of the Nietzsche circle, Paul Rée, a young philosopher who was shocking many by his militant positivism. Although in her youthful addiction to virginity she had refused to live with Rée, she did not feel free at any time to give him up for the sake of his extraordinary friend. But Nietzsche seems never to have understood this. He followed her around with dog-like persistence. Utterly fascinated by his intellect, Lou no doubt seemed to give more than she actually intended; and when Nietzsche finally realized that she preferred Rée to him, he was hurt, insulted, enraged, and defeated. Though we cannot follow Bernoulli when he writes: "He [Nietzsche] desired Lou hotly but not of course sensually," we can accept his report when he says: "The disappointment that Lou had not chosen to join her intellect with his, Nietzsche called the greatest of his life." Lou was to have been daughter and disciple as well as wife. She had proved an apt pupil, and Nietzsche snatched at her as at a straw; it was his last attempt at intimate union with a human being.

The first period in which Nietzsche experienced the extremes of joy and misery, hope and despair—namely, his days with Cosima at Triebschen—was formative; the second such period —his capture and loss of Lou Salome—was creative. In both periods Nietzsche was inspired and drawn on by a hero. The name of the first hero was Richard Wagner; of the second, superman. The first hero was alive and successful. The second was an idea. Nietzsche was a personal failure. He failed in health, in his profession, in love. He had no power over men. Within his breast was a conflict which he expressed differently at different times. He strove to unite Dionysos and Apollo, Dionysos and Ariadne, Dionysos and Christ. An offshoot of this struggle of masculine and feminine, the idea of the superman partakes of both halves of Nietzsche's sundered psyche. It is at once a religious aspiration and a plan of *real politik*. Where you expect to find him practical Nietzsche is a dreamer, but where you yourself are most a theoretician you will find Nietzsche remorselessly realistic.

In 1877 Wagner had published the libretto of the opera he was about to compose, *Parsifal.* Nietzsche received a gift copy, and it was clear to him that the masculine mind of Siegfried had in this neo-Buddhistic work been converted to a feminine ideal of purity and compassion. Wagner represented to Nietzsche that part of himself, the feminine, which he wished to exorcise. His vehemence is self-flagellatory. Nietzsche saw *Carmen* at Genoa in 1882 and he felt himself liberated by its fierce paganism from the seductions of Wagnerism. The words of the opera rang in his ears. "Yes, I have killed her, my Carmen, my Carmen, whom I have adored." This, he felt, was the way to cope with adoration. Nietzsche suffered from music, he tells us, as from an open wound.

He had no patience with those who wished to make the crooked straight and the rough places plain. Opposed to all uniformitarianism, he found that the best had its roots in the worst and that joy was the twin of sorrow. The year 1882 must have seemed to him one of his best, uniting, as it did, the joys of music with the sorrows of life. He so far denied his power-craving as to write: "I don't want to be lonely any more. I'll learn to become a man again." But Lou Salome preferred his friend Paul Rée, and Nietzsche lost them both. A support beyond the stings of man and time, a religious solace, however incompatible with political realism, now became an urgent necessity. In his teaching, he would become more harsh. And he would be revenged upon the female intelligentsia whose company he had sought. He would advise a young man: "You are visiting women? Don't forget your whip!"

After a period of deep depression, in which his family feared he would either go mad or kill himself, Nietzsche found confidence and renewal in another Dionysian experience at Rapallo in the mild January of 1883. The story of ecstasy on Portofino mountain, near Rapallo, is told in a poem oddly labeled *Sils-Maria* in print, though the manuscript bears the title *Portofino.*

All at once Nietzsche ceased to act, to think, to be. He was merged with the mountain and the landscape. He became the sea and noon and pure unmeasured time. In the moment of consummation Zarathustra touched him; then passed on.

These apocalyptic years (1882-83) following upon the years of sickness and suffering provided the motive force for all Nietzsche's subsequent writings. A fire had been lit that could be put out only with life itself. Nietzsche has measured for us in his autobiography the temperature of his spiritual furnace. His conception of human and superhuman nature will never be understood except by those who know his conception of inspiration such as his own: "An ecstasy whose frightful tension is occasionally released in a stream of tears. . . . One is completely beside oneself. One is distinctly conscious of countless delicate tremors and thrills down to the very toes . . . an instinct for rhythmic relations. . . . The whole process is in a large measure independent of the will, yet in that tempest one feels free and entirely unconditioned, mighty and godlike. . . ."

10

Upon the loss of his health, his academic chair, and many of his friends, followed the loss of his sister, to whom he was strongly attached, however much hatred mingled with his love. In 1884 Elisabeth became engaged to Bernhard Foerster, whose pan-Germanism and anti-Semitism were alike repellent to Nietzsche. In the following year, the married pair went to colonize Paraguay and Nietzsche never saw his sister again until after the debacle of 1889.

Nietzsche had a talent for friendship, but he was harassed by his inability to find mental equals or even sympathetic admirers. The well-known Hellenist, Erwin Rohde, and the loyal Franz Overbeck had been good friends, but neither could accompany Nietzsche on his journeys to the end of the night. Nor could Nietzsche's Horatio, Peter Gast. The case of Gast proves only that what Nietzsche craved was love, respect, and recognition. In return for these he was willing to confer upon Gast, who was just a third-rate musician, the title of greatness which he in the end denied to Wagner. No other friendship meant so much. The only man who might have given Nietzsche the spiritual companionship he craved was Heinrich von Stein, a brilliant youth who met Nietzsche in 1884. But Stein let Nietzsche know that nothing could be dearer to him than the memory of Wagner. The acquaintance of Nietzsche and Stein was short-lived.

Happiness was despaired of. In the end, according to Nietzsche, a man does not love happiness. He loves only his child and his work. Since Nietzsche's child *was* his work, his affections were focused upon one point. More and more with the years, he felt himself to be a destiny, not a man but a symbol, not a teacher but a portent. He tried completely to identify himself with his message. He taught that the Christian epoch was disintegrating but that a new and glorious epoch would take its place. Therefore, he would himself enact the tragedy of the age in his own head and his own heart. He would disintegrate but he would preach faith and hope in a new gospel. He would be a Dionysos, torn to pieces that there might be more abundant life.

Like Carlyle, Nietzsche felt homeless. "From first to last," says Frau Foerster, "we find the sense of loneliness, of having no home, of being strongly drawn towards Nature; a peculiar musical and lyrical mood, a yearning for sympathetic friends, a painful sense of being cut off from all that men are wont to take delight in, to love, desire, reverence and fear." In the eighties the specter of madness drew nearer with every year that passed. His despair after the Lou Salome affair made Nietzsche in his own eyes a "semi-distracted lunatic," a victim of "megalomania and wounded vanity." His relations with his mother and sister became strained, as Nietzsche dimly realized, perhaps, that they had shaped his affective life until he was unable to adjust himself to other women. He admitted that only a native incapacity for hatred prevented him from hating his own family. During this period of tension his mother was tactless enough to call Nietzsche an insult to his father's grave.

The very thought of his father was a stab. Had he not died too early, leaving his son a prey to women and to feminine ideals,

leaving no masculine vicegerent except a visionary hero? Nietzsche made a resolve to receive no more family letters but broke it
because he lacked the necessary hardness of heart. In the first
two days, however, of his last disastrous malady, inhibitions
disappeared and his terrible pent-up hatred of his mother passed
the censor. This was Nietzsche's last rebellion against the piety
of Naumburg, against the fatherless home, against omnivorous
motherhood and the eternal feminine.

Nietzsche shored up the fragments of a public destiny against
the ruins of his inner self. Every six years, he wrote in the middle
eighties, his life took a step forward, though now it was crumbling
before his eyes. 1870, 1876, 1882—these had been years of renewed effort. A final stage was expected around 1888. From
1870 dated his hopes in the reform of educational institutions,
in a new palace of art, and in Richard Wagner. From 1876
dated his faith in the independent, positivistic, intellectual. By
1882 he took a decisive step away from historical actuality to
the shadowy superman. The step he took in 1888 led to the
asylum.

The final step had been fully prepared. As early as 1883
Nietzsche deliberately removed himself from men, characterizing
his attitude as *Menschenscheu*—shyness of mankind. If a man
is the sum of his social relations, Nietzsche was trying not to be
a man. He kept himself alive not by personal relations but by
a sense of destiny. He was a natural force, the lightning of
Zarathustra. He was borne up by the groundswell of prophetic
indignation. This indignation, like Carlyle's, was essentially
chiliastic. The world would be redeemed, but first at Armageddon
there must be universal destruction. In 1887 he wrote: "in me
a catastrophe is being prepared." Late in 1888 he resolved to
inaugurate the millennium. He worked at a memorandum to
be sent to all European courts. He wrote to August Strindberg:
"I have summoned a council of princes to Rome. I will have
the young Kaiser shot." To Peter Gast he announced: "The
world is transfigured and all the heavens rejoice."

After this high talk the words of the Turin doctor who examined Nietzsche are sadly prosaic: "Maintains that he is a famous

man and asks for women all the time." Sometimes he thought he was Dionysos, sometimes Christ. The choice between the two had even yet not been made. The masculine and the feminine were still at war even when darkness had fallen on the intellect. The fact seems to be a proof of Nietzsche's theory that a man's conscious thoughts are merely a fantastic commentary on his unconscious conflicts.

No German has ever united so powerful an intellect with so fine a sensibility. A born artist and a born prophet, he was not allowed to live his life. Society provided no man to father him, no woman to marry him, no credible God to protect him, no fame to flatter him. A thwarted Samson, he brought down the building on his own head. But others, he gave assurance, would not escape the consequences of living in the modern world. Nietzsche would rather have been a Basel professor than God, would rather have won a woman's love and submitted to a woman's care than have sought out the secrets of heroic power and the mastery of the world. But turning in disgust first from common men, then from the elite, turning from leaders and friends and admirers, turning from mother and sister and sweetheart, turning from his home and his profession, in the end Nietzsche found no chair empty but that of the dispossessed deity, in which a man sits at his peril.[5]

[5] One thinks of D. H. Lawrence. And after I wrote the present book my attention was directed by Kenneth Burke to an analysis of Lawrence that resembles this chapter on Nietzsche much more than it resembles my chapter on Lawrence below. This is William Troy's essay "The D. H. Lawrence Myth," *Partisan Review*, 1938, reprinted in *The Partisan Reader*, 1946. The essay begins with this sentence: "Of the many examples of the artist as 'suffering hero' thrown up by the nineteenth century and afterwards (Blake, Hölderlin, Baudelaire, Wagner, Melville, Van Gogh all belong to the tradition), D. H. Lawrence is perhaps the only one who took the next logical step and identified himself overtly with a mystery god." (Note added in 1957.)

"Dies Lied ist aus, der Sehnsucht süsser Schrei Erstarb im
    Munde:
Ein Zaubrer that's, der Freund zur rechten Stunde,
Der Mittags-Freund—nein! fragt nicht, wer es sei—..
Um Mittag war's, da wurde Eins zu Zwei . . .

"Nun feiern wir, vereinten Siegs gewiss,
    Das Fest der Feste:
Freund Zarathustra kam, der Gast der Gäste!
Nun lacht die Welt, der grosse Vorhang riss,
Die Hochzeit kam für Licht und Finsterniss." [1]
        —NIETZSCHE, *Aus hohen Bergen.*

1

So great is the temptation to use Nietzsche as the cue for one's
favorite lecture on Nazis and proto-Nazis that it will be a salutary exercise to recall, quite simply, what Nietzsche said. One
way of doing this is to comb Nietzsche's works for all the most
aggressive remarks he ever made and then to call the anthology
What Nietzsche Really Meant. It is surely preferable to present
an exegesis of the one book in which the superman is most in
Nietzsche's thoughts. For it is not the force of Nietzsche's remarks
that has been misunderstood but their context and associations.

Thus Spake Zarathustra is built round the twin ideas of the
superman and the Eternal Recurrence. The word *superman*
(*Übermensch*)—by no means a new word in German—was first
used by Nietzsche when he was fourteen to characterize Byron's

[1] "This song is done, the sweet cry of yearning died on the lips: a wizard
made it, the timely friend, the noonday friend—no, ask not who it was—at
noonday it was when one became two.

"Now, confident of our common victory, we celebrate the feast of feasts:
friend Zarathustra came, the guest of guests! The world now laughs, the
great curtain was rent, the marriage of light and darkness took place."

heroes. But to the end his use of the word was elastic: Christian poets have not defined God, nor has Nietzsche defined the superman. *Thus Spake Zarathustra* states the need for a superman by describing European civilization in the nineteenth century. In so far as the book pierces the mists of the future at all it asks: How shall the superman be brought into being?— rather than: What will the superman do, say, and be? On the subject of the superman, Nietzsche's language is at its most figurative. Those who read it in English in order to discover Nietzsche's "Nazism" will find it involved, pretentious, and queer. Translations are the chief hindrance to a sound understanding of Nietzsche, and translations of *Thus Spake Zarathustra* have been outstandingly inadequate.[2]

Like many masterpieces, *Thus Spake Zarathustra* belongs to an art form of which it is the sole example. The lyric chapters recall the Psalms and perhaps also the free verse of Novalis' *Hymns to Night* and the free prose of Rimbaud. Throughout the book there are reminiscences of the *Hyperion* and *Empedokles* of Friedrich Hölderlin, who was Nietzche's favorite poet as a boy, and a major influence on both him and Stefan George. Nietzsche himself described *Thus Spake Zarathustra* as a fifth gospel, and its mingling of philosophy and poetry recalls the fourth. The book, however, is not only a gospel but a countergospel. It contains satire ranging from flickering irony to out-and-out invective. According to Nietzsche, Luther's Bible was the best book in German; his own gospel is an ironical homage to Luther.

The title of the book is based on the Sanskrit *Iti vuttakam,* which means "Thus said the holy one." Zarathustra is the Iranian name of a Persian prophet who is better known by the corrupt Greek denomination of Zoroaster. Out of his love of wisdom, the prophet withdrew to a mountain, and this is one of the few facts known about him which Nietzsche utilized. Nietzsche, who wanted a dancing god, may also have been interested in the fact that, according to Pliny, Zoroaster laughed

---

[2] Until the appearance of *The Viking Portable Nietzsche.* (Note added in 1957.)

the day he was born. But the historical Zoroaster was for Nietzsche a symbol of what he did not believe, a symbol of primordial religion, Indian, Jewish, or Christian. His own Zarathustra on the other hand is a spokesman for a counter-religion.

How did Nietzsche approach his task? He had for a long time toyed with the idea of writing a drama in defense of heroism. Among his notes we find "ideas for a Prometheus" and "Empedocles, a sketch for a drama"; but neither plan got very far. Stefan George maintained later that Nietzsche ought to have written poetry, not polemics, yet, though he was as much a man of poetic imagination as of abstract thought, he always failed in his more literary efforts. Almost all his poetry is second or third rate, and his dramas remain notes and sketches. What did evolve was neither—in a departmental sense—literature nor philosophy but a strange combination of the two, a combination characteristic of a man who could begin a paragraph with lyrical praise of a mountain and end it in philosophic technicalities.

Nietzsche made several plans for *Thus Spake Zarathustra*. The extant version was planned as three books; the fourth, which was later added, was intended as the first of another three. Five plans exist for the two books which were never written. Book six was to end with the death of Zarathustra, an event which in some of the plans is a defeat, in others a triumph. Nietzsche simply did not know how to end the work. So he merely breaks off. It is clear that his conception was much more polemical than tragic, since a tragic dramatist does not leave the death of his hero to be settled later.

It is therefore quite legitimate to seek in *Thus Spake Zarathustra* only aphorisms, or at most individual chapters, without looking for a more general structure. The Decadent School maintained that in their work the larger, classic unity was sacrificed to a finer unity of the page, the paragraph, or the sentence; they have therefore good reason to claim Nietzsche as their own. The structure of *Thus Spake Zarathustra* is not entirely non-existent, as we shall see, but it is very loose and not of much importance.

The story of Nietzsche's book is that Zarathustra, at the age of thirty, went up into the mountains, where he remained for ten years. He then descended to convert the common people to the gospel of superman. But the common people derided him, and Zarathustra withdrew. Zarathustra next attempted to launch his gospel by means of disciples, but this attempt also failed, and in the end, Zarathustra, now white-haired, was left to launch it alone. Such is the main myth. Fused with it is a myth of sun-worship. At the very beginning, Zarathustra prays to the sun before undertaking his mission among men. The consummation of his task is called "the great noontide." It is not reached in the book itself. Nietzsche breaks off the narrative as follows:

" 'This is *my* morning. My day is at hand. Rise, then, rise, thou great noonday!'

"Having said this Zarathustra left his cave, glowing and strong. He was like a morning sun emerging from dark mountains."

Under the sun the proudest creature is the eagle, and the wisest is the serpent. The union of these two, an emblem which D. H. Lawrence later discovered to his great joy in Mexico, is the emblem of Zarathustra. Lawrence, too, connected them with sun-worship. The symbolism is admirably expressive of Heroic Vitalism.

2

If Nietzsche had been judged less by philosophers and more by literary critics, more would have been said before now of his remarkable, if not always successful, imagery.

In the Prologue to *Thus Spake Zarathustra*, Nietzsche tries to create, in a succession of images, a vivid impression of his idea of the superman. Man is a sea, he begins, which reaches its full-tide in superman; he must try not to be the ebb of that great tide. The argument continues: As man is to the ape, so shall superman be to man. The world hitherto has been a dispiriting place; it is impossible to believe in anything that has existed: therefore the meaning that must inhere in this vast creation is in the future, not in man but in superman. Man is half plant and half phantom, a hybrid of the degraded and the unreal. He will have meaning only when his discords are resolved in superman. Man, the metaphor changes yet again, is a polluted stream. The Christian remedy is to eliminate the pollution; but when this is done there is hardly anything left. The true remedy is the superman, who is so large a sea that he can accommodate polluted streams without hurt. The superman, in less figurative language than Nietzsche's, relieves man of his disgust and his boredom, the prime sufferings of the nineteenth-century intelligentsia (Baudelaire and Huysmans come to mind). The superman frees man, on the other hand, from the intellectualism of the positivists of eighteenth-century tradition who forget passionate experience in their prostration before reason, virtue, and happiness. Man, says Zarathustra, should be touched by lightning and inoculated with frenzy. The superman *is* lightning and frenzy. Zarathustra is not the superman. He is the prophet who reminds man that he is not a goal but a rope stretched between beast and superman, a rope over an abyss; the superman is thunder and lightning, Zarathustra a premonitory drop from a thunder-cloud.

The fourth section of the Prologue consists of Zarathustra's beatitudes, beatitudes not of Christianity but of Heroic Vitalism. The Christian is meek and possesses, above all virtues, charity; the Heroic Vitalist is noble and possesses above all virtues, courage. The Christian is humble, compassionate, and untouched by the world; the Heroic Vitalist is proud. If he is generous, it is not through compassion but magnanimity. The heroic chieftain giving of his bounty is not to be equated with Jesus washing the feet of his disciples. Zarathustra, consistently with this philosophy, which is not so far from Carlyle's *Frederick*, recommends despising your fellow men and not having too many virtues. What he adds to his Machiavellianism is a new altruism, altruism on behalf of future generations. The ethics of Zarathustra are based on a hatred of nineteenth-century Christianity and nineteenth-century materialism. The old aristocratic modes of feeling are to be grafted on to the thought of a new evolutionary futurism. This is the way history is moving: towards superman.

The analysis of the age corresponds roughly to Carlyle's. An era is drawing to a tumultuous close and signs of a new era are awaited. The old era is characterized by atrophy and triviality. Man has become analytical, rational, mild, weak; but these diseases will be ended by the searing-iron of war and revolution. Born a generation later than Carlyle, Nietzsche feels a greater need for laying the moral foundation of a new age. He enjoins upon men both the recognition of life's catastrophes and the duty of confidence in the future. Courage involves the frank confrontation of the obscene and the terrible, and also the determination that man shall advance to superman. This idea is advanced in several metaphors. Man, says Zarathustra, must plant the seed of his hopes, fix his goal, launch the arrow of his longing into the unknown region beyond present humanity. Men must have chaos within them, he says, to give birth to the dancing-star of the superman.

When Zarathustra descends to the market-place he finds, as prophets do, that mankind has forgotten its purpose. He fears— we can again follow Nietzsche's own metaphors—that the string of man's bow has forgotten to whirr. He finds the ice of hatred in men's laughter. They prefer to watch a buffoon knocking a tightrope-walker off his rope. Zarathustra knows that man himself is such a tightrope-walker and that a buffoon is causing him to lose balance. Nietzsche has himself suggested that the buffoon is another incarnation of Zarathustra, but he might also be identified with the Last Man of whom Zarathustra speaks. The Last Man is the nineteenth-century intellectual, the only surviving mentor of mankind, himself effete and empty. As spokesman of the people, and especially of the respectable ("the Good and the Just"), the buffoon advises Zarathustra to leave the town. Dragging with him the corpse of the tightrope-walker, which represents defeated mankind, Zarathustra departs. A second stage in Zarathustra's spiritual progress is reached when he leaves the corpse in a hollow tree, gives up hope of converting the people or the respectable and resolves to address himself next to a few select comrades. They will help him to break the old and create the new tables of value. He will show them the rainbow and all the steps to the superman.

In short, the Prologue relates how Nietzsche despairs of our civilization in general but proceeds to seek salvation through the select few.

3

The subject of Part One of *Thus Spake Zarathustra* is the need for regeneration. The opening chapter states in allegorical terms the principle which Nietzsche, in *The Will to Power,* expressed explicitly in these terms: "We would like to recover the pristine purity of the stream of becoming." The official ethics of the West had, according to him, exalted the saint, the anchorite, the ascetic, in a word, abnormality, on the assumption that life itself is involved in guilt. Nietzsche taught that life, for all its agonies, is guiltless, that, contrary to the Pauline view, human nature is innocent. This is not a new doctrine and it might be asked: how then is Nietzsche differing from Rousseau, who also believed in the innocence of human nature and who also asserted that natural innocence was besmirched by the ideas and prejudices of the modern world? In these beliefs, and in the belief that human nature is active and emotional before it is contemplative and intellectual, Nietzsche is the continuator of Rousseau. He differs only in his general contempt for man, which demands superman as counterweight. But this is to anticipate.

Before the spirit can regain its guiltlessness—and all secular philosophies aim at the elimination of Christian "guilt"—it must learn to carry heavy burdens instead of practicing evasion. The idea is expressed in another series of singular images. Having learned to serve and to carry—the office of the camel—it can then learn to give orders and to rule by strength. Through leonine strength, the spirit acquires nobility and freedom. But this is not, as some suppose, the consummation of Zarathustra's ideal. The camel changes to a lion, the lion to a little child. The

lion defeats the dragon *Thou Shalt!* with its defiant affirmation
I will! But new values are the creation of newborn innocence.
Becoming again like a little child—the doctrine seems Christian.
But the evocation of the New Testament is a typical piece of
Nietzschean irony. The innocence for which Zarathustra strives
is not abstinence from evil, an abstinence based on the axiom:
who touches pitch shall be defiled. Zarathustra teaches that
there is no defilement in pitch and that the child knows this.
So-called "Evil" is necessary. Like Jesus, Zarathustra is tempted
to swerve from his path. His despondency is represented by
the youth on the hill ("The Tree on the Hill"). The hard
realization for the youth is that he must have hope and yet
plunge into evil without misgiving: "Yes, into evil!" The phrase
die Unschuld des Werdens ("the innocence of becoming")
implies acceptance of the world, without bitterness, without
recoiling from horror, without supernatural consolation, yet in
a tragic, or not even a tragic, but only a solemn, spirit. Nietzsche's
belief in the superman is extreme optimism; his "tragic acceptance" is very close to the pessimism of Richard Wagner's *Ring,*
which is the classic defense of the "innocence of becoming,"
symbolized by the Rhine. Extreme optimism is closer to extreme pessimism than it is to any intermediate view.

So Zarathustra plunges into our evil world. He observes the
professors whose god is sleep, the backwoodsmen of the mind
lost in thickets of theistic superstition, ascetics who turn from
mother earth and from their own bodies, cowards sterilized by
their refusal of struggle, pietists insulated by their fear of evil,
the respectable hidden behind cardboard walls of fantasy.
All—to Zarathustra—is weakness, abnegation, and avoidance.
There are preachers but they preach death: "Life is suffering,"
"Giving birth is too much trouble," "Pity is necessary. I yield."
There are worshipers but they worship the State and its venal
bureaucracy. There are "leaders" and "great men" but they are
demagogues, busybodies, and careerists. There are moralists
but their outward propriety conceals inner filth. All are dissatisfied with life and hostile to heroic activity. At the antipodes
of Heroic Vitalism they represent *Gemütlichkeit,* stagnation, and

anæsthesia. Their sympathy is weak because they are incapable of enmity. They try to smooth all things into one thing. Their women are null because they strive to be like men. Their leaders are futile because they take their cue from the led. If they fight it is always for a sacred cause.

Against this mode of behavior Zarathustra makes a perfectly serious point. It is an empirical fact that men fight and especially in ages of achievement like the Renaissance. That they fight for sacred causes is not an empirical fact. "You say: the good cause sanctifies war. I tell you: the good war sanctifies every cause." Of what use would it be, in the world revealed by Western history, to turn the other cheek? The enemy, according to Nietzsche, would only be abashed. Be angry, says Zarathustra, and he will understand. Vindicate heroic life by denying that he has hurt you. Let the serpent that has bitten you crawl back and lick the wound.

Life, as history and evolution reveal it, is justified only by its occasional nobility and grandeur. The continuance of life is justified only by increased nobility, with its corollaries of courage as the prime virtue and recognition of difference between sexes and individuals. Life has been prosaic and monotonous. It must become poetic and varied. Love itself—this is the gist of Nietzsche—will surpass the spiritual adoration of the romanticists, the intellectual companionship of the rationalists, and the sterile sensuality of the birth-controllers, for love will be a generous yearning for the superman. The sorrow of the judge passing sentence, the friendship of man for man, must be love— so Nietzsche concludes—for the superman.

All of which is brilliant reasoning. But just as we found that Carlyle would follow up brilliant criticism of his age with the most outrageous conclusions, so we find that Nietzsche has, by his trenchant criticisms of life, led us into two tacit assumptions: first, the assumption that the doctrine of progress, which he claims to despise, is really true on an infinitely bigger scale than the previous apostles of progress had ever dreamed, since man is to progress to superman; second, that the human ideal is "the complete man" who has all experiences and includes everything in himself. The superstition of the Whole had been the constant idol of the metaphysicians whom Nietzsche rejected, yet he preaches it himself—with a difference. The complete man of earlier traditions was replete with virtues; Nietzsche wants to have the vices too. That is indeed the crux of Nietzscheanism. What Catholics say of Rousseau, that in countenancing the instincts he approves evil, is untrue of Rousseau, but true of Nietzsche, whose naturalistic ethics are vitiated by his utterly religious view of nature. In this respect he should be linked not with Rousseau but with Baudelaire. The Catholics maintain that on the purely human level there is no way of distinguishing the divine from the dæmonic. One need not agree with them. One need not even accept their categories. But Nietzsche and Baudelaire accepted their categories and agreed with them. *Thus Spake Zarathustra* and *The Flowers of Evil* are the result.

4

Part One describes the unregenerate world and announces the need for regeneration. Part Two describes Zarathustra's struggles and temptations at his present level of understanding. He is now a conscious aristocrat speaking to aristocrats. Yet, though the camel has become a lion, Zarathustra feels ("The stillest hour") that he lacks the lion's voice of command. His terrible mistress, "the stillest hour," informs him that the voice of command will come only when he loses all sense of shame and becomes like a little child. This final metamorphosis Zarathustra refuses as yet to attempt.

The troubles of Zarathustra are presented in two extraordinary dreams. In the first ("The Child with the Mirror") a child shows Zarathustra his face in the mirror of public opinion. Appalled at the misrepresentations of his doctrine, Zarathustra returns to the society of his friends. None saw more clearly than Nietzsche that his philosophy, though not confused or involved, would meet with misinterpretation. Hence the subtitle of *Thus Spake Zarathustra: Ein Buch für Alle und Keinen* ("A Book for All and None").

Zarathustra's second dream ("The Soothsayer") is hard to decipher. He dreams that he is a guard in the mountain-fortress of Death, along with three women, Midnight-brightness, Loneliness, and Death-rattle Stillness. When a prolonged silence is at length interrupted by a thunderous noise at the gate of the fortress, Zarathustra hurries to the gate to admit the new corpse. But he cannot open the gate. Then a roaring wind tears the gate open, and a coffin is whirled into the fortress amid peals of laughter. Zarathustra sees the caricatured forms of children, angels, owls, fools, and butterflies as large as children, mocking and shouting at him. He is awakened by fright. The disciple whom he loves most (another Biblical touch) interprets the mockery to be Zarathustra scoffing at death; but the prophet gazes in his face and shakes his head. What then is the true interpretation which Nietzsche does not supply? Before dreaming, Zarathustra had been listening to the words of the nihilistic Soothsayer (Schopenhauer), words that recall the pessimistic book of *Eccleciastes*. After the dream, he calls the soothsayer to sup with him in order to "show him a sea to drown himself in." The dream itself, therefore, probably expresses the doubts, planted in Nietzsche's mind by Schopenhauer, as to the truth of his own gospel of superman. The kingdom of death is the world of Schopenhauer. Nietzsche stands in this Schopenhauerian world, his own body appears in a coffin, and his images of strange new forms of being seem no more than stage properties, angels, owls, and fools.

The two dreams are cryptic confessions of Nietzsche's two deepest misgivings, each of which opens our eyes to his complexity and his greatness. One is the feeling that his work would be misunderstood. Nietzsche's strange style—grotesque in *Thus Spake Zarathustra*, disjointed and ejaculatory in his later works—reflects the difficulty he, like some other great teachers, faced in having to communicate what was not yet communicable. The other misgiving, which it is natural he should shroud in symbolism, is the astonishing suspicion: Perhaps my gospel is false! By his own implication Nietzsche is not a theologian but an explorer. In his company we discover unfamiliar and amazing regions; also pitfalls, deserts, and swamps.

In Part One, Zarathustra overcomes the respectable and the religious. In Part Two, he fights more distinctly modern enemies: the "rabble" and their spokesmen, the democrats. The argument of Heroic Vitalism against democrats is that they have what Spengler calls the frog's perspective; they believe in equality and thus in the masses; in breaking down barriers and identifying the leaders and the led. The Heroic Vitalist always wastes many words attacking the belief that all men are equal, being ignorant, apparently, of the democratic doctrine—clearly enunciated by Locke in the seventeenth century—that all should be regarded as equal *under the law,* unequal as their talents may well be. The fear of radicals as destroyers comes strangely from an arch-destroyer like Nietzsche, yet this fear is typical of the destructive anti-democratic intellectual. The assumption that there are two essentially different kinds of people, the leaders and the led, we have already found in Carlyle; we would find it in every Heroic Vitalist; and we are far from convinced by the analogy of a ship which cannot round Cape Horn, says Carlyle in the *Latter-Day Pamphlets,* without a rigid division of function and status as between commanders and obeyers.

Nietzsche makes such points, as Carlyle had before him and as D. H. Lawrence would after him; Lawrence's doctrine that power is good but that Communism is anti-power is pure Nietzsche. The Heroic view, in Nietzsche's view as in Carlyle's, is that democracy is pusillanimous and ignoble; it levels and belittles where the Heroic Vitalist seeks to differentiate and enlarge; its aim is destruction of authority, redistribution of material goods, and a petty happiness. Heroic Vitalism proclaims an end to economic man, a beginning of tragic man. The liberal democrat of the old positivist school believes that man is good and that the universe is mere matter in motion; the Heroic Vitalist believes that the great man is noble and that the heart of the earth is of gold ("Great Events"). These are the lessons which Nietzsche preaches through the primordial image of the descent to the underworld. The underworld where Zarathustra meets the revolutionary Fire-dog (a clever inversion of a Water-dog in the story of Zoroaster) is a volcano.

The volcano story enables Nietzsche to combine with an attack on revolutionism one of the positive points of Heroic Vitalism. To the amazement of the onlookers Zarathustra *flew* to the volcano. The feat symbolizes the emancipation of Nietzsche from the force of gravity. Gravity (*Schwere*) means either dull seriousness (for Nietzsche the Devil was "the spirit of gravity") or the attraction of matter towards the center of the earth. It is characteristic of his thought that he thinks of gravity—especially in "The Vision and the Enigma" (Part Three)—as at once physics and psychology: he was eager, for instance, to support his psychological hypothesis of the will-to-power by the animistic physics of the contemporary scientist, J. C. F. Zoellner.[3] Zarathustra's immunity from the force of gravity is prelusive of his immunity, stressed in Part Three, from the injuries of time. *Thus Spake Zarathustra* becomes progressively more subjective, by which is meant not only more autobiographical but more relevant to the individual and the discipline of the self than to politics. Hence the doctrine of Eternal Recurrence, which was a poultice to Nietzsche's tender heart rather than a necessary part of his social doctrine, is reserved for the last two books. The chief doctrine enunciated in Part Two ("Self-Surpassing") is that whoever cannot obey is commanded; that commanding is more difficult than executing; and that life is not will-to-survival but will-to-power.

The doctrines of Part Two are a more than Carlylean jumble of acuteness and perversity. On the positive side, there is the realism that demands leaders as well as followers, the high purpose that derides mechanical materialism, the aristocratic taste which cannot ignore the vulgarities of the modern world. On the negative side, there is the hasty conclusion that socialist or democratic ideas mean destruction of authority as such, that the happiness of the people must necessarily be a petty happiness,

[3] Author of *Über die Natur der Kometen*. Leipzig, 1871. See Charles Andler: *Nietzsche, sa Vie et sa Pensée*. Paris, 1920-31, Vol. II, p. 315ff.

that redistribution of property must be purely "material" and external in its consequences, that the only alternative to Darwinian fatalism is dæmonic assertiveness.

5

In Part Three, the chief teachings of Zarathustra are reviewed, especially in the chapter called "Old and New Tables." Increasingly, as the book progresses, Nietzsche turns from particular satires on decadence to his own spiritual problems. The devil which he calls the Spirit of Gravity has created constraint, law, necessity, consequence, purpose, will, good and evil, above all Time, and the problem is to get on the other side (*jenseits*) of all of them. How Heroic Vitalism attacks the problem of Time we have seen in the case of Carlyle. Nietzsche's arguments are substantially the same. The pattern of all experience is not monotonous happiness but ebb and flow, exhaustion and renewal, systole and diastole. The pattern of all life is one of birth, growth, and decay, the pattern of the seasons. The first of these two principles is implicit in all Nietzsche's poetical chapters in *Thus Spake Zarathustra,* the second is stated by the animals in "The Convalescent." Heroic Vitalists from Carlyle to Spengler insist not only on the image of the seasons as an historical principle (as they insist on the image of the ship or the army as a symbol of class structure), to this cyclical theory of evolution they add another image which we have noted in *Sartor Resartus:* that of the phœnix. For them evolution, individual and social, is saltatory. In "The Way of the Creating One" (Part One) Nietzsche tells the creative genius, whose experience corresponds to the social process, that he cannot be renewed without first burning in his own flame. This phœnix-principle is restated in Part Three. Zarathustra surveys the great city which dominates our culture (the Megalopolis of Spengler) and reflects that the great noontide must be preceded by the consuming of the city in pillars of fire. The image changes, though the idea remains, in the eighth of the Old and New Tables. Sleepers and loungers by the fireside, says Nietzsche, believe in permanency when, for the winter season, the land is ice-bound; but in spring comes a thawing wind and the "permanent" gangways and railings are swept away. Spring is a furious bullock with angry horns; and spring is the prototype of all renewal.

So far Nietzsche's theory is objective and might conceivably be part of a social program. But there is a subjective side to the theory of time, which is not only separable from the objective side but incompatible with it. In fact this subjective side, the theory of Eternal Recurrence, represents the feminine and religious side of Nietzsche's mind as the power philosophy represents the masculine and secular side. The ambivalence of the religious longing for immortality and the worldly longing for success is the same as Carlyle's. The philosophy of Heroic Vitalism is the product of the worldly longing, the historical imagination, the evolutionary appetite, yet, though Heroic Vitalism takes over some of the affects of religion, there has often been in Heroic Vitalists an urge to escape from the consequences of living in the inexorable time-sequence of history, an attempt to escape the dog-fight of natural selection. This urge finds expression in a doctrine of immortality.

The poetic statements of the doctrine of Eternal Recurrence which occur in *This Spake Zarathustra* are probably more valuable than the philosophic statements of *The Will to Power*. Zarathustra climbs a mountain, which is for him, as for Wordsworth, a symbol of maternity, and its height represents freedom from earth and from gravity. As he climbs, a dwarf, speaking for the defeatist nihilism that always lies in wait for him, reminds him mockingly that every thrown stone must fall. This time Zarathustra demonstrates his emancipation from gravity not by the simple gesture of flying but by a parable of Eternal Recurrence. The dwarf has the necessary knowledge (necessary to Heroic Vitalism and objective, masculine thought) that truth is crooked and that time itself is a circle, but the circle is an iron ring and a fetter to Zarathustra. Where a road passes under a portal, it stretches to infinity behind and on to infinity in front. The portal is This Moment. If there is an infinity of time behind the portal of This Moment and an infinity in front, must not everything have already happened an infinity of times and will not everything happen another infinity of times? (The assumption is of course that matter is finite.) Zarathustra sees a young man—and Nietzsche subsequently admits that he is a projection of Zarathustra himself—into whose mouth a snake has crept. The snake is historical time and no amount of manipulation can loosen its grip. There is one way to break free. The youth must bite off the snake's head. When he does so, he hears an unearthly laughter, feels an unquenchable thirst, and knows that he cannot bear to die.

At one or two points, Nietzsche links Eternal Recurrence to Heroic Vitalism. Men are supposed to do only such things as may well be done an infinite number of times (though since they have already done these things an infinite number of times the incentive to resolution must be slight); the conquest of death is supposed to be a supreme act of courage, for courage says: "So that was life? Very well: repeat the performance" ("The Vision and the Enigma"); the cyclical account of history is merged ("The Convalescent") in the doctrine, dear to the nineteenth century, to Shelley, to Yeats, of the Great Year. The Great Year is the period, in the cosmology of Heraclitus, which elapses before the seven planets again find themselves in the same signs as they were in when it began, a period sometimes estimated at 10,800 years. The commencement of a new Great Year is an idea which has appealed to the chiliastic imagination of the poets.

Critics have made very little of Carlyle's "empire of silence" and Nietzsche's "terrible mistress," the Stillest Hour. It is not simply a matter of loneliness. It is not simply a belief that great things happen without *éclat.* In silent meditation, in the intuition of eternity, they find a refuge from their visions of harsh historical reality, a refuge which perfect sexual union might have equally well supplied. For if the hero is a substitute for God and the father, the consolatory belief in Eternity (not personal immortality, but just the Infinite) is a substitute for Our Lady and the mother. The involuntary happiness, more than Benthamite happiness, that comes to Zarathustra ("Involuntary

Bliss") comes because, he says, he does not run after women. "Happiness, however, is a woman," and apparently an adequate substitute for all others.

The Heroic Vitalist seeks power and pretends, before the world, to be self-reliant, but he keeps a secret mistress and finds fulfillment in mystical experience:

"O how should I not lust after Eternity and after the wedding-ring of rings—the ring of the Return?

"I have never yet found the woman by whom I should like to have children unless it be this woman whom I love: for I love you, O Eternity. For I love you, O Eternity!" ("The Seven Seals").

6

In Part Four the spiritual progress of Zarathustra enters upon two further stages. The first is comradeship, the second, solitude. In the Prologue, Zarathustra had appealed to the populace and had made friends with a corpse; in the first three parts, we continually hear of disciples; in the fourth book, Zarathustra proceeds towards mastery of the world by the selection of suitable comrades. These comrades are Higher Men, the best of the old order, the only men who provide a hint of the superman. They consist of the soothsayer (Schopenhauer); two kings sick of the vulgarity (*"ach!* loathing, loathing, loathing!") which makes the meanest into rulers; a scientist who stands with the Nietzsche of "The Gay Science" for sincerity of spirit, for determination to press ruthless investigations despite the ravages of bloodsuckers; a musical magician (Richard Wagner) who preaches penitence in perfervid accents, but in the end confesses that he is not great; the last Pope, who is out of service, because he knows that, after a period of vindictive harshness (the Old Testament), God has become weary of will and weary of the world and has at length suffocated from excessive compassion; the ugliest man, ugly because it was he—the atheist—who murdered the God whose interloping and pity had become intolerable to man, ugly because he is a despiser and an outcast; a voluntary beggar, who is part-Buddha (he has discarded riches) and part-Jesus (*der Berg-Prediger*), an aristocrat of the spirit, driven by loathing of plebeianism and plebeianized rulers ("plebs above, plebs below") to leave mankind for the sacred kine. Is it possible that Nietzsche had in mind Tolstoy? Part Four of *Thus Spake Zarathustra* was written in 1885; Tolstoy's *Confession* had been published, though in Russian, in 1884, and in the same year Tolstoyism had become an organized sect. (However this may be, the Heroic Vitalist's wrath at Tolstoy is patent enough in the final page of D. H. Lawrence's *Fantasia of the Unconscious.*) The last of Zarathustra's guests is his own Shadow, a puzzling character who seems to signify the personal fret and frustration which dog Zarathustra as he pursues his noble aims.

The story of Part Four is simple enough. Zarathustra assembles the guests in his cave. Having played the part of Moses with his tables (Part Three), he soon is in the position of Moses finding the Israelites worshiping the golden calf. For the calf Nietzsche characteristically substitutes the ass, and from Moses the ironic allusion crosses to Jesus. Watching the Higher Men reveling at the ass-festival (based on the *festum asinorum,* at which the congregation responded with cries of *I-a*), Zarathustra thinks how right Jesus was when he said: Except you become as little children you shall not enter the Kingdom of heaven. "But we do not in the least wish for the Kingdom of heaven. We have become men. Therefore it is the Kingdom of earth that we wish for" ("The Ass Festival"). Higher Men are only less inadequate than the populace, the buffoon, and the corpse. In the end, when they see Zarathustra with the lion and the encircling doves, symbols of the new day, they flee in terror. Without reluctance Zarathustra resigns himself to labor quite alone. Fellow-suffering with the Higher Men is the last infirmity of noble mind.

"'Very well. The lion has come, my children are near, Zarathustra has grown ripe, my hour has come.

"'This is *my* morning, my day is at hand. Rise, then, rise, thou great noonday!'

"Having said this Zarathustra left his cave, glowing and strong. He was like a morning sun emerging from dark mountains" ("The Sign").

The symbolism of this final passage is both complex and magnificent. In the phrase "the lion has come, my children are near," there is a hint that, having earlier turned from camel to lion, Zarathustra is now to experience the final metamorphosis into a child. Children are also a symbol for Zarathustra's achievements and thus for Nietzsche's works: in *Ecce Homo*, Nietzsche speaks of the time when he composed *Thus Spake Zarathustra* as a period of gestation. Zarathustra is, on the one hand, mother and life-giver; on the other, he is the child that is born.

The cave is a common symbol of the creative womb of the mother. Nietzsche's use of the symbol is significant. Zarathustra says: "My cave is large and deep and contains many nooks and crannies. There the man who is most hidden finds his hiding-place" ("The Ugliest Man"). The cave of Zarathustra is primarily the creative mind of Nietzsche. The womb of his genius is impregnated by the genius of Schopenhauer and Wagner, by all the Higher Men of the past. Only miscarriages result. The fact that Zarathustra is left alone at the close symbolizes the failure of Nietzsche to join in fruitful union sperm and ovary, male and female, a failure already illustrated. The womb is a constantly recurring image in the fantasies of those who, in their desolation and homelessness, yearn for the primordial repose of the embryo. *Thus Spake Zarathustra* grows steadily more subjective in that this regressive fantasy, alongside the marriage-surrogate of Eternal Recurrence, occupies more and more space as the work proceeds.

7

Thus Spake Zarathustra is not an unequivocal exposition of Heroic Vitalism. It is an honest presentation of ambivalence in the mind of one Heroic Vitalist, of his divided aims, of the struggle not finally resolved, between masculine and feminine. (In this it is similar to Carlyle's *Heroes*. Odd that Carlyle and Nietzsche should be best known by their most ambiguous works.) The philosophy of the Heroic Vitalists with all its hard realism might be characterized as masculine. The longing for felicity, repose, return to the womb, immersion in eternity, mystical communion with nature might be characterized as feminine. It may be worth noting that Nietzsche was always splitting himself into two. He is Zarathustra and he is Zarathustra's interlocutor at "the tree on the hill." He is Zarathustra and he is the man whom Zarathustra sees attacked by a snake. Zarathustra says later ("The Convalescent") "—und wie jenes Untier *mir* in den Schlund kroch und *mich* würgte! Ach *ich* biss ihm den Kopf ab. . . ." [4] Zarathustra converses with his own soul, with his Stillest Hour, and with his shadow. Appended to *Beyond Good and Evil*, there is a poem called *Aus Hohen Bergen* ("From High Mountains") in which Nietzsche speaks of the midday and the midday friend:

> *The noonday friend—no, do not ask me who.*
> *It was at noon, when one turned into two. . . .*

The poem ends with a wedding feast; when Zarathustra, the guest of guests arrives, light and dark are married. All this may be far from clear in detail, but it is clear at least that, while in Nietzsche's mind one becomes as two, Zarathustra turns duality into unity. In short, Nietzsche's was a divided mind, but Zarathustra is the symbol of his striving for unity. Since, however, Nietzsche did not see his way to a synthesis, when he had pushed Zarathustra out of the market place, out of the company of his disciples, friends, and higher men, out of this world into the ring of Eternal Recurrence, there he had to leave him, unless the ambiguity of the whole scheme were to be unveiled. After a fashion, then, the work is finished. Nietzsche's homelessness, at least, is carried to a conclusion.

Thus Spake Zarathustra is conceived to make you long, if you are an heroic soul, for the superman. But exactly what are you to long for and with how much confidence? You are

---

[4] "—how that monster crept into *my* throat and strangled *me!* And *I* bit off its head. . . ." (My italics.)

to wish yourself into the world, into the seat of power, into the main stream of history, and you are to wish yourself out of the world, into the seat of mystical bliss, out of history altogether. You are to be Cesare Borgia and Buddha at the same time. In this implied proposal of Nietzsche's lies the chief contradiction in his personality, a very similar contradiction to that in Carlyle's. If Nietzsche is Zarathustra then Part Four of *Thus Spake Zarathustra* means that nobody but Nietzsche can work towards superhumanity; and a solitary individual, even if he be Nietzsche, cannot procreate. This is one conclusion. But if Zarathustra is also a symbol of the unity of masculine and feminine, dark and light, history and religion, Heroic Vitalism and Mysticism, then the book is an exhortation to effect an impossible marriage. In Nietzsche's refusal to admit that to be hyper-mystical and hyper-mundane is to try to move in two directions at once, there is a hint of his failure to define the role of thought, such as his own, in history. It will be said that Nietzsche declared emphatically that the creator of values is the ruler of the world. This is true. But he never explained the position of the creative philosopher *vis à vis* Cæsar. Had Nietzsche taken over Carlyle's unsubstantiated belief that great men are great in any direction in which the wind blows? Carlyle sometimes regarded the writer as the director of men's destinies. At other times, Cæsar won his unqualified adulation. Nietzsche is equally undecided. Zarathustra praises cruelty, struggle, and worldliness, all as a prelude to a prayer-meeting with the animals. Can any amount of interpretation remove the dubiety which the two-sidedness of *Thus Spake Zarathustra* sets up in the mind?

In Nietzsche-criticism there have been two traditions. The one, consisting of German militarists and Germanophobes, sees only the masculine Nietzsche in whom the German militarist rejoices and against whom the Germanophobe inveighs. The other, consisting of generous—over-generous—souls, sees only the feminine Nietzsche, the pathetic invalid who sought a purely personal, purely spiritual, and entirely harmless freedom. *Thus Spake Zarathustra* is Nietzsche's greatest work because it is his most heroic attempt to unite the dark hero and the fair goddess.

All of Nietzsche is in this book. "I know both sides," he announced on the first page of *Ecce Homo*, "because I am both sides." It is important not to overlook either side, for to do so is to overlook the struggle for impossible union which is Nietzsche's life, the life of his will, his heart, and his intellect, the life of a private individual seeking happiness and of a public destiny seeking fulfilment.

CHAPTER VI

The Philosopher of Heroism

"For everything now awaits the man of action who strips from
himself and from others habits which have lasted thousands of
years and sets a better example for posterity to follow."

—NIETZSCHE.

1

Outside Germany, Nietzsche has not had his due, because
those who soften his teaching blunt its cutting edge and
therefore defeat its purpose, while those who see nothing in
Nietzsche but brutality are undone by their own indignation.
The "soft" school of critics has not recognized the importance of
Heroic Vitalism in the modern world. The "hard" critics, if
German, are too rhapsodic; if Germanophobe, too prone to
sarcasms and debating points. There are some who consider
Nietzsche brilliant but erratic and, therefore, not to be taken
seriously. Nietzsche is so "abnormal" and the critic is so "normal" that the latter has little difficulty in proving his own
superiority. The philistine's impression that there is nothing in
Nietzsche but a string of random *aperçus* is all but confirmed by
the widely accepted view that Nietzsche made radical changes
in his philosophy according to the books he happened to be
reading at the moment; that there is no Nietzschean philosophy
but only a series of Nietzschean philosophies, all intriguing and
none serious. Nietzsche is now a Schopenhauerian, now a
positivist, now a creative evolutionist. It is possible to spend
more time dividing up Nietzsche into periods than discussing what
he had to say.

There are, doubtless, many convenient ways of parceling up
the works of Nietzsche, but the chronological division is one
of the most misleading. Instead, two dichotomies might be
proposed as aids to the understanding of his total achievement.

The first is the one which has been proposed in the two preceding chapters, the dichotomy of the masculine and the feminine, which, on the plane of philosophy, is the opposition, very marked in Carlyle, between an Heraclitean power-philosophy[1] and a poetic mysticism. The second dichotomy is that between the published and unpublished works of Nietzsche, that is, between the works he himself prepared for the press and the notes which executors published after his death.

This second dichotomy requires some explanation. It is not factitious. The published works were campaigns in a war against the age, campaigns in which Nietzsche would use any weapon, mystical or Heroic Vitalist, in the struggle against the old ideologies, radical and reactionary. The published works were propaganda, pamphlets designed to make enemies and influence people; the most systematic of Nietzsche's published works, *The Genealogy of Morals*, is subtitled "a polemic." One of the chief devices of warfare is camouflage, and in this department Nietzsche was so far a master that the kind of people he despised are still taken in. Where the soldier speaks of erecting camouflage, Nietzsche, in artistic metaphor, speaks of a foreground (*Vordergrund*) which conceals the more significant background from vulgar eyes. Or, Nietzsche adds in *The Will to Power*, the writer may be said to wear a mask: it would never do for his face to be visible to the uninitiated. "We take over accidental positions (compare Goethe and Stendhal) and our own experiences as 'foreground' and underscore them so that we deceive ourselves concerning our 'backgrounds.' . . . All strength is devoted to the development of strength of will, an act which allows us to wear masks."

Ever ready to regard himself as a duality, Nietzsche was particularly fond of regarding himself as a face covered by a mask, as a background obscured behind a foreground. Interpretation enters into discussion as soon as one tries to say which

[1] Twenty-five centuries before Nietzsche, Heraclitus wrote: "Men should know that war is general and that justice is strife. Good and bad are the same. War is the father of all and king of all; and some he has made gods and some men, some slaves and some free. To me one man is ten thousand if he be the best." (Dicta, 62, 57, 44, 113.)

is face and which is mask in Nietzsche's work. The implication
of Germanophobe criticism is that Nietzsche's religiousness is
mask, his militarism the hidden reality. The "soft" critic, on
the other hand, regards Nietzsche's harsh masculinity as mask,
his tender woman's heart as the hidden reality. This was the view
of Frau Foerster whose explanation of Nietzsche's character is
summed up in these verses of his:

> Dass sein Glück uns nicht bedrücke
> Legt er um sich Teufelsstücke,
> Teufelswitz und Teufelskleid.
> Doch Umsonst! Aus seinem Blicke
> Blickt hervor die Heiligkeit.[2]

Frau Foerster thinks the philosophy of Heroic Vitalism is a
trick played by her brother in order that we should not be embarrassed at his holy joy. In support of this "soft" criticism, she
might have urged that Nietzsche hated anti-Semites, hated the
Kaiser, hated Bismarck (off and on), hated the Reich, hated
patrioteering (Vaterländerei), hated the apotheosis of the state.

Those, however, who have agreed that in Nietzsche the masculine and feminine were in constant collision will not want to make
our two dichotomies into one by calling the masculine element a
mask and the feminine a face, or *vice versa*. The mask was a
wholly conscious device, whereas the struggle of masculine and
feminine was seldom conscious at all. It was not because his
message was too soft or too hard that Nietzsche wore a mask, but
because it came too early (he was one of those, he said, who are
born posthumously) and because it was not intended for the
vulgar.

> Wer sich einst zu verkünden hat,
> Schweigt viel in sich hinein.
> Wer einst den Blitz zu zünden hat,
> Muss lange—Wolke sein.[3]

[2] "Lest his joy should distress us he puts on devil's things, devil's wit and
devil's clothes. But in vain! From his eyes holiness shines forth."

[3] Quoted by Alfred Rosenberg, *Der Mythus des 20. Jahrhunderts.* München, 1934, p. 423. "Who has one day to speak keeps much locked in his

The tendency of the creator of new values to hide behind the mask of parable should be familiar.

Zarathustra was a simple mask for Nietzsche himself. Dionysos was not so easy a proposition: this mask was more like a shirt of Nessus. The last mask that Nietzsche tried on was that of Jesus Christ, but by this time the face behind the mask was glazed with insanity. These are only the most celebrated and most obvious of Nietzsche's masks. In truth, when, in the early campaigns, Nietzsche sheltered behind the name of Wagner, the great musician was just as much a mask as Zarathustra. Naturally Wagner soon began to feel that he was a stalking-horse, under cover of which Nietzsche was shooting very strange barbs; and since Nietzsche could never understand why Wagner should not enjoy being a stalking-horse, estrangement followed. Schopenhauer was another mask and Nietzsche's use of his name is best expressed by the note in the *Ecce Homo:* "Schopenhauer and Wagner, or—in a word—Nietzsche."

In his published works, Nietzsche wore a mask which only the discerning could pierce. It is possible to see Nietzsche without his mask only in the various collections of posthumously published notes which comprise Volumes IX to XVI of the collected German edition and of which *The Will to Power* is the only well-known extract.[4] These notes not only provide more direct statements of Nietzsche's philosophy: they enable us to discredit the division of Nietzsche's career into three philosophies (involving two *voltefaces*) and to establish not merely continuity but consistency throughout Nietzsche's literary life. It is no praise of a man that he never changed an opinion—Nietzsche did change many opinions—but the main principles of the power-philosophy were in his mind from 1870 onwards, that is, from the very date of his alleged "Schopenhauerian phase." The year of 1871 was that of *The Birth of Tragedy,* which is the classic statement of the first of Nietzsche's supposed three philosophies. But 1870

---

breast. Who has one day to kindle the lightning must long be—a cloud." The lines were written on the title page of a copy of *Die fröhliche Wissenschaft.*

[4] One of these volumes (XV) contains a work Nietzsche had published: *Ecce Homo.*

was the year of conversion to the power-philosophy, a conversion effected by the sight of charging cavalry, and 1871 was the year of many notes (especially *Werke* IX, p. 144ff.) explicitly stating the philosophy of Heroic Vitalism.

Posthumously published notes leave no doubt that Heroic Vitalism, the philosophy of Nietzsche's masculine mind and his public destiny, was the philosophy of all his mature years from 1870 onwards. He did not vacillate or betray. The later notes (in *The Will to Power*) simply carry the investigation further and it may be said that, however much Nietzsche's eyesight improved, he looked steadfastly in the same direction. Inconsistencies arise where the mask compelled him to say something that was not consistent with his own character: that is why Nietzsche often felt a loathing for the characters he impersonated, the higher men he kept in his cave, and in solitude tried to rediscover his real self. There are things in *The Birth of Tragedy* that could scarcely be reconciled with Heroic Vitalism. Whether such behavior on Nietzsche's part amounts to deception we can scarcely say. In mitigation of the offense it might be urged that every artist contains multitudes and contradicts himself, that Nietzsche did explain the nature of his masks, and that, finally, Nietzsche had no more pretentions than Marx to "immaculate perception," having no faith in non-participant objectivity and inert analysis. He was organizing his own life and seeking to organize the life of others. He was in the realm of action, not of contemplation. Above all, he wished to create a band of destroyers, seekers, good Europeans, free spirits, higher men, and when he spoke in their name he was using them as his rallying cry, his oriflamme, his mask, without insincerity.

He wore first the mask of Wagner, but the new era did not arrive. The mask was changed for that of a Free Spirit, not because Nietzsche had changed his philosophy, but because he had chosen another group of men to work towards the new age. Like Zarathustra, he found adequacy in none of his comrades and in the end bequeathed his philosophy as a free gift to those who should come after. He wore no mask in *The Will to Power* because the notes of which it is made up were not prepared for publication. Moreover, after *The Twilight of the Idols* (1888), in which Nietzsche wore the mask of the iconoclast and the enemy of the epoch, there was no mask left that Nietzsche need wear. The masks had failed: no man heeded the rallying cry, and Nietzsche's situation is correctly described by Stefan George:

> *Du hast das naechste in dir selbst getötet*
> *Um neu begehrend dann ihm nachzuzittern*
> *Und aufzuschrein im schmerz der einsamkeit.*[5]

2

A great part of the preceding chapters on Nietzsche has been occupied with his feminine side, his soft-heartedness and mysticism. Most of what follows is occupied with Nietzsche's Heroic Vitalism, the philosophy not of a phase but of a career, the philosophy to which he was called. Psychological studies of Nietzsche may fairly describe the tragic conflict of Nietzsche's destiny with his private desires, but students of his social philosophy should study the destiny alone. Nietzsche was trying to give this advice in *Ecce Homo*. If the inviolable soul of Nietzsche wore a mask in this work, the mask was Nietzsche's own public destiny. "I am a destiny" (*Verhängnis*), Nietzsche wrote; and his destiny was to advance a philosophy which horrified his own heart. *Ecce Homo* is not simply an exercise in egoism. In an age when men were writing confessional autobiographies, Nietzsche wrote an autobiography from which the author's ego was substantially excluded. The book was written not to explain the struggles of the psyche but to announce the public importance of Heroic Vitalism. The autobiography tells why Nietzsche wrote such good books, what their import was, and why Nietzsche was a destiny. There is no more pregnant chapter in all Nietzsche than "Why I Am a Destiny," where he deliberately lures the reader from the study of the personal Nietzsche to the study of the Heroic Vitalist.

Admitting the discrepancy between the heroic philosophy of

[5] "Within yourself you have killed what is nearest to you, only, desiring it again later, to tremble after it and to cry out in the pain of loneliness."

Nietzsche and his feminine temperament, we need not admit that there is anything fragmentary about the heroic philosophy itself. Let us turn to some of Nietzsche's accounts of the superior man.

We Philologues (1874) is characteristic of Nietzsche's early unpublished writings. It is infused with the spirit of Schopenhauer, and there are statements in it which Nietzsche would not have written after he discarded the mask of Schopenhauer. For instance: Nietzsche maintains that the whirlpool in the midst of which man stands is wholly irrational, but that man's only happiness depends on reason. The highest reason, he says, is to be found in the work of the artist. There follows the hope, which is echoed in all Nietzsche's work until *Thus Spake Zarathustra*, that an amalgamation of the learned for the breeding of better men should be formed. Nietzsche speaks with respect for the saint in this work, but even here suggests that Schopenhauer's saint is too passive and renunciatory.

What we may call Nietzsche's futurism is a device by which Nietzsche sought to enlist altruism and religious fervor in support of Heroic Vitalism. A man should live for the future, for his children and his children's children. This idea, already pervasive in the earlier seventies, is what leads Nietzsche to praise the Schopenhauer man; to the end he recognized that Schopenhauer had played a hero's part in the war against the age. In *Richard Wagner in Bayreuth* (1876) Nietzsche speaks of Wagner's generous impulses towards mankind and adds in a phrase which is printed as a separate paragraph: *"aber zu Menschen der Zukunft"* ("but to future mankind").

Towards the end of the sixth part of *Schopenhauer as Educator* (1874), Nietzsche lists three characteristics of the good scholar. They are as follows:

(1)   An adventurer's love for new discovery.

(2)   Enjoyment of the dialectical chase like the desire of the hound for the hunt.

(3)   Love of battle and victory; as against the professor who

enlists the *Truth* in support of the ruling classes, churches, and governments.

The first attempts of Nietzsche to sketch the features of the man of the future are not, it may be thought, very thorough, but we should be aware at once that Nietzsche *never* gave a complete portrait of his ideal man. He explained what the hero would have to destroy, and what his attitudes must be to good and evil and to other men. But Nietzsche is primarily concerned with mobilizing the energies which will drive master-natures towards superman, whose face is too bright to be visible. By 1875 Nietzsche has told us a good deal.

The early works of Nietzsche, even when they are not lectures, are very much concerned with the nature of the scholar. The goal is a new Hellas; the means, the student group. The cultural richness of Germany in the nineteenth century has to be taken into account, for Nietzsche's noble aspirations had been planted in his heart when he was an undergraduate. Leo Berg described Nietzsche's philosophy as primarily a friendship cult.

Nietzsche's days at Pforta had been brightened by a literary club known as Germania, at whose meetings Nietzsche lectured on subjects ranging from Hölderlin to Napoleon III. At Bonn, Nietzsche was an enthusiastic member of a less serious fraternity (which he soon tired of, to be sure), the celebrated Franconia. At Leipzig, he returned to academic sobriety in a Philology club. Music festivals were not the invention of Wagner: Nietzsche was an enthusiastic visitor at the Lower Rhineland Festival at Cologne in 1865.

With this background, Nietzsche came to have a lofty conception of the scholar's position and a high opinion of the achievements of cultured minorities. Foreign critics forget that Nietzsche was not brought up in a democracy. He found the best things in life among an intellectual aristocracy whose activities seemed to be threatened by the new industrial society.

When Nietzsche changed the Schopenhauerian mask for a Voltairean mask in *Human All-too-Human* (1878), *Dawn of Day*

(1881), and *The Gay Science* (1882), the portrait of the superior man was also changed. He is no longer the conscientious scholar, the historian, the musician, or the poet, but the independent intellectual: "the free spirit," "the good European," "we fearless ones," "we homeless ones," "we immoralists." [6]

The presentation of an ideal of manhood in these works should be a useful corrective to the popular view that Nietzsche depreciated intelligence. For while he always insisted that consciousness is a small part of a larger whole which is life itself, and that the greater should not be sacrificed to the less, Nietzsche insisted also that morality is to be recognized by knowledge, not blindly accepted. The analysis of knowledge would come later. For the present, he would teach men to flourish: "We must learn from the beasts and plants what it is to flower."

These changes of mask and of polemical method are a revelation of Nietzsche's mind. It is as a change in his own temper that Nietzsche explains that the subtitle "A Book for Free Spirits," to *Human All-too-Human,* must not be understood as anything else than a changed voice in the author. It was a homage to Voltaire on the centenary of his death. Very clearly from this time forward, Nietzsche's "destiny" was a vindication and a progressive understanding of "the innocence of becoming" (a phrase which was once intended to be the title of his master-work, surviving only in the fragments known as *The Will to Power). Dawn of Day* and *The Gay Science* each close with a peroration of futurism, an ecstasy of hope, for they are Nietzsche's most joyous work, the fruit of the euphoria of convalescence. Nietzsche can no longer be depressed by the thought that his own generation stops short: "other birds will fly further." The free and fearless spirit represents Nietzsche's new-found buoyancy, his resolve to press forward to further effort. "We homeless ones" are reconciled to our position outside orthodox educational institutions, outside conventional thought; "we immoralists" have joyously abandoned the herd to its morality.

---

[6] The expression "we immoralists" does not itself occur till 1886, in *Jenseits von Gut and Böse,* 226, but "immoralists" are mentioned, *Der Wanderer und sein Schatten,* 19.

This phase of Nietzsche's writing does not require distinct treatment in an examination of Nietzsche's ideals of superior manhood. All the essentials are carried over into the writings of the final phase. The best description of the Free Spirit, for instance, is the second chapter of *Beyond Good and Evil* (1886). An exact perusal of the text confirms the thesis that the *social philosophy* which Destiny thrust upon Nietzsche is constant and contradicted only occasionally in the early polemical works. From this point on, we can ignore Nietzsche's hankerings after Christianity, Schopenhauer, and Wagner, and stick to his Heraclitean philosophy.

3

The statement of this philosophy provided by Nietzsche's little-read notes of the years 1870-71 is one of the most lucid. The following account is chiefly based on these early notes.

Society cannot take root, or reach beyond the family, until the inevitable *bellum omnium contra omnes* has been checked by the invention of the state. But, says Nietzsche, war does not thereupon cease. War gathers in states like rain in the clouds. Men still strive for mastery, and life remains dangerous. Out of the tension comes great art, the tonic *par excellence* which preserves men from pessimism. The embodiment of an abundant vitality, art cures the devitalized.

Out of the bitter struggle for survival and mastery, Nietzsche's theory continues, a few individuals emerge with the full stature of manhood. The struggle is mitigated by no human rights. Conflict is the law of life, from the conflict of the white corpuscle with the typhoid germ to the conflict of embattled nations. The protoplasm itself sends out its pseudopodia in its effort to absorb and overcome. Life is defined as a lasting form of force-establishing processes, in which the various contending forces grow unequally. If we are to *accept* the nature of the world instead of flying in its face, we must, according to Nietzsche, recognize that power confers the first right, and that there is no right that is not at bottom usurpation. The state is the objectification of the predatory instinct.

"War is just as necessary to the State as the slave is to society."
The army, says Nietzsche, is the prototype of the State. It consists of a pyramidal caste system in which the slave is the base
and the superior man the apex. A general cannot treat his men
as ends in themselves. He must *use* them for his own purpose,
that is, for victory. What is the result of victory? The general
has vindicated his virile nature, has followed his destiny, has
brought health to the social organism. His men have behaved
honorably too, for they have been the *means* used by better men.
The slave is a piece of machinery operated by the superior man.

One need not at this point refute these arguments. The identification of might and right is not an invention of Nietzsche's.
Belief in slavery cannot be challenged if the believer postulates
two species of men. Let us provisionally accept such postulates, since Nietzsche's subsequent social writings must be regarded as an amplification of them. He amplified his ideas of
the nature of the physical world, the nature of the State, the nature of the slave, the nature of art. The amplification which concerns us here is that of the idea of the superior man, especially
the man of action and the philosopher.

What, to begin with, is the superhuman? The term is poetical
and emotive. The superman was a substitute for God, and God
can only be respected while he remains infinite and therefore
incomprehensible. Without mystery, the superman too would
evaporate. None the less, in the final philosophy of Nietzsche, as
we piece it together from his notes, the superman is fitted into
the scheme of things. The pivotal concepts of Nietzsche's philosophy are Life, Will-to-Power, and Valuation. The superman is
related to them as follows:

We do not know enough, Nietzsche says, to make the Kantian
distinction between Noumenon and Phenomenon, that is, between
an intuited reality and an actuality apprehended by the senses,
much less to assert its truth. We can be convinced of nothing but
our own life and our own striving. But since action is necessary
to life, we are compelled to form opinions of the outer world.
Let us therefore be empirical and start from what we are most
sure of, our own striving. Let us assume nothing in the outer

world other than a similar striving for mastery. Biology and history provide abundant evidence.

A principle of integration is implied which Nietzsche calls *der Wille zur Macht* (the will-to-power). The word *zur* is misleading because it suggests that power is a final goal for the will. The thing ought to be expressible in one word. The will-to-power is the ceaseless process of Becoming which, though it is ever in conflict, has no stopping points and no final goal. It is similar to, but more than, the *élan vital* of Bergson and the Libido of Jung.

The principle can give direction to our behavior only by the Values it establishes. Value is immanent in life, bound to life by creative intelligence; in Platonic terms, by Reason and Eros. But Nietzsche is not an idealist like Plato, and his Reason and Eros do not lead to a realm of universal forms. They lead to the realm, not of the supernatural, but of the superhuman. The will-to-power fares on towards the superman.

Is this view deterministic? Seeking to avoid teleology (the idea of progression to a definite goal) Nietzsche seeks also to avoid determinism (the idea that progression is completely controlled by antecedents). He believes that while events group themselves in regular configurations, Reason and Eros enable the superior man to *use* these groupings for his own purposes. Destiny proposes, man disposes: this is the transvaluation of the older values. Man, or rather the great man, is supreme.

Is not the argument ingenious? It must surely be among the most intricate of the many intricate defenses of free will which men have devised. Is it convincing? No more perhaps than the others. It relies too exclusively upon two conceptions whose credentials are little better than Deity and Idea, which he is avoiding, namely, Destiny and Superman. When those affairs which are not explained by the common-sense part of the theory are handed over to these bizarre concepts, we proceed from the unknown to the more unknown. The argument is against fatalism. We are enjoined to rely on Destiny and await the Superman. But is this really preferable to being enjoined, say, to rely on God and await the Messiah?

4

Epistemology, cosmology, and biology confirm the cult of the great man, and history is not behind. According to Nietzsche there are three legitimate kinds of history, the monumental, the antiquarian, and the critical.[7] Each ministers to the needs of a different type of man. Monumental history is the history of examples, teachers, and comforters, and it ministers to the need of the man of action and power. The soul of history is found in the impulse it gives to a powerful spirit.

Antiquarian history is the history of such things of beauty as appeal to the man of reverent and conservative nature. The patriot greets the soul of his people across the centuries. Goethe stands brooding before the tomb of Erwin von Steinbach, the Italians of the Renaissance before the ruins of ancient Rome.

Critical history is also necessary. It breaks up the past and applies it to life. It questions. It judges. Finally, it condemns: for former standards must be surpassed. Is history not to be impartial? No, for the truth of a judgment made by so frail and unreliable a thing as a man's mind can be of small importance beside the life of which the mind is a mere fragment. Is circumspection good? No. "It is not caution, detachment, or objectivity that enables the fittest to survive, but alacrity, strength, and intuition. Rather act and take the consequences than refrain from doing a good thing because one cannot do it better."

Nietzsche's philosophy of history is not conceived, any more than Carlyle's, purely in terms of individuals. The tools of his historical analyses are such concepts as moral type and epoch, and his ideal is always the enrichment of life. He insists, however, that since the aim of mankind can lie ultimately only in its greatest examples, the time will come when historians will ignore the masses, the evolution of man and the world, to look only at individuals who form a bridge over the stream of Becoming. The devil and statistics, says Nietzsche, can fly away with the masses, who remain of interest in three respects only: first, as the copies

[7] *Vom Nutzen und Nachteil der Historie für das Leben* (1873), 2.

of great men, printed on bad paper from worn-out plates; second, as a contrast to the great men; and third, as their tools. The great man is the chief determinant in history. The *direction* of his power is often conditioned by his surroundings (hence the erroneous belief that he is the expression of his time), but his power adapts itself to the surroundings and then molds them.

All three types of history are to be found in Nietzsche's own work. Historical personages find their way into his pages chiefly as *exempla,* as monuments; he rifled the history of Europe for teachers and comforters. The "antiquarian's" attitude is exemplified in his love of the Renaissance and the Greeks. The history of Christianity presented in *Antichrist* is an astonishing piece of critical history.

The great men of the past spoke to Nietzsche, and when they spoke he listened and obeyed. His reverence for them was the rock upon which his hopes for a better humanity rested. More: while Nietzsche followed Rousseau, Kant, and Fichte in basing his values on feeling or intuition, and for him words relating to values were merely "banners planted on spots where a new blessedness was discovered," he insisted, as only Carlyle had done before him, on the supreme value of the hero: the blessedness discovered in the lives of heroes was the origin of his chief judgments of value. The Nietzschean ethic of masters and slaves was the banner planted on the spot where the Greeks were discovered.

Nietzsche's account of Western history goes something like this. The earliest society we commonly study, pre-Socratic Greece, was healthy and wise. Wars were frequent and they made possible the efflorescence of great art. The Greeks were athletic and æsthetic. They were cruel and they were fair. They had visions of Apollonian grace and they plumbed the depths of Dionysian horror. They could be sad without mawkishness and joyous without restraint. Their philosophy had not taken refuge in the idea, their behavior had not been tamed into morality, their religion had not been devitalized into piety. In Athens before Socrates, there was heroism, there was hierarchy, and there was *hubris.* The Greeks were on the other side of good and evil. They are the highest point yet reached by men, a necessary example to the fathers of the superman.

The slave-mind, Nietzsche continues, erupted into philosophy with Socrates, in whom the Hellenic equipoise of body and mind was upset. Thought was overrated, a transcendental world was invented, life ran at a slower pace, and blood turned to water. If the Romans restored manhood, the rise of Christianity, the religion not of Jesus but of Paul, effectively tainted man for more than a millennium. The Christians could not abolish the will-to-power, but they could assert their own will-to-power by seizing control of the Roman Empire itself, and converting the church into a political force, in order to corrupt mankind in a denial of the very force by which they themselves triumphed.

Yet the hero, Nietzsche feels, cannot perpetually be ousted. Even the Middle Ages produced Frederick II of Hohenstaufen. Finally the Italian Renaissance cut the noose of morality from the neck of the ruling classes. Cesare Borgia, Leonardo, and Michelangelo were such men as justify life. Greece rose again.

Then Luther, a slave-mind like Socrates and Paul, came to Rome, where Christianity had been choked at its source, where paganism flowered in sweet and bitter blossom. Luther was the philistine who could not see beauty, the boor who could not admire manners, the bucolic who could not comprehend etiquette, the plebeian who must envy the great, the priest who must hate himself for loving pleasure: in short, the moralist. He reinstated the Christian genealogy of morals and set the yoke of piety upon the neck of Europe for another four hundred years.

There followed various forms of transmogrified Christianity: the counter-reformation with asceticism and the *auto-da-fe;* the enlightenment with its rationality and its Christian morals; Romanticism, Evangelicalism, Socialism, Democracy. Leibnitz and Kant replanted the Christian tree, and Rousseau watered it with his tears. The weak, by their numbers and their revolutionary Pauline Christianity, came to be masters of the strong. Which is why we have to fight against the eighteenth century. First in the fight was Napoleon Bonaparte. Over the corpse of the slave, Robespierre, Napoleon willed his path to power and scaled the topmost height of heroism. He was brilliant, cruel, unscrupulous, successful, contemptuous of his age, and aloof from his peers: a man of destiny.

The role of the hero or genius in Nietzsche's scheme of history should now be clear. He is not to be viewed sociologically. We are not to ask: What did he do for his people? How did he serve common humanity? There is an older attitude to the hero than this, one of simple admiration for the marvelous. We would marvel at the beauty of a speeding planet, though by collision it caused some cosmic disaster. Plutarch felt an unfeigned admiration for a Master, irrespective of his services to others. The hero is a magic personality. He is "what he is." The French have very generally revered Napoleon, though few would say he had been useful: the hero, it is assumed, justifies himself.

The hero is not necessarily a leader. Nietzsche promulgated no *Führerprinzip*, nor did he insist that one man must be elevated above the other members of the ruling class. Whatever the connection between Heroic Vitalism in general and the regimes of modern Europe, our dictators of today resemble Plato's tyrants, thrown up by the chaos of democracy, while Nietzsche's conception is more like Plato's Timocracy where the rulers, though governed by honor, do not claim to lead or support the populace.

Nietzsche extended his history of the West into a prophecy. He felt that with socialism and democracy, Christianity had prolonged itself to the limit. We are, he said, now on the ice-floes of the stream of the Middle Ages. This explains, says Nietzsche, "why I am a destiny." Nietzsche enacted in his life and work the end of an epoch. We feel the full force of the pronouncement he makes to his sister in December, 1888: "You have not the slightest idea what it means to be next-of-kin to the man and destiny in whom the question of epochs has been settled. Quite literally speaking: I hold the future of mankind in the palm of my hand." He had transposed to the personal plane all the struggles of the political world. "Great politics," he said with what proved to be prophetical accuracy, "date from me." In him the transition from decadence, through conflagration, to health is made flesh.

Nietzsche's humane and generous nature, excessively weak and compassionate, is the Christian culture which he believed was being broken as the Heraclitean life returns. In him the ice of the passing winter cracked and splintered as the spring floods swept onwards.

The twentieth century, Nietzsche prophesied, would be the classic age of war. Christianity dies hard. When the floods subside, a renewed humanity, a superhumanity, strengthened by conflict and sweetened by suffering, served by a neo-Buddhistic slave-class, may bask in the sun of a new renaissance.

Such is Nietzsche's picture of human history. Clearer, more brilliantly critical than Carlyle's,[8] it is yet a series of overbold generalizations and begged questions. One need not in this place supply a less tendentious interpretation of Socrates, Paul, Luther, and Napoleon, but one should note in passing that Nietzsche's æsthetic, non-social approach to the hero is not extended to villains. Napoleon is justified on æsthetic grounds, but Socrates, Paul, and Luther are condemned on those social and historical grounds which Nietzsche affected to despise. This is not playing fair. Nor is Nietzsche's boasted *amor fati* (love of fate), that is, his insistence on accepting the hard fact, compatible with his resentment against Socrates, Paul, and Luther, who, according to Nietzsche, have perverted whole epochs. If such "weak degenerates" can control whole epochs, why should we stand in awe only of Cæsars and Napoleons, much less of Cesare Borgias? Nietzsche's historiography is that of a certain type of poet: valuable only for its significant attitudes.

Nor is his vision of the future beyond criticism. By all means he saw, with many of his contemporaries, that the liberal optimists were deluded and that the future would be violent. But will the violence yield a breed of supermen? Will a new culture rise like a phœnix from the flames? In our time we have seen too many men of war to believe in supermen and too many conflagrations to put much faith in phœnixes.

[8] See above, p. 40ff.

5

Nietzsche's theory of value has implications. The will-to-power gives direction to our lives by the values it establishes. The will-to-power assures victory to the qualities which, discovered by the emotions and approved by the intellect, it calls *valuable*. The difficult problem of the Order of Rank, which Nietzsche puzzles out in his posthumous work, is solved. The man who creates values must be the highest in rank.

Plato's great peroration is again pat: "Until philosophers are kings. . . ." But Nietzsche is not echoing Plato. He is answering Plato. In those difficult and penetrating jottings, like the ruins of some great château, that compose the fourth book of *The Will to Power,* Nietzsche distinguishes two classes of philosophers: first, those who wish to expound a system of values and, second, those who are the *Lawgivers* of such values. The second class dominates history. But how perilous is the path of such a philosopher! He is quite alone, outside the boundary set by the last great lawgiver and enforced by rigid custom. Plato, says Nietzsche, was such a one. He covered his eyes when he saw how narrow was the strip of land that separated him from the abyss. Lacking supreme courage, Plato persuaded himself that "the good" as he wanted it, the good as he might have seen it had he used his eyes, was not the "good in itself." He consoled himself with "eternal values" as others console themselves with God. Plato is not the highest man. "The man who establishes values and controls the wills of epochs in that he controls the highest natures is the highest man."

Talk of Nietzsche's vanity has not been ungracious only; it has obscured issues of the first magnitude. Nietzsche understood himself and his destiny. He knew he was not the "highest man"; he felt himself more in the position of the "last man" in *Thus Spake Zarathustra.* He had divined some of the things that lay hidden in the soul of the highest man. "Perhaps everyone perishes who learns the secret of the highest man. But whoever has seen him must help to make him possible." Nietzsche philosophized with a hammer and planned a Transvaluation of All Values, but he himself went no further than Moses, to whom he often compared himself, towards the promised land.

He who wishes to find a compact description of the great man according to Nietzsche will search in vain through the works of Nietzsche and his critics. Nietzsche composed no programs and formulated no politics. He planted dynamite in the world's cellar and brandished his hammer in the face of the gods. There are scattered *aperçus* throughout his works on the character of the man of art, the man of action, the man of religion, but the qualities of all these are fused in his idea of the philosopher. Nietzsche, it might be said, begins and ends, like Plato, with the philosopher, the student of life. But he tries to get beyond Plato's belief that philosophers *ought* to rule, with the belief that philosophers *must* rule, that they *are* the legislators of the world, though unacknowledged.

Nietzsche changed his mind as to the mode of development from the nineteenth century to a higher humanity. But from his early days he passionately admired two qualities in man: strength and beauty. He felt, like Hedda Gabler, that is was necessary to shoot, and to shoot beautifully. It was the fusion of strength and beauty in the lives of such young men as Baron von Gersdorff that had endeared them to Nietzsche. The question Nietzsche always put to himself, in searching for an ideal of personality, was: *was ist vornehm?* (what is noble?) From the start he found the answer in the flower of German manhood in and around the universities. In von Gersdorff, he said, delicacy was grafted upon force, the outward discipline of martial training had produced an inward athleticism.

In European tradition as far back at least as the Middle Ages, there are three moral planes. First, there is the good *in æterno*, exemplified in the renunciatory virtue of Sir Galahad. Second, there is the good *in sæculo*, the worldly strength and grace of Sir Launcelot. Third, there is the bad, the bald baseness of Sir Breuse-sans-Pité.

Nietzsche publicly repudiates Sir Galahad, though with an internal struggle that was never resolved. His philosophy is chiefly, though not merely, a vindication of Sir Launcelot, and his immoralism will never be understood by those who make him the champion of Sir Breuse. Nietzsche justifies a secular life. Life is innocent. The Nietzschean philosophy is a philosophy of cleanliness, of "the innocence of becoming." Man is to be accepted whole, not negated by a doctrine of sin, but surpassed by an exercise of strength. History is to be accepted, not blindly as by optimists who court disillusionment, but with a Dionysian outlook that accepts tragedy joyously. Nietzsche shocks "the good and the just" not, it must be admitted, because he is less virtuous than they, but because he lets his right hand know what his left hand does.

The world is waiting for a man, Nietzsche wrote in 1873, who will destroy the habits of thousands of years and replace them with better. Nietzsche awaited the great man. For a long time, he entertained the Messianic Hope of Germany, familiar to him since childhood in the works of Hölderlin, the hope that the new strength and the new beauty would be German. This idea is set out in an originally unpublished Preface to *The Birth of Tragedy*, addressed to Richard Wagner. The preface is worth careful study. "I would like nothing better than to meet a man with whom I could not talk this way, a being of angry greatness, with the bravest eye and the keenest will; at once warrior, poet, and philosopher; one whom you could imagine striding over serpents and monsters."

"The hero of the future will be a man of tragic awareness. The light of Grecian joyousness will be on his brow, the glory with which the rebirth of antiquity—hitherto lingering—will be inaugurated, the rebirth in Germany of the Hellenic world."

All this, except for the hero's angry greatness, is pure Hölderlin, and could now be called pure Stefan George. And this German Messianic Hope is Nietzsche's most deeply rooted political idea. Later, of course, Nietzsche lost patience with the Germans, and nowhere is the German character so belabored as in his last works. Horizons broaden and all Nietzsche's later plans are pan-European. Europe will become one politically, because it is rapidly becoming one economically and culturally. National

States are an anachronism. But the "good European" does not —as soft critics of Nietzsche have supposed—hanker after a pacifist federal union. He desires a pan-European *power* which will avoid the stagnation of Chinese civilization[9] on the one hand and the money-grabbing of American civilization on the other. Nietzsche did not despise China in the offhand manner of Houston Stewart Chamberlain,[10] but Heroic Vitalism, far from being "a war against the West," regards itself as an expression of the aristocratic mind of Europe as against both the Orient which, according to Nietzsche, lacks vitality and the New World which lacks heroism. In order that Europe might enter the battle for the mastery of the world with good prospects of victory, Nietzsche recommended a union with Russia and an "understanding" with Britain. Within fifty years Britain would crumble because of the impossibility of shutting out *homines novi* from the government, the small nations of Europe would all be mastered, and (a hint of twentieth-century economics) provided the "good European" was a soldier first and foremost he would keep his credit as a merchant.[11]

The great man must be "a good European"—which is almost the opposite of a good Wilsonian—but of what stock? The potentialities of many breeds are considered: Spaniards, Arabs, Corsicans, French, English. The conclusion is that the best Germans are leaving Germany, that Germany is the door to a pan-Slav-Europe; Asiatics are a hundred times more magnificent (*grossartiger*) than Europeans. As to the master-classes in particular, the future of German culture is found to lie with the sons of Prussian officers. Who shall be found worthy mates for

[9] For Nietzsche's opinion of China, see (e.g.) *Jenseits*, 267, *Die Fröhliche Wissenschaft*, 377. Note that in a list, often cited by propagandists, of "magnificent barbarians," Nietzsche includes the Japanese alongside the Homeric heroes, Scandinavian vikings, and the Roman, Arab and German nobility (*Zur Genealogie*, I, 11).

[10] *Die Grundlagen des neunzehnten Jahrhunderts*, München, 1903. Vol. I, p. 42. "The nations which do not even to-day belong to Christendom—the Chinese, the Indians, the Turks, etc.—have none of them as yet any true history. . . ."

[11] This and the succeeding paragraph are based on a set of notes in the *Nachlass* (*Werke*, XIII, p. 330ff.).

them? The Jews are the oldest and purest race in Europe. Their continued existence as a race after dispersion proves their health and strength. "Therefore the highest beauty is found in Jewesses." Is there not, Nietzsche hints, a gleam of hope? If Nietzsche was seduced by the nineteenth-century pseudo-science of eugenic breeding, whose foolishness should be apparent in the last few sentences, at least he did not reach the conclusions which this pseudo-science was to popularize in the days of Adolf Hitler!

We can distinguish chronologically two sets of Nietzschean superior men. First, there are the free-spirits of today, the home-less ones, good Europeans born before the age of a united Europe. Next, there are those who will inherit the new Heraclitean continent after the age of great wars and great politics, namely, the twentieth century.

The free-spirits, as they are described in *The Gay Science* (377), acknowledge a debt to Schopenhauer whose philosophy was "a European event" and who dreamed of a kingdom of higher men, and to Hegel, who was, says Nietzsche, a true German in his distaste for the concept Being as against the concept Becoming. The fearless ones are "unfavorable to all ideals," that is to all notions outside the possibilities of history. They oppose liberals and Utopianism. If the ice wears thin, they break it. They hate compromise and love adventure, danger, and war. They regard modern ideas as a symptom of exhaustion and look forward to a new Order and a new Slavery. As "good Europeans" they are heirs of millennia of European thought. While they intend to forfeit no crumb of this heritage, they are not benefactors of Mankind, whom they regard as an old woman like the philosopher's "Truth." While they approve morality that is associated with the gregarious instinct, for themselves they oppose Christianity and say Yes to sin, Yes to man, Yes to history, and Yes to life. They possess *la gaya scienza*.

When the wars of the twentieth century are done, the peoples of Europe, in the age of "great politics," will be reduced to what Nietzsche frankly calls *slavery*. They may, of course, be happy, and they will believe in a neo-Buddhist, neo-Christian quietist slave-religion. But they will be a means to ends pursued by a race of masters, "the lords of the earth." It is for them that Nietzsche was preparing his final work, *Die Umwerthung aller Werthe* (The Transvaluation of all Values).

This final work was never written. But *The Will to Power* is full of suggestions. The lords of the earth do not require extreme forms of belief, which would blind them to actual conflicts. They do not resent, and may even welcome, a modicum of chance and the irrational in human affairs. They do not exaggerate the importance of mortality, yet they are not weak and self-effacing. Abounding in health, they are equipped to face suffering and sorrow. Of one thing they have no doubts: their own power.

Such is the sketch provided in the first book of *The Will to Power* (55). The fourth book recapitulates and elaborates: Able to discount small things, the great man can extend his will over vast stretches of his life. He is indifferent to public opinion, neither respected nor respectable, hard. He spares himself the luxury of compassion, and is not above thinking of himself in moments of danger. A mask shields him from other men; he wishes not to help but to use them; his strength of will emanates in mendacity. But he is too intelligent to be a bigot. Because he lacks convictions, he is strong. Because he is strong, he makes of the intellect a good servant.

It is true that a great man may become identified with a people and with a century, though this does not mean he is altruistic. The energy of greatness is needed to model the man of the future. But the effort may involve the annihilation of millions of the misbegotten. Human instincts are at war in all of us, but most of all in the noble. The great man is an arch spanning the banks called Good and Evil. In him is celebrated the marriage of heaven and hell. If he is magnificent, he is also the highest manifestation of injustice, falsehood, and exploitation. A great man is not a freak. He is neither a sport of nature nor a gift of God. He is the result of breeding. He is an aeronaut of intellect and a capitalist of power. He is a Destiny.

These Nietzschean descriptions—I have stuck close to the text —read less like philosophy than like notes for a heroic poem. Is not the Nietzschean attitude richly expressed in the tragedies of Kleist, the fiction of Hölderlin, and the poems of Stefan George? Nietzsche's notes are more explicit and various than these and consequently more incriminating. This hero of his is not likely to affect our opinion of any concrete social problem. Only the Nazis would profess an admiration for such a one, and they only for their own un-Nietzschean purposes. The errors we have noted in passing—the identification of might with right, the postulate of two species of men, the infusion of æsthetic standards into social and moral phenomena, the Baudelairian diabolism which results from Christian premises without Christian convictions—these pervade and vitiate the whole argument.

Yet, as with Carlyle, the critic who only scolds misses an extraordinary storehouse of thought. The hero of Heroic Vitalism is a product of the errors just listed, but on the other hand the positive content of Nietzsche's hero-worship is even greater than Carlyle's. Carlyle's contribution was to base nature upon the concept of organism and not upon that of matter, to grope toward a new sort of naturalism not confined within the bounds of mechanics, to justify the superior man by a vitalistic and pragmatic standard. All this is true *a fortiori* of Nietzsche. The upshot of the theory of value which we have looked at is that values are "free," are created, are man-made. Thus the dignity of which man had been deprived by eighteenth-century science and Darwinism alike is restored to him by Nietzsche, as by William James, without recourse to the word *neo*. Though Nietzsche had his antiquarian side, his theory of values does not have a romanticized Renaissance or a romanticized Hellas as its necessary base; the positive aspect of the superman doctrine is that the creative man *makes* value and truth; that, since man is eternally creative, values and truths will change. The neo-Thomist, the neo-Platonist, the absolutist of every sort retorts that this doctrine is a surrender to chaos, meaninglessness, and disvalue, for once the postulate of absolute truth is abandoned, there is nothing left but the relative and the subjective. Nietzsche replies that, to be sure, there is nothing left but the relative, but that the relative may be entirely *ob*jective; and, as to the psychological appeal of such a doctrine, there is nothing less inspiring about a doctrine of diversity and ever-changing truth than about the fixities of Platonic and Christian tradition.

This being Nietzsche's view of truth, it would be stupid to regard his works as articles of a fixed faith; they invite an active intellect and a precise, lively sensibility to sort out this from that. Nietzsche's conception of the Complete Man, for example, is close to the neo-Hellenic cult of the Whole and not devoid of diabolism; but it is also an un-Greek recognition of the unity of theory and practice. Nietzsche's abasement before the great man shows an undemocratic contempt for common humanity; but it is also a reminder—William James, to name a very gentle man, knew how much it was needed—of the necessity of leadership, personality, and superior brains. Nietzsche's identification of might with right is often a mere reiteration of the cynicism of Machiavelli and Hobbes; but it can also be, when less savagely asserted and less flippantly illustrated, the germ of a more moral view of might and a more pragmatic view of right, the germ of a view which will not make an antithesis of morals and actions. Nietzsche's psychology inherits much from the brilliant negativism of Schopenhauer and La Rochefoucauld; it also serves the good purpose of helping to destroy the naïve, narrow, rationalistic, mechanical conception of man which was the heritage of the eighteenth century.

One substantial portion of Nietzsche's teaching, like a substantial portion of Carlyle's, is hostile to civilization itself. That is clear. If we had, in absolutist fashion, to accept or reject a philosophy *in toto*, we would have to reject Nietzsche for his anti-humane sadism, his anti-democratic hero-worship, and his anti-civilized diabolism. But we need not demand of a philosopher either a party-line or a religious dogma. We can take what is fruitful and leave the rest. And, since Nietzsche himself encouraged such an attitude, he could scarcely complain if we apply it to him.

"Out of him [Carlyle] *flows most of the philosophy of Nietzsche."*—G. K. CHESTERTON.

1

In many respects, Carlyle and Nietzsche differ *toto cælo*. Except in connection with the subject of this book, there would probably be nothing to learn from a comparison of them. The outstanding difference is one of merit. It is now undeniable, though the contemporary overestimation of Carlyle and under-estimation of Nietzsche long obscured the fact, that, alike as artist and philosopher, Nietzsche stands head and shoulders above Carlyle. The next most obvious difference between the two is that, while Carlyle philosophizes and Nietzsche is not innocent of history, Carlyle was by profession an historian, while Nietzsche, though nominally a philologian, was primarily a philosopher.

No purpose would be served by a prolonged contrast of the cottage at Ecclefechan and the parsonage at Rœcken; the grammar school at Annan and the college at Pforta; the lectures of Dr. Thomas Brown and the discourses of Friedrich Ritschl; the journalistic problems of the young hack and the pedagogic problems of the young professor; the marital relations of the literary lion and the celibate strivings of the peripatetic invalid. The wider scope of his life, the superior richness of German, Swiss, and Italian culture—at least when a man could have all three— are almost enough to explain Nietzsche's personal superiority. His intellect and his sensibility were much more highly educated. It would be churlish to compare his masterly and imaginative understanding of the classics with Carlyle's clumsy efforts or to compare his absorption in great music with Carlyle's boorish railings against Mozart and Beethoven. Let us turn rather to significant similarities between the two.

159

Carlyle and Nietzsche spent a great deal of their lives trying to understand their epoch. Many have found their conclusions capricious or even crazy, yet we should have been given pause by the strange coincidences in the life-work of the two men, different as were their premises, their environment, and their style. At least we should by this time have been disturbed by the fulfilment of their craziest forebodings.

Nietzsche was still a schoolboy at Pforta when Carlyle left Germany forever in 1858. The two never met, and the only person who ever saw them both, so far as I know, was Mazzini, who in a railway carriage recited to Nietzsche (with whom he was not, however, acquainted) the lines of Goethe:

> *Im Ganzen, Guten, Schönen,*
> *Resolut zu leben.*

Frau Foerster says these lines had a profound effect upon her brother. They certainly had an effect on Carlyle who emended them to

> *Im Ganzen, Guten, Wahren*[1]

because he was no æsthete. Both Carlyle and Nietzsche seem to have feasted on Byron and to have hated Hegel. They happened to agree in some of their oddities of opinion, such as that Socrates was a decadent. But these are merely picturesque details.

A psychologist might make something out of the fact that both our Heroic Vitalists were born in pious homes and intended for the church in an era when the church was losing its grip. Their fathers played a part in their development. Nietzsche felt the need of a substitute from the day that the old pastor was buried in 1849. Carlyle's father died in 1832 and we know the blow was a heavy one. Since, as we have seen, Carlyle lost his spiritual father, Goethe, in the same year, it is not unnatural that it was precisely in the years which immediately followed that the Hero came to prominence. The puritan religion from which both

---

[1] Goethe wrote: "In the whole, the good, the beautiful, resolutely to live." Carlyle wrote: "In the whole, the good, the *true*."

Carlyle and Nietzsche were destined to be emancipated was personified in their mothers, to whom both were strongly attached. It was the spirit of his mother within him that forced Carlyle into phrases and attitudes of pietism. Even Nietzsche had not wholly put off the mantle of Naumburg, and his mother learned in 1889 how he hated her. Both Carlyle and Nietzsche were, as far as one can make out, sexual failures, though both were sustained by the society and letters of well-bred women: Jane Welsh and Lou Salome, Lady Ashburton and Malwida von Meysenbug. It is possible that sexual frustration was the mainspring of their adulation of virile potency.

Allied with sexual frustration, there was in both men a deep sense of social frustration. Each was ambitious and each had been seriously balked. Each was intensely lonely and each felt himself to be a charge of electricity in the heavy air of society. Each felt himself to have a mission that kept all thoughts of personal happiness from his doors. Each felt himself to be a destiny whom a decadent generation was too busy about its frivolous business to recognize. From the time when each arrived at the university to discover that philosophy there was effete, each felt himself to be enacting the end of an old era and the beginning of a new. Carlyle once looked at a blackened fingernail which remained in place until the new and living nail had grown beneath it. The social process, he thought, is similar. Nietzsche watched the apples fall in the season of autumn, and decay. It was also, he thought, seed-time. When one says that Carlyle and Nietzsche felt themselves to be living in a transitional era of decay, catastrophe, and the promise of a new life, one must have in mind the metaphors by which they imaged the historical process.

A general study of the two men might stress their religious background, their sexual life, their isolation, their environment, but, whatever the emphasis, two words would recur, whether the interpreter liked them or not: *frustration* and *compensation*. Nietzsche says that Carlyle killed something inside himself in his anxiety to hide (from himself, as we have seen) the tendency of his thought.[2] Both Carlyle and Nietzsche were forever doing violence *to themselves*. In their later work, *The Twilight of the Idols* or *Latter-Day Pamphlets*, they shriek, bully, and exaggerate because no one will listen. (No one would listen at all to Nietzsche except close friends and, at the end, Brandes, Taine, and Strindberg. The English read Carlyle, but laughed him off.) If the frustrations are obvious enough, one might instance as compensation a factor which some might think crucial for both men: their aggressive manner.

Both were, by nature, highly passionate and, further, highly *com*passionate. Neither, as we have seen, could bear the thought of even an animal in pain, yet both are famous for the brutality of their political doctrine, their advocacy of slavery, and their admiration for bloody tyrants. Yet it would be a mistake to pass off the teachings of Carlyle and Nietzsche with a sneer. It is partly because Carlyle and Nietzsche were more highly sympathetic than the rest of us, because they were more sensitive both to pleasure and pain, that they sensed the impotence of compassionate, modern man in the cruel processes which historical study was revealing, that they felt a need for personal renunciation and expiation, a need to be twice-born. Their philosophy was, among other things, a means of self-conquest, a philosophy of personal courage, of *Entsagung* (renunciation) and *Selbsttödtung* (self-killing). When Nietzsche saw cavalry galloping to their death, he did not damn their general for cruelty; he condemned himself for sympathy, for being above the battle, for being too cultivated and too compassionate to face the facts of living as the historians and biologists seemed to have established them. Since they were honest enough to accept the new world opened up by historical imagination, they must—even if it meant killing something inside them—adapt themselves, their weak, puritan, Protestant, Christian selves, to this world, though it would have been easier to shout an everlasting No or to rest at the center of indifference.

[2] *Götzendämmerung*, Streifzüge 12.

2

Carlyle groped towards a philosophy which I have called Heroic Vitalism; Nietzsche openly brandished this philosophy and shook it in the face of the world. Despite important differences Carlyle and Nietzsche are significantly akin both in their political philosophy of Aristocratic Radicalism and in their poetic phenomenalism or Supernatural Naturalism. On the negative side, they were both involved in an internal fight against Christianity which they always seemed to be winning, though it is hard to say whether in the end either of them won.

Let us examine the analogy between their political philosophies. It has been said that they are completely dissimilar and that, while Carlyle was a collectivist who loved his fellow men, Nietzsche was an individualist and an anarchist who hated them. In replying to this contention, one hesitates whether to declare that Carlyle was not a collectivist or that Nietzsche was not an individualist. Carlyle's love for common men was intermittent and so was Nietzsche's contempt for them. Carlyle preached the "individualist" doctrine that history consists either of the sum of all biographies or of the sum of heroes' biographies. Nietzsche preached the "collectivist" doctrine that society coheres by an order of rank (*Rangordnung*) and that Benthamite social atomism and social hedonism were symptoms of decay. Manifestly, the words *individualist* and *collectivist* are mere noises that do not help us to consider the problem: what is the analogy between Carlyle and Nietzsche?

Carlyle and Nietzsche both start from what might be called the classical social analysis with its triple standard of Order, Hierarchy, and Obedience. And, as Machiavellians, they part company with the classical tradition over the question of justice. A representative of this tradition, Shakespeare's Ulysses, has it that if Hierarchy (*Rangordnung*) is upset and respect for superiors (hero-worship) disappears:

> *Force should be right; or rather, right and wrong—*
> *Between whose endless jar justice resides—*

> *Should lose their names, and so should justice too.*
> *Then every thing includes itself in power,*
> *Power into will, will into appetite;*
> *And appetite a universal wolf,*
> *So doubly seconded with will and power,*
> *Must make perforce a universal prey,*
> *And last eat up itself.*[3]

Justice adjudicates between right and wrong, but, says Ulysses, were order in the universe upset, right and wrong and justice would all be meaningless sounds. Now with the strange advent of the historical imagination in the eighteenth century, with the new interest in psychological and social origins, with the doctrine of progress and the rapid development of pragmatic philosophies, the universe Shakespeare speaks of *had* been upset and the planets, so it seemed to classicists, had run amok. Hume had proved the inability of reason to discover what Ulysses thought she could discover; man ceased to press forward to a Celestial City and, should he look behind, no golden age was to be seen: an ape, as Nietzsche put it, stood grinning in the path. At such a time, according to Ulysses, "everything includes itself in power." The poet adds a prophecy that the primacy of power leads to the primacy of will, which in turn yields to mere appetite. At the last, appetite, will, and power are universally destructive.

Such is Ulysses' analysis of Heroic Vitalism, and many of our modern neo-mediæval and neo-classical critics will think his verdict just. For the Heroic Vitalist "everything includes itself in power," or as Carlyle phrased it: "All power is moral," or as Nietzsche phrased it: "The universe is will-to-power and nothing else." And, to be sure, Nietzsche followed the argument through to the Shakespearean conclusion: Life on Heroic Vitalist premises makes of appetite a universal wolf. Nietzsche himself, that is, forces a choice between Christianity and the worship of appetite; and this pleases Christian critics. But we have already seen it as Nietzsche's great limitation that he could see no middle

[3] *Troilus and Cressida,* I, iii, 116-24.

ground between the absolute of religion and the absolute of power worship.

Was Carlyle less religious? Carlyle's Hero, we are told, was one who benefited mankind; and Nietzsche, therefore, despised Carlyle. But Carlyle was at least half-emancipated from this moral prejudice by the time he wrote *Latter-Day Pamphlets* and *Frederick the Great*. He continued to use the moral phrases, to pretend that the tyrant bullied people for their own good. In the Inaugural Lecture (1866) which is for the most part unctuous and assiduously respectable (he calls the university he had so much loathed "my dear old *Alma Mater*"), Carlyle describes the "extremely proper function . . . of a Dictator" as the wielding of power without responsibility to any man, power of life and death over everything. This doctrine is not very far from Nietzsche's. Nietzsche was willing to grant a docile happiness to the masses, who were to keep their quietist religions. But it is the great man and his power who justify existence and constitute history. This is a fair conclusion from *Frederick* as well as from *The Will to Power*.

In forming his political opinions Nietzsche began where Carlyle left off. There is a similar story to be told of their anthropology, their psychology, their cosmology, their religious ideas. Carlyle hovered (in anthropology) between a Hobbesian-Darwinian view of "nature red in tooth and claw" and a homely affection for human frailty. Nietzsche forced himself to regard the mob as mere means to the ends of the higher man: for life is a process of exploitation. As for psychology, there were for Carlyle two sorts of mental constitution, the slave and the free. Every man is born, according to Heroic Vitalist dogma, in one group or in the other: "Slave or free is settled in Heaven for a man." [4] Democracy is the desire of Judas to slap Jesus Christ on the shoulder, while true government is the regimentation of the majority by the few, of the bores, blockheads, and blackguards by the wise and noble. As for Negroes, they are slaves by their very nature as assuredly as British West-Indian Governors are Kings. Carlyle

[4] *Latter-Day Pamphlets*, "Parliaments" (No. 6), p. 248.

was not as outspoken as this until his later years; Nietzsche, however, began here, and his dichotomy of master and slave was so rigid that he built up a separate system of morality for each.

The essence of the epistemology of both men is that they believed knowledge to be riveted to need, that, in pragmatic fashion, they discounted metaphysical speculation and sought a world-view that starts from one's own strivings and actions. This epistemology fits their predilection for action. It is also the germ of their cosmology. Ignorant of Schopenhauer, Carlyle does not speak of will. He imagines a world made up entirely of Force, and the historical process is the conflict of forces in flux. Nietzsche develops the Schopenhauerian concept of will until his own cosmology might be described as: the World as Will-to-Power and Value-Judgment. In Carlyle there is only an inchoate striving towards such a cosmology.

Carlyle and Nietzsche envisaged a world-process that had no goal and was not wholly determined. Because it had no goal, they had to turn to the highest examples of man for their ideal rather than to a heavenly destination. And it was owing to these highest examples of man that the process was not wholly determined. The higher men are the free spirits. They justify history by their grandeur but more by the fact that it is they, and they alone, who prevent history from being the completely predestined enactment of a plan. Carlyle was an equivocator, and not all his remarks tally with this view. But there is no doubt about Nietzsche.

3

Yet we have also seen that both Carlyle and Nietzsche are inverted Christians. If Carlyle's mysticism is not wholly convincing it is because he tries to lift himself by his own bootstraps. No man ever wanted more vehemently to be a mystic, but the heavenly powers seem to have been unresponsive. Carlyle shrieks where he should sing. In *Sartor Resartus*, for instance, he had tried to force himself into belief. Time is unreal. "This is no metaphor, it is a simple scientific *fact*." The tone becomes dithyrambic: "And seest thou therein any glimpses of IMMOR-

TALITY? O Heaven! . . . Is the lost Friend still mysteriously here, even as we are here mysteriously, with God! Know of a truth that only the Time-shadows have perished or are perishable. . . ." No one would be surprised to learn that the writer of these lines lived to doubt if there was any immortality at all. The grim actualities of Frederick's battles seemed much more like "simple scientific facts."

There would be no reason to stress Carlyle's desire for eternal life were it not so strangely paralleled in Nietzsche, were it not so strangely connected in the minds of both men with a desire for personal courage and an aspiration towards a higher humanity, and were it not a symptom of a deep spiritual *malaise*. Nietzsche's Leith Walk, as we have seen, was the rock near Lake Silvaplana, where what he calls the fundamental idea of *Thus Spake Zarathustra*, namely, Eternal Recurrence, came to him. Nietzsche's is the more candid voice and the more penetrating eye. In both men, the doctrine of immortality is chiefly subjective. It is the device by which they protected themselves from loneliness. It is a sop thrown to their essentially religious natures. In *Heroes* and *Thus Spake Zarathustra* an attempt is made to reconcile religious nature, *anima naturaliter christiana*, with Heroic Vitalism.

The feminine world of ecstasy and personal nonexistence, in which all conflict and antithesis is washed away as in an ocean of Wagnerian music; the masculine world of conflict and antithesis, the world of endless change and limitless force. Two worlds, and how much to be said for each! Carlyle and Nietzsche began by insisting that a choice must be made between the two and ended by trying to have both. It is worth noting the effect that this had on their own happiness and on their view of happiness.

It was a prime doctrine of the Romanticists that happiness should not be the direct aim of living, but that a Faustian interest in work—Goethe's Faust dies planning a building project—will confer happiness as a by-product. But happiness remains the ultimate goal, as it must in any humane scheme of values. Carlyle and Nietzsche, however, invert the error of those who make happiness both a direct and an ultimate goal. They make of work an ultimate. This is a subterfuge. A man who has failed in the quest of happiness drowns his sorrows in alcohol or—in work. (Or, it might be said, he finds a "higher happiness" in work. But this reduces the discussion to a verbal quibble: read "higher happiness" for "work" and you are back at the start again.) Dissatisfaction with happiness as an ideal is a symptom of a general rebellion against all temporal rewards and all temporal commitments. In Carlyle and Nietzsche it is symptomatic of their difficulties in putting religion out of their lives, of their homesickness for the old religion and their reaching out for a new. The argument for work and against happiness is a highly ingenious link between their mysticism and their pragmatism.

Ingenious as such contrivances may be, however, neither Carlyle nor Nietzsche finally resolved the conflict. Carlyle fought hardest in *Frederick* and described his state of mind on the completion of the work: "A gloomy but quiet collapse there is in mind and body—a world left very *vacant* in comparison, and much less lovely to me than it once was." Carlyle's last years were a period of fretful skepticism and wistful defeat. Nietzsche, on the other hand, flung himself into the vortex. He never extricated himself to shiver regretfully on the shore. The waters closed over him.

Part Three. From Richard Wagner to D. H. Lawrence

"*For us, who happen to live while the World-Phœnix is burning herself, and burning so slowly that, as Teufelsdröckh calculates, it were a handsome bargain would she engage to have done 'within two centuries,' there seems to lie but an ashy prospect.*"—THOMAS CARLYLE.

CHAPTER VIII

Richard Wagner, Siegfried, and Hitler

"Der von mir erkoren, / doch nie mich gekannt, / ein kühnster Knabe, / meines Rathes bar, / errang des Niblungen Ring: / ledig des Neides, / liebes froh, / erlahmt an dem Edlen / Alberich's Fluch; / denn fremd bleibt ihm die Furcht. / Die du mir gebar'st, / Brünnhilde, / sie weckt hold sich der Held: / wachend wirkt / dein wissendes Kind / erlösende Weltenthat. . . . / dem ewig Jungen / weicht in Wonne der Gott." [1]—Wotan forecasts the career of Siegfried.

"Aechter als er / schwur keiner Eide: / treuer als er / hielt keiner Verträge: / laut'rer als er / liebte kein And'rer: / und doch alle Eide, / alle Verträge, / die treueste Liebe— / trog keiner wie er!" [2]

—Brünnhilde reviews the career of Siegfried.

1

There is one man who has been more often mentioned in recent times for his hero-worship and his vitalism than either Carlyle or Nietzsche, and that is Richard Wagner. But the name of Wagner is one to conjure with. He has been excessively praised and excessively condemned. His interests were varied, his gifts uneven, his temper erratic, and Wagner criticism is sheer

[1] "Chosen by me, though he never knew me, a valiant lad, without counsel from me, seized the Nibelung's ring, free of envy, rejoicing in love. The curse of Alberich grows lame before this noble one, for fear is alien to him. Her whom you [Erda] bore me—Brünnhilde—the hero lovingly wakes; awaking, your child in her wisdom achieves the world's redemption . . . enraptured, the god gives place to the eternally young."

[2] "Truer than he none ever swore oaths; more loyal than he none ever kept compacts; more proudly than he none ever loved, and yet all oaths, all compacts, the loyalest love, none betrayed as he did!"

confusion. Some dislike the man because of his work, others dislike the work because of the man. Some dislike the philosophy because it is embedded in music and drama, others dislike the music because it is associated with philosophy. Wagner's first critics accepted or rejected his work *in toto*. Later it was the fashion to ignore everything save the music. Recently several critics have merely included the music in a condemnation of Wagner's ideas.

Recent anti-Wagnerians make one point to which all others are subordinated: Wagner is a "proto-Nazi." The point is elaborated according to the prepossessions of the particular historian. If he thinks like Peter Viereck that Nazism is essentially romantic, then Wagner is convincingly equated with romanticism. If like Jacques Barzun he thinks that Nazism is essentially materialistic, then Wagner is equated with materialism. The historians are agreed in assuming that since Hitler was an acknowledged disciple of Wagner, Wagner's ideas cannot be dismissed as trivial. Fair enough. The question is whether a man can justly be called a proto-Nazi because Hitler liked him, whether what Hitler liked about him is the whole truth, and whether searching the nineteenth century for proto-Nazis is a very significant or useful pursuit.

What does Wagner's "Nazism" amount to? In his book *Metapolitics*, Peter Viereck has provided the best summary of Wagner's ideas as found in his prose. The ideas are those of Rosenberg's *The Mythos of the Twentieth Century* and *Mein Kampf*, that is, Heroic Vitalism colored with racism. The concepts of *life* and *dynamism* are basic. For Wagner they are manifest not merely in the hero but also in the race, particularly in the German community. Wagner's Teutonism is a familiar pattern. He postulates a race-soul; he grows to hate French and "Mediterranean" ideas; he champions culture against civilization. Above all, though probably Jewish himself, he is fanatically anti-Semitic.

Lenin's dependence on Marx was not more openly professed than Hitler's on Wagner; the *mæstro* was imitated, even down to his eccentricities such as vegetarianism and teetotalism. Wagner's son-in-law and chief disciple was Houston Stewart Chamberlain. Chamberlain came of a British military family, renounced a military career because of ill health, traveled on the continent, and began to feel about Germany as a Rhodes Scholar feels about England. During the First World War, he was given German citizenship; after it he endorsed National Socialism, and, via Rosenberg and Rudolf Hess, gave his ideas to Hitler. Among Chamberlain's few British friends were the Redesdales. Lord Redesdale wrote the preface to the English edition of Chamberlain's most important book. One granddaughter of this Lord Redesdale married Sir Oswald Mosley, leader of the British Union of Fascists; another, Unity Mitford, became one of Hitler's few female friends.

If, then, Hitler said that nobody can understand Nazism without understanding Wagner, if there were busts of Wagner at Berchtesgaden and allusions to Wagner in the Führer's speeches, it will not be surprising. But was Hitler always right about Wagner? *Mein Kampf* relates how Hitler heard *Lohengrin* at the age of twelve; and one thinks of Dorothy Thompson's allegation that Wagner's music has deluged Europe in blood. Unfortunately, however, the music and libretto of *Lohengrin* are much more innocent than, say, Swinburne's poetic dramas; if Hitler's sadism was thereby increased, his response was quite arbitrary. Stanley Baldwin's favorite author was Mary Webb, but if he considered his policies intelligible only to readers of *Precious Bane* he was wrong. Hitler and Miss Thompson are wrong if they think ideology or musical taste is the foundation of fascism.

It is conceivable that some strange youth hungry for fancies might read *A Vision* by W. B. Yeats, accept Yeats's views, and make them the basis of a political ideology. Would Yeats's poetry be less good? Obviously not. Another modern myth-maker, D. H. Lawrence, says: "This pseudo-philosophy of mine . . . is deduced from the novels and poems, not the reverse." If the same is true—and I think it is—of Wagner's pseudo-philosophy, does that mean that Nazism is embedded in his music-dramas? Not necessarily. Ernest Newman, who has studied the life of Wagner more thoroughly than anyone else, confirms my impression that Wagner's prose was chiefly a purgation of the intellect. Being a German intellectual, Wagner liked to have a "profound" philosophy. He prepared himself for creative work by erecting a pseudo-philosophic scaffolding which could be knocked away later; it is simply unfortunate that some people have been more interested in the scaffolding than in the edifice. "My literary works," said Wagner in a letter to Rœckel, "were testimonies to my want of freedom as an artist; it was dire compulsion that wrung them from me." This being so, it is not surprising that the prose works are pretty uncouth. Wagner was not a competent philosopher. If in some sense he embodied Schopenhauer's philosophy in *The Ring*, it should be recalled that the work was planned before he read a word of Schopenhauer.

In all this I am allowing the reader to assume the worst of Wagner's prose. But this is giving too much away to his critics. Wagner, like Nietzsche, George, and Lawrence, is a many-sided —or more precisely, a two-sided—writer. He contradicts himself. If a fascist can find solace in his prose, so can a democrat. In *What Is German?* for example, Wagner speaks of the tendency of a people to identify itself with its great men. This tendency, he says, is sheer vanity and, moreover, *"diese Neigung ist grunddeutsch"* ("this tendency is fundamentally German"). In the same essay Wagner speaks scornfully of those who wish to make Germany a new Roman Empire controlling other peoples. There is much also in *The Artwork of the Future*, with its prefatory dedication to the great free-thinker Feuerbach, that would today be judged decidedly libertarian. And in his notes for this work, now available in the *Collected Works*, Wagner declares that real history will begin under a "communist" new order when men will be governed by a genuine historical understanding and not by myths such as divine right and the sanctity of property. Richard Wagner, in such articles as "Programmatic Demands for a Democratic Germany" (*Dresdener Anzeiger*, July 14, 1848), was a pioneer of German social democracy; that he was also a pioneer of Nazism is a paradox that only a more intimate study of his mind and art can help us to understand.

2

In his early operas, Wagner examines the efforts of heroes to push back the boundaries of necessity, but he finds the hero doomed at the start (*The Flying Dutchman*) or misunderstood in the end (*Lohengrin*). The major spiritual problem, as most would admit, was faced only in *The Ring Cycle*, which, whether it is the most perfect, is certainly the richest and the most problematic of Wagner's works. It is Wagner's *Hamlet*. I shall here interpret *The Ring* as an epic of Heroic Vitalism, or rather an epic *manqué*.

In *The Ring* Wagner sought, or so at first it seems, to embody the new heroic religion which, with Carlyle and Nietzsche, he found to be a necessary successor to the Christian epoch. Wotan, the old god whose tenure has always been insecure, is dethroned by Siegfried, the hero who can neither be helped nor hindered by the gods. The theme is worked out with the utmost variety of character and incident.

The old world, as Wotan explains to Mime (*Siegfried*, Act I), consists of the dwarfs and of Alberich; of the giants, Fasolt and Fafnir; of the gods and Wotan. The earth contains riches which are innocent enough when in the protection of the auroral Rhine-maidens but which, in the hands of the loveless dwarfs and giants, became the cause of endless and purposeless strife. Wotan, who heads the hierarchy of the gods, is not omniscient or omnipotent. He forfeits one eye as the price of marriage with Fricka, whose dowry is the power of Law. He forfeits the Rhinegold and the magic ring in order to have his castle built without losing Freia, Fricka's sister, whom he has pledged to the builders of the castle, the giants. Freia is a symbol of love—she possesses golden apples —and godhead has been able to retain the attribute of love (Freia) and law (Fricka) only by humiliating barter. So much for the limitation of Wotan's power. His wisdom is limited by his unruly temper, which drives him to quarrel with the giants who thus learn that he is not perfect. The giants represent stupid insurgent humanity as the dwarfs represent shy, treacherous humanity. One is reminded of Nietzsche's opinion of the mob.

When, assisted by his cynical intelligence, personified by Loge, the god gives away the Rhinegold, Fafnir kills Fasolt rather than share the booty, transforms himself by the use of the Tarnhelm, a magic helmet, into a dragon and sits guarding the gold. That is: the richness and the meaning of the earth were, in the course of history, claimed by man himself, but, far from rising to wisdom and nobility, man became a slavish and sleepy monster while God was an increasingly harassed elder statesman. Man has bought the ring and the gold by sacrificing love.

The symbols are primordial. The ring is a time-honored symbol for man's goal, his union with what he most needs. It is often a female sexual symbol—as in the final lines of *The Merchant of Venice*—but, here in Wagner, the ring is what Fafnir prefers to woman: namely, the key to worldly power. The helmet represents the dexterity and adaptability of man, a dexterity and adaptability which can easily be misused. The hoard reminds us of Nietzsche's belief that the heart of the earth is of gold. It is important to note how Wagner demonstrated the necessity of godhead's preserving love and handing over earthly power to mankind. Erda, Mother Earth herself, the personified life-force, rises from her bed, warning Wotan to yield the ring to Fafnir. The demands of the life-force are final. *Das Rheingold,* which I have been sketching, closes with rejoicing over Freia. Intelligence (Loge) has the last word on the gods: "They hurry to their end, who boast of such great strength."

The Christian story passes from the failure of Adam to the triumph of the second Adam. In *Die Walküre* and *Siegfried,* Wagner describes a not wholly dissimilar process, the failure of Wotan and the triumph of Siegfried.

Feeling the insecurity of his position, Wotan buttresses his divine power with a bodyguard of fallen heroes whom his Valkyries have borne to Valhalla from the battlefield. These buttresses of Deity symbolize the churches or any organized support of the old order. Fearing that Alberich will wrest the ring from Fafnir, Wotan prepares plans for the future. His conclusion is that only a higher nature than has previously existed can recover the ring. This higher creation is the hero, the germ of whom he feels in his own godhead. The Wagnerian hero, like the Carlylean and the Nietzschean, is the legitimate successor of the old god. As Zarathustra strives towards superhumanity by his love of the earth, Wotan impregnates Erda herself. The fruit of this union is not the hero but true will, directive *Wille zur Macht* (as against the merely rational Loge). True will, which is also the eternal image of woman drawing men on to high endeavor, is called Brünnhilde.

The breeding of the hero is indirect and slow. Wotan cannot father him. He fathers, by a mortal woman, the twins Siegmund and Sieglinde. Contravening human laws against adultery, for Sieglinde is by this time married to Hunding, and contravening also holy ordinance against incest, the pair engender the hero, Siegfried: the old order is broken by immoralists. The sexual potency and creative power of Siegmund are suggested by the myth, familiar to readers of Malory, of the sword which can be drawn only by the hero. But Siegmund has to atone for his temerity by death; and (a highly imaginative stroke) Brünnhilde flees carrying on her war-horse the fragments of Siegmund's broken sword and Sieglinde pregnant with the hero. Siegmund's death, required by the ancient law (Fricka), was redeemed by the resentful will of Brünnhilde.

Brünnhilde's rebellion, threatening the status of Wotan and the old order, is punished, not with death, for Wotan cannot kill the emanation of his own union with the life-force, but by her being thrown into a deep sleep. Like Snow White and other heroines of the folk imagination, Brünnhilde can be awakened only by the advent of the hero. The creative will of humanity is imprisoned, though the circle of flame that encloses her is a mirage. Since only the hero has courage, a mirage is enough to deceive unheroic mankind.

The delivery comes in *Siegfried*. Wagner portrays his hero as the iconoclast. By a Christian criterion, he is too loud, too violent, too arrogant: an unregenerate pagan devoid of compassion. Siegfried agrees with Carlyle that one need not act charitably to the contemptible and treats Mime as roughly as his anvil. But the *hubris* which the ancients considered a fault is a virtue for

Wagner, as for Nietzsche; and it is by his boundless confidence
that Siegfried recreates Nothung, the sword of Siegmund. Siegfried is a crude emanation of the vital energy which for Carlyle,
Nietzsche, and Wagner has superseded the divine idea. He is
irreverent and, like Zarathustra, is more at home with the beasts,
and especially the birds, of the forest than with men. For Nietzsche, men were a cross between monster and phantom; for Wagner, at this time, they were either dolts or knaves. Siegfried
slays the dragon, seizes the ring and helmet, leaving the earth's
riches undespoiled. A friendly bird whispers to him in sleep
that on a mountain peak Brünnhilde awaits him within a ring of
fire.

The climax of the death of Fafnir is prefatory to a higher climax.
At the foot of Brünnhilde's mountain, Siegfried meets Wotan.
They converse and Siegfried explains that he has a healthy contempt for the old and effete. Wotan summons all his divine
grandeur to impress the youth. But Siegfried reverses the fate
of his father (who had broken Nothung across the spear of
Wotan) by breaking the spear of Wotan with Nothung. After
this, Wotan disappears from human history. God, as Nietzsche
put it, is dead. We await the superman. The myth of Heroic
Vitalism ends in the prologue of *Götterdämmerung*, where Siegfried and Brünnhilde exchange symbols, a male one for a female,
Brünnhilde's horse for Siegfried's ring. The quest is achieved.
On the horse of Brünnhilde, Siegfried is master of the world.
Meanwhile Wotan has tried to mend his spear with a bough from
the World Ash. The ash withers, for now that the hero has freed
mankind from divine shackles, its day is done. Wotan's heroes
cut it down and prepare to burn Valhalla with the faggots. Night
will fall on the gods.

What happens to the allegory in *Götterdämmerung?* In
1898 Bernard Shaw maintained, in *The Perfect Wagnerite,*
to which the present analysis is greatly indebted, that it simply
disintegrates and that this final part of the trilogy declines into
mere Italianate operatics, complete with coloratura singing and
a stage-villain. Shaw pointed out that Wagner had sketched a
Death of Siegfried at the age of thirty-five and suggested that,

when he turned to the old libretto at the age of sixty, he had lost interest in the myth of revolution.

Now everyone would agree that with the entry of Siegfried into the court of Gunther there is a change of tone. But Shaw, for the moment a Heroic Vitalist, too readily despises Wagner's apostasy from Heroic Vitalism. *Götterdämmerung* (*The Twilight of the Gods*) is Wagner's palinode. It is a picture of life after the triumph of heroism. The hero finds himself the dupe of villainy and corruption, because he carries with him the ring and its curse. The ring is a symbol of power as the gold is a symbol of wealth. Alberich is economic man, the victim and incarnation of Mammonism; Siegfried is power man, the hero of the new post-capitalist epoch. According to the Wagner of *Götterdämmerung* power man is doomed no less than economic man. Siegfried is given a chance to restore the ring to the Rhine-maidens, but he is too proud or too ignorant to yield to their entreaties. Moreover, night has not yet fallen on the gods. They linger on until the final consummation. And the final consummation is reached through the sacrificial love of Brünnhilde. In the closing bars of *Götterdämmerung* is heard the motif of redemption by love. The ring returns to the Rhine, and reconcilement is reached through love and sacrifice. The Siegfried-ideal, evidently, is not enough.

Bernard Shaw was angry with Wagner for the same reason as Nietzsche. He thought he had found in Wagnerism an expression of the power-instinct, only to discover in the end that for Wagner love and not power was primary. All Shaw's arguments against *Götterdämmerung* are answerable, and here it is relevant to mention one of them. Shaw argues that there is no point in Siegfried's getting back the ring from Brünnhilde and that the incident is a bit of muddled melodrama. Now the whole tetralogy is an attempted answer to the question: What must a man do to be saved? The old deity, Wotan, is dying a not ignoble death. The new hero is trying his hand. In Siegfried's endeavor, a first stage is reached when he rides in triumph down the Rhine on the horse of Brünnhilde, the dynamic of human will. Is this the answer to Wagner's chief question? For a time it seems that it may be, and one of the Valkyries, having missed the irony of

Wotan's comment that gods and men will be redeemed (*erlöst*) when the ring is given back to the Rhine, is of opinion that men and gods might continue to live happily if Brünnhilde restores the ring to the Rhine-maidens. But Brünnhilde, believing that a final solution has been found in her living union with Siegfried, refuses to comply with her sister's request. No sooner has she done so than it turns out that, drugged and deceived by the Gibichungs, Siegfried gives her away to King Gunther and reclaims the ring for himself. A dupe of knaves, the hero loses his pure will and arrogates to himself the symbol of power. This, the beginning of the end, is the second stage of Siegfried's attempt to work out the salvation of the world.

"In the original draft of Siegfried's death," says Shaw in *The Perfect Wagnerite*, "the incongruity is carried still further by the conclusion, at which the dead Brynhild, restored to her godhead by Wotan, and again a Valkyrie, carried the slain Siegfried to Valhalla to live there happily ever after with its pious heroes." The significant fact is that Wagner eliminated the incongruity by canceling this conclusion. Night does fall on the gods and a solution is found, not as yet in complete Christian innocence, but in the annihilation of will, human and divine, by the flames of love. The hero is helpless, when severed from pure will.

"Death and vulgarity," says Lord Henry Wotton in *A Picture of Dorian Gray*, "are the only two facts in the nineteenth century that one cannot explain away." In *The Ring*, Wagner had accommodated vulgarity with some success (Alberich, Mime, Fafnir, Fasolt, Hagen), but there remained death, the death of the hero. Shaw, obsessed with politics, lacks the tragedian's concern with death; to him death is simply an inconvenience. Not so to Wagner. The death of Siegfried was literally his first and last interest. From his plan of *Siegfrieds Tod* in 1848 he was led back through the story of what is now Siegfried to *Die Walküre* and *Rheingold*. In 1853 the libretto of the tetralogy was complete. Shaw's argument about a change in conception can only hold for the score, incomplete for over twenty years. *Siegfrieds Tod* was transformed into *Götterdämmerung* in the early fifties.

What is the real significance of the transformation? There is no truth in the theory that, while the optimism of *Siegfried* reflects the revolutionary Wagner of 1848, the pessimism of the final *Götterdämmerung* (revising the earlier *Siegfried's Death*) reflects the counter-revolution of Napoleon III, the Hagen who stabbed European revolutionism in the back in 1851; for we now have documentary evidence that the pessimistic end was planned before this.[3] Even if the theory were true, it would not be any more illuminating than, say, the theory that Shakespeare wrote problem plays when Jacobean England was passing through a phase of disillusionment. Actually there is other evidence. Wagner did not, as many since Nietzsche have imagined, evolve from world-embracing Heroic Vitalism to Buddhistic nihilism. The two opposite philosophies or attitudes, Heroic Vitalism and Buddhist-Christian religion, coexisted in his breast as they did in Carlyle's and Nietzsche's. If Nietzsche was angry with himself for not seeing this before he received the libretto of *Parsifal*, it was because he did not know how old the *Parsifal* project was or that in 1848 Wagner had planned a Christian drama on the subject of Jesus himself.

The two Wagnerian philosophies are brought together in *The Ring* by a device as daring as the maestro's musical technique. Since the Siegfried story is nowadays known to us chiefly through Wagner, we tend to forget his most audacious act: the conflation of the myth of Siegfried with the myth of the fall of the gods. The twilight of the gods was not part of a story imposed on Wagner by his sources. It is an alien element which only an urgent sense of purpose and a considerable genius could fuse. The idea that heroism is ultimately worthless, that the "innocence of becoming" can only be restored through sacrifice, is what Wagner substitutes for the happy ending which Shaw rightly ridicules. But why does Shaw ignore the meaning of the substitution? Perhaps because he could not see how a man can affirm and deny the life-force in the same work. Shaw himself was to be a "perfect Wagnerite," a Wagner without negation or nihilism, without Schopenhauer, Buddha, and *Götterdämmerung*. But Wagner remained an imperfect one.

[3] Newman's *Life of Richard Wagner*, Vol. II, Ch. 17.

3

Siegfried is, manifestly and *par excellence,* the hero of Heroic Vitalism. How does Wagner interpret him and how did he arrive at his conception?

The starting point is to be found in his earlier heroes and hero-ines; the evidence is to be found not only in the operas and music-dramas themselves but in such theoretical lucubrations as *Eine Mittheilung an meine Freunde* ("A Communication to my Friends").

Through the fog of Wagner's prose, one can dimly descry the intention. The Flying Dutchman, Tannhäuser, and Lohengrin are all seeking redemption (*Erlösung*) through the eternal femi-nine. Wagner's magniloquence—Senta is "the Woman of the Future," Tannhäuser "the spirit of the whole Ghibelline race," Lohengrin "the type of the only really tragic material, of the tragic element of our modern life"—convinces us at least of his serious intentions. The Siegfried idea came from the heroine of *Lohengrin,* Elsa. She made Wagner, he says, a full-fledged revo-lutionary. He was yearning for redemption through the spirit of the Folk, and Elsa was the incarnation of that spirit.

Elsa was the incarnation of Wagner's personal and social ideals, of all his life-affirming ideals. At last he had arrived at a con-clusion. But Elsa was a woman, and Elsa's life was a failure. It was necessary to present the idea again. The Ring Cycle springs from this need. The character of Siegfried was a necessity of Wagner's development, Siegfried the hero in his fullness, the doer of deeds, the complete man. "It was Elsa," Wagner says, "who taught me to discover this man."

"*Dem ewig Jungen / Weicht in Wonne der Gott*" ("enrap-tured, the god gives place to the eternally young"): Wagner was once present at a rehearsal when these words of Wotan's were sung. He is supposed to have shouted: "It should sound like the announcement of a new religion." "Siegfried," he wrote, "is the man of the future whom we have wanted and desired but who cannot be made by us and who must create himself through our annihilation." This conception has been well digested by those who write about Wagner and Hitler. One thing is forgotten: that Wagner himself rejected it. *Siegfried* has one of the grimmest, most ironical endings in all drama, no less ironical for the fact that the audience goes home thinking it has witnessed a happy ending. Bernard Shaw, revolted by passion, turns away his gaze. One widely used English translation reads "laughing at death" for *lachender Tod* (at the end of *Tristan* the words *Unbewusst, höchste Lust* are translated "In a Kiss, highest Bliss"). The words of Siegfried and Brünnhilde are ambiguous. Consider the final line: "*Leuchtende Liebe, lachender Tod!*" [4] This means that salvation is to be found in love and death, love being associated with light, and death not with decay but with laughter. The statement as it stands is not very different from the conclusion of the whole tetralogy. But the context is different. Siegfried is not yet the dead hero who has paid the price. He is overcome with *hubris;* he is on the brink of his downfall at Gunther's court. The irony here consists in his utter unawareness. Brünnhilde on the other hand is, until the last moment, overcome with foreboding. Each ecstatic thought of Siegfried's she has capped with a despairing thought. He speaks of life, light, day, creation; she of death, darkness, night, annihilation. Logically there is no contradiction, because he is speaking of their own future, she of the end of the gods. But the gods cannot die while Siegfried keeps the ring. Brünnhilde knows this and cries out in deliberate forgetfulness, Siegfried in involuntary joy: "*Leuchtende Liebe, lachender Tod!*" *Götterdämmerung* is foreshadowed.

Ambivalence is the cardinal characteristic of Wagner's mind, and the natural outlet for such ambivalence is irony. Irony and *double-entendre* are carried over into the music itself when the orchestra plays such themes as World's Heritage at the very time when Brünnhilde, full of foreboding, feels that she will not inherit the world. *The Ring* concludes with the leitmotif of redemption through love. Whether Wagner rejects his Siegfried philosophy or merely moves away from it would be hard to determine.

---

[4] "Gleaming love, laughing death."

4

Like other Heroic Vitalists, then, Wagner is involved in ambiguity and personal conflict. In his life, as in Nietzsche's, masculine and feminine were at war. Why did the two men not agree? Was it not partly because Wagner actually let his feminine nature speak in his works, thus giving utterance to what Nietzsche most loathed not only in Wagner but in himself? To be sure, Wagner had conceived "the young Siegfried," and precisely at the time when Nietzsche met him. But not only does Siegfried come to a bad end, Wagner's other heroes are the very reverse of pagan supermen. Tannhäuser is a voluptuary redeemed only by the intercession of a virgin. Lohengrin is a Christian emblem of chivalry. Hans Sachs, the real hero of *Meistersinger*, believes in Renunciation, as Wagner, the least restrained of men, liked to think he himself did.

Two significant heroes remain, Tristan and Parsifal, who can be discussed only in relation to the works from which they are taken. For most people *Tristan* is the quintessence of Wagnerism; for the musician it is the great step towards modern atonality. For the historian, however, it represents—unlike *The Ring*—only one side of Wagner: Wagner the nihilist. That it should be precisely this opera that brought Nietzsche to Wagner is of course a paradox, and we must assume that it spoke to the nihilist who was resident also in Nietzsche's spirit. *Tristan* speaks in a voice of command. You have either to flee or capitulate. An early German Romanticist had described music as "the land of faith where all our doubts and our sorrows are lost in a sea of sound." None but Wagner ever quite realized this idea, and he nowhere but in *Tristan*.

The piece is a landmark also in the history of the drama. The bourgeois epoch, since Lessing and Diderot, had developed its own non-tragic drama based upon two psychological factors: the Illusion that the characters on the stage were real, and Suspense as a magnet to draw the audience. Far from restoring that tragic dignity which sets the audience at a distance, Wagner exploited the technique of illusion and suspense to the utmost. His stage at Bayreuth was known for its "mechanical wonders" and its realism. Effect is piled on effect to secure the surrender of the audience. It is a total surrender, a surrender of all the faculties, to a magician. Unfortunately if we are to judge Wagner, we are bound to use in sober analysis those faculties of which, in the theatre, he robs us.

We are confronted with Tristan, a great example of a hero whose existence justifies life, "the miracle of all kingdoms," as Brangaene says, "the highly praised man, the hero without peer, the treasury and seat of fame." But from the first he moves in an atmosphere of fret and fever, of billowing, sinister emotion and talk of feud and death. The time-honored conflict of love and honor is transmuted into something macabre and morbid, for though honor remains honor, love is equated with death and, worse still, is found the better for being equated with death, just as the love of Siegmund and Sieglinde grows more confident and ecstatic when they know it is incestuous. Tristan stands to Frau Minne, the divine patroness of love, as Tannhäuser did to Venus, but Wagner's Tristan not only surrenders as did the Tannhäuser of mediæval tradition, he surrenders in the belief that she is not only deadly but the more exciting and desirable for being deadly. This is Wagner's very un-Nietzchean transvaluation of values. Darkness and night, primordial symbols of evil, become symbols of goodness, which is equated with extinction; day is an object of dread. This inversion of symbols is not limited to the famous *"unbewusst, höchste Lust"* ("highest joy, to be unconscious"), it is the imagery of the whole drama. Its meaning is brilliantly hit in a single sentence of Nietzsche's in which he isolates the essence of passionate pessimism: *"Denn der Mensch will lieber noch das Nichts wollen als nicht wollen"* ("For man would rather desire nothingness than *not* desire"). The Buddhistic-Schopenhauerian philosophy advocated the annihilation of desire; and Wagner was soon desiring annihilation.

Tristan has a crude sexual basis. The world knows how it had its origin in Wagner's love for the wife of a silk merchant, Otto Wesendonk. But that is not all. The love duet is a not very indirect representation of the sexual act. More than that: the idea of ecstasy followed by extinction follows the sexual pattern. The whole of *Tristan* is a celebration of the sexual act in the terms of music-drama, as *Lady Chatterley's Lover* is such a celebration in realistic terms. The celebration might be cleanly pagan as in primitive, ancient, and Renaissance poetry. But in Wagner it is not. His love is greasy with self-conscious sex. He performs moral gymnastics and ends standing on his head. Which is no doubt what critics mean by inverted puritanism.

What happens to the Wagnerian hero? He goes to his death not with Hellenic cheerfulness but with orgiastic pleasure. Wagner's "religious" resolution to extinguish desire led him to an attitude that was neither pagan nor religious. He took what was piquant in both schemes of life and accepted the responsibilities of neither. His hero is not a great exemplar of *any* view of life. His heroic tragedy is neither tragic nor heroic.

Wagner conceived Siegfried and Tristan. Then, so popular legend has it, he repented and conceived Parsifal, the Christian hero. Actually *Parsifal* was conceived in 1845, before either *The Ring* or *Tristan*. The different ingredients of Wagner's strange brew were present all along; his career shows musical development but little development of ideas. In 1865 the libretto of *Parsifal* was sketched, and perhaps it was in Wagner's mind when a few years later he was discussing the lack of popular support of his operas with Nietzsche and he said: "The Germans don't want to hear about heathen gods and heroes now. They want to see something Christian." The man who was too Bohemian to live with his age, too Schopenhauerian to have sympathy for it, was not above coming to terms with it.

Parsifal is ostensibly the completest renunciation of worldliness and thus of nineteenth-century civilization. It is a return to that defense of spirituality as against the flesh and the devil which had been the subject of *Lohengrin* and *Tannhäuser*. Like Lohengrin, the hero is a stainless, saintly knight with an aura of the supernatural about him. Like Tannhäuser, he is tempted by a sensual sorceress. Unlike both other heroes, however, Parsifal

succeeds in his mission, and the drama ends with the very
Wagnerian words:

> *Höchsten Heiles Wunder*
> *Erlösung dem Erlöser!* [5]

Parsifal is of all Wagner's works the most extraordinary and
the most unacceptable. In *Tristan* the code of chivalric heroism
is fused with nineteenth-century sex and nineteenth-century
nihilism; in *Parsifal* it is chivalric religion which he fuses with
these. In *Tristan* the Launcelot-type is degraded, in *Parsifal* the
Galahad-type is degraded. The second degradation is the more
drastic and the more disastrous.

Like most Wagnerian protagonists, Parsifal is searching for
redemption (*Erlösung*); like them, he relies upon miracles
(*Wunder*); like them, he lives in a world of phantasmagoria,
the strange Wagnerian world where everything is mythic and
unreal yet solid and substantial as a Victorian drawing-room.
Redemption, in this context, has less the force of a religious experience than of a superb thrill. The miracles which bring redemption have less the force of sublimity than of magic for
magic's sake. One has the feeling that an obsession with this
sort of redemption, a dependence upon this sort of miracle, a
penchant for this sort of phantasmagoria are fundamental traits of
Wagner's mind, reflecting his compromise with his age. They
offer solace without solution, excitement without order.

In *Götterdämmerung* we see Wagner in retreat from Heroic
Vitalism; in *Parsifal* we see him stating an alternative that reveals only his mental confusion. The virtues by which Parsifal
succeeds are: virginity, simplicity, and compassion. These qualities Wagner most sadly lacked. The virginity is like the renunciation of Hans Sachs, a piece of wishful thinking. The simplicity
is also a fantastic overcompensation. The compassion comes
oddly from the man who cracked jokes when four hundred Jews
were burnt to death in a theatre fire. Perhaps if Wagner had
really been capable of making sacred drama out of virginity,

[5] "Miracle of highest salvation, redemption to the redeemer!"

simplicity, and compassion, we could take these virtues seriously. But he was not. He could not even imagine what the words meant. Why, then, was he interested in them? The immoralist, in search of the abnormal and the illicit, makes of vice his first subject of study, but when in time vice becomes normal, virtue in its turn acquires a morbid fascination, and normality seems Bohemian. This is the stage Wagner has reached in *Parsifal*. Once his conception is taken seriously, it is a matter not for the church or the theatre, but for the clinic.

One need not ask why Nietzsche hated *Parsifal,* which he judged from the libretto, not from the score. He hated in Wagner what he hated in himself and his own background: venal piety, abasement before sheer size, the willingness to compromise or to be merely clever. These are the fundamental faults of which Wagner's jingoism and anti-Semitism are mere offshoots. Seeing such faults, Nietzsche finally saw little else. That is not surprising. But for us the amazing and almost incredible thing about Wagner is that he is far from a total failure. No great artist is open to so many objections. But he *is* a great artist.

The Composite Artwork (*Gesamtkunstwerk*)—the Wagnerian conception *par excellence*—did not quite come off. Wagner was not much of a poet; he was still less of a philosopher. His music, for all its influence, is more a résumé of the past than a model for the future. There is truth in Nietzsche's withering words: "Wagner as musician is reckoned among painters, as poet among musicians, as artist generally among actors." Yet though Wagner's mind was fundamentally a theatrical one, his greatest achievement was not in the sphere of drama but in the sphere of music. That is one typically Wagnerian paradox. Another is that, despite waves of nihilism and vulgar Teutonism, he could on occasion affirm life, crave excellence, and admire the hero. That is why the term Heroic Vitalist fits him better than the term proto-Nazi.

CHAPTER IX. Oswald Spengler and German
Historiography

*"For man is a beast of prey. . . . Ideals are so much coward-
ice."*—OSWALD SPENGLER.

*"Spengler said before he died that for the world's sake the
Pope should excommunicate Hitler."*
—*Mein Kampf.* New York, 1941.
(Editorial footnote, p. 761.)

1

The study of the German thought of recent generations is one
of curious difficulty. One discerns several strands, often quite
distinct, but sometimes meeting in a disconcerting fashion.
Working through the thought of the century is like driving out
of New York City. Many magnificent highways open up ahead,
but when you think you are bound for Connecticut you find
yourself on the way to Schenectady. Highways branch off above
and below, to right and to left. For a time two highways run
parallel, then diverge. It is confusing. One speaks of the socialist
road which, one supposes, branches out to the left towards Marx;
yet another socialist road bends to the right towards Lassalle
and Hitler. The anti-Semitic highway, one is told, is a right-
bend, yet on it one discovers the anarchist Max Stirner. A
magnificent highway, sweeping broadly to the right, leads to
Heinrich von Treitschke. To reach Nietzsche one follows the
Treitschke road a little way before taking so violent a fork that
one is not quite sure whether it is left or right. As to Hegel,
even the signposts are not agreed on his position. He is not to
be found to the left with Engels, straight ahead with Feuerbach,
or to the right with Bernhardi. Some advise taking the Nietzsche
road, though it is notorious that Nietzsche could not bear to be
in the neighborhood of Hegel. And so forth.

189

The attack on liberalism brought together the strangest bed-fellows. Liberalism was too comfortable and mild for Karl Marx as for Ferdinand Lassalle, whom Marx called the "Jew-Nigger," for Hegel the idealist as for Clausewitz the military historian, for Treitschke the nationalist as for Nietzsche the "good European," for bureaucrats like Bismarck as for Junkers like Ludendorff, for Thaelmann the communist as for Hitler who put him in jail. Closest to the heart of all these men was the dream of a new Germany redeemed from liberalism. This dream was not confined to ambitious politicians. It dominated the thought of intellectuals such as Otto zur Linde, whose review *Charon* gathered round it writers who wished to regenerate Europe and usher in a new Dionysian age, and Rudolf Pannwitz, who has looked forward to a Europe united under Franco-German domination.

Two factors help to explain these branches of German thought: first, the historio-geography of Germany in the eighteenth and nineteenth centuries; second, the religiousness (itself partly the product of historio-geography) of the German intellectual. German culture before 1870 was more like the Swiss than like the French in that it was municipal rather than national or metropolitan. When Fichte addressed *die deutsche Nation* he was addressing a body of very vague outlines, *das deutsche Volk,* a body of men which contrived to build up a sense of kinship through such emotive terms as *Rasse, Blut, Volk,* for lack of clear political boundaries such as those of the French and English. Our knowing ethnologists have "exposed" the German myths of race, but their attitude of indignant superiority has prevented them from recognizing the nature of German national-ism. Scientific ethnology can expose only the least important part of racial myths, just as Victorian scientists could expose the least important parts of Christianity. In its failure to explain how racial myths grew up and why people still believe them, scientific ethnology has been as much a display of arrogance as the Aryan myth itself.

Since so many Germans, especially middle-class Germans, are religious in their modes of thought, it is natural that the new

religion founded on historical imagination should have found its
most fervent adherents in Germany. While in the nineteenth
century Anglo-Saxons, Frenchmen, and others turned increasingly
from the Christian religion to a secular liberalism, many Germans
felt the need, if they could not cling to the old faith (as most of
them could) for a counter-religion. (One recalls Blake's remark
—very applicable to all the inverted Christians of this book—
that if men will not choose the religion of Jesus, they will choose
the religion of Satan.) The faiths which non-Christian Germans
have lived by in the past century have often been surrogates
for Christianity: attempts to find, not a new logic or even a new
metaphysics, but a form of living and feeling and thinking that
would be to the modern world as Catholicism was to the Middle
Ages. Most of the relevant conceptions have been historical
and evolutionary, but the *metapolitical* attitude to history and
religion, to adopt Mr. Viereck's term, has itself been religious.
To the metapolitician the historical process is, in Max Eastman's
metaphor, an escalator: a man can cooperate with it by walking
forward or vainly protest by walking in the opposite direction;
the escalator moves inexorably on. It is easy to see how unim-
portant, in this respect, are the differences between idealism and
materialism in modern thought. Marx and Hegel are agreed
upon the metaphysic of the escalator. What they both deny is
the metaphysic of the Platonists and Christians on the one side
and the free-will of pragmatism on the other. As Nietzsche said,
the doctrine of *der werdende Gott* (the developing God) in Hegel
is a mythological representation of the historical process. When
the same mind was so religious as to demand a God and so
historical as to demand an evolutionary philosophy, the natural
result was Hegelianism.

2

As a previous generation in Germany had been intoxicated
with Protestantism, so are modern Germans with history. Oswald
Spengler (1880-1936) and Heinrich von Treitschke (1834-1896)
are classic examples. They are the dipsomaniacs of historiog-

raphy. They reel through the corridors of the past with a lucidity
and eloquence that only drunken elation can attain. They have
this in common with the paranoiac: that, while they are careless
as to the accuracy of their statements, they build up a consistency
of interpreted facts, a consistency that is luminously clear. Carlyle
always called for a bible created out of the historical imagination
which should possess all the ardor of religion and all the information of the encyclopædias, a poetic emanation of a people and a
race. Treitschke wrote such a bible for modern Germany; Spengler for all Western culture.

Spengler took up the tools of a century of metapolitics and
used them without fear or favor. In his equipment I find eight
important ideas.

(1) The seasonal metaphor as a description of human history.
Within this guiding conception, Spengler manipulates his notion
of "culture" (the summer of an era) and "civilization" (the
autumn). Starting from the metaphor of the tree Igdrasil,
symbolic, in Spengler as in Carlyle, of the organic nature of social
development, and from a cyclical theory of history, Spengler
pushes vitalist interpretation to the utmost limit in his seasonal
charts on which the life and death of cultures, each analogous
to the other, are traced in detail.

(2) The modern repudiation of metaphysics in favor of
history is restated in Spengler's antithesis of Truth and Fact.
Truth is the possession of the passive, contemplative mind which
is, as far as possible, outside the march of historical events. Truth
is the solace of the impotent who compensate for their inability
to act by knowing and analyzing. Fact is that which the active
man recognizes and confronts. It is the element he lives in. The
man of Truth *knows*, but his knowledge is inert, though (or
because?) immutable and timeless. The man of Fact does not,
perhaps, know, but he lives. Jesus is the prototype of men of
Truth, Pilate of men of Fact. Pilate's question "What is truth?"
is significant because Pilate did not stay for an answer. Spengler's
antithesis is a brilliant oversimplification of Carlyle's predilection
for Frederick the Great who "gravitated towards facts" and of

Nietzsche's comments on the powerlessness of contemplative intellect.

(3) Spengler seeks to give the historical imagination primacy by removing the last vestige of philosophy. In sociology, if we are to believe him, "political science" is a mere offshoot, a rather morbid offshoot, of the tree Igdrasil in the sere and yellow leaf, a sign that a civilization is drawing to a close. The man of Truth has a God; the man of Fact, and such admirers of the man of Fact as Spengler, prefer the non-theological, non-philosophical term, *Destiny*. History is basic. History is the evolution of life. The living organism cannot be comprehended by static Cause and Effect. Let the driving force in history, a force which is undoubted because intuited by the man of Fact (e.g. Napoleon), be called Destiny. (It was in *Frederick the Great* that Thomas Carlyle, having deserted the God of his fathers, appealed to "the Destinies.") The term *soul* is used by Spengler to characterize a state of mind appertaining to an epoch (e.g. Magian, Apollonian, and Faustian souls).

(4) Carlyle and Nietzsche had, on the one hand, worshiped Cæsar and, on the other, asserted that the greatest man was the thinker who created new values. Not, apparently, being involved, as Nietzsche was, in internal conflict, and not being concerned to create new values himself, Spengler has no hesitation in granting to the great soldier and statesman priority over all other men. The indecision of Carlyle and Nietzsche is abrogated, if not resolved, and in this as in other respects Spengler picks up one of their ideas, drives it to an unequivocal conclusion, and makes of it a tool of historical interpretation.

(5) Nietzsche is more lavish, Spengler more consistent. Spengler's idea of the hero is less various and suggestive but more clear and precise. The Spenglerian man of Fact has not much control over the destined course of history, but he is the necessary instrument of Destiny. The two chief types of hero are the Alexanders and the Cæsars. (Mommsen had worked out the antithesis in his Roman history.) The Alexanders are the embodied spirit of youth and yearning, of gallantry and unquenchable will to power. The Cæsars occur at a much later

phase in the cycle of time. In an age of decay they bring life and discipline to disintegrated democratic society. Alexander stands for youth and romance, Cæsar for age and realism. If the formula be applied to the present cycle, it is evident that Napoleon is our Alexander, planting the hope of conquest and empire in the hearts of modern Europeans, and that Spengler, throughout the twenties, was awaiting the new Cæsar.

(6) Spengler elaborated Nietzschean ideas of the period between Alexander and Cæsar, the period of contending states. Rationalism, sentimentality, hedonism, analytic philosophy, vulgarity, commercialism, belief in the common man, are the symptoms of decline. But decay is also seed-time. A second religiousness appears as democracy declines. A Cecil Rhodes arrives to announce the impossibility of liberal monotony: "expansion is everything." Instead of *happiness* and *salvation*, instead of money-values and truth-values, there reappear *honor* and *nobility*. Nietzsche had asked: *Was ist vornehm?* (What is noble?) Spengler's answer is that the noble man of Fact is not a thinking machine but a highly trained organism—trained by praxis like an athlete or a race-horse. The man of Fact is not mentally analytic, impassive, and *hors de combat*. He is "in form," "in training." The timing of his actions (one thinks of Hitler) is judged instinctively. He walks, says Spengler, with the sure tread of a somnambulist.

(7) Instead of moral philosophy, said Nietzsche, we want naturalistic values; instead of sociology, a doctrine of the forms of dominion; instead of "society," the complex whole of a culture; instead of epistemology, a valuation of the passions; instead of metaphysics and religion, Eternal Recurrence. This is Spengler's starting point. The unconfessed argument of his books is *for* "life-values" (and his conception of *life* is corybantic) *against* money and against religion. His idea of a healthy society comes wholly out of Nietzsche, though it does not, any more than Stefan George's philosophy, lay under contribution anything like the whole of Nietzsche. Spengler insists that man is a beast of prey and that greatness and happiness are incompatible; his work is relieved by no ray of Nietzschean sunshine.

(8) Carlyle believed that most people need drilling and dragooning, and Nietzsche's ideal society (if the phrase is not, for Nietzscheans, a violent oxymoron) is modeled on a military hierarchy. Spengler takes this conception seriously. Having written a Ph.D. dissertation on Heraclitus, the great exemplar of Heroic Vitalism, he inverts the dictum of Clausewitz that war is a continuation of politics by other means and declares that politics is a continuation of war by other means. The severity and sourness of his mind attracted him to the myth which caught the imagination of all Heroic Vitalists (Carlyle, Nietzsche, Stefan George, D. H. Lawrence), the myth of Armageddon and the millennium, or, in its northern form, *Götterdämmerung*, which is Armageddon without the millennium. Some have argued that the title *Der Untergang des Abendlandes* (The Decline of the West) is misleading in that the book is chiefly an exposition of a cylical theory of history. But when Spengler chose his title he knew that the work was a polemic against the plutocratic democracy which, *he hoped,* was on the decline; the book is a philippic against England and France and an elegy on the Kaiser's Germany. The apparatus of historical analogy is a persuasive strategy.

3

The poet and the paranoiac find connection where the logical mind finds none. The assumption of German historicism is that all things are knit together by bonds which the intuition, if not the intellect, can discern. Defining a man as the sum of social relations, Marx, for instance, gives the cue to Engels, who, while he denies the manifold interconnections of classical metaphysics, makes of the universe a complex of systematically interacting forces. But in practice the historiography of Marx and Engels is kept pretty firmly anchored by their common sense and their materialism. Spengler's ship has no anchor.

Spengler assumes that cultures develop in identical cycles, that there is always an exact analogy between, say, the painting of a period and its mathematics, between its political system and its

physics. Is this a rigid determinism? Religionists of the Middle
Ages always found the doctrine of free-will hard to reconcile with
the omniscience of God, and historical religionists like Spengler
find the doctrine of free-will hard to reconcile with the determinism of their escalator theory. The Christian solved or evaded
the difficulty with a paradox: In Thy service is perfect freedom.
The same paradox (except that *Thy* refers to the process of
history) underlies the philosophy of Nietzsche and Spengler.

Mediæval discussions of the hierarchies of angels are often
considered funny, but cosmic forces as remote from scientifically
verified experience are taken seriously by German historicism.
As Wagner postulated a primordial conflict between North and
South, so Bachofen, at one period a friend of Nietzsche's and
subsequently admired by members of the Stefan George Circle
and by many Nazis, postulated a primordial conflict between East
and West. It is hard to see what truth there is in such theories.
They are offered here as typical products of a new pseudo-
religion. The chief categories of the influential thinkers of this
type are strange to non-German ears and no easier to define
than the terminology of the Declaration of Independence would
be for a Hindu or a Mohammedan. Gobineau, a Frenchman
chiefly read in Germany, divides men in White, Yellow, and
Black races, names which bear less relation to the color of the
skin than to Gobineau's moral preconceptions. Through Alfred
Rosenberg's *Der Mythus des 20. Jahrhunderts* (*The Mythos of
the Twentieth Century*) stalk ghostly figures like "the race-
soul," "the Jewish mythos," "blood and honor," "the German-
nordic law." Rosenberg's book, the most complete statement of
Nazi ideology, is the culmination of the historical development
which we have traced. Rosenberg acknowledges his debt to
Bachofen, Paul de Lagarde, Wagner, and Stewart Chamberlain.
He brings together the theories of his predecessors in the school
of intuitional historicism into a vitalistic philosophy that is built
round the words "race-soul," "nationality" (*Volkstum*), "personality," "cycle of culture" (*Kulturkreis*). The old order will
fail, and a new order will create "a nation of brothers." Rosenberg aligns himself with the humanists against the "obscure men"

of the age and with the Greeks against the Barbarians. The mythos of the Middle Ages was Catholicism with Rome at the helm; the mythos of the twentieth century is "Aryanism" with Berlin at the helm.

Rosenberg's myth did good service for Rosenberg, for many a muddle-headed mystagogue is a clear-headed go-getter. It made him a leader of what was called culture in Hitler's Germany. But Oswald Spengler could not stomach it. If he was eccentric and superstitious, at least his eccentricities and superstitions were disinterested. The quiet, cultured historian who had graciously entertained a Jewish publisher from New York, who had politely and wistfully answered an American lady's query: "Would peace prevail in the modern world?" was profoundly disturbed and shocked by National Socialism. His last published work was a cautious criticism of the new regime; an official rejoinder was issued. Spengler discovered that the defeatism of *The Decline of the West* was a luxury permitted only by the decadent republic which he had condemned; from now on, optimism was compulsory.

Perhaps the old historian told himself that if this was the new order he preferred the old. It is said that he hoped the Pope would excommunicate Hitler; the papacy at least had not put pessimism on the index. Spengler stood by his vision, individualistic as any liberal bourgeois. Like the last guardian of Pompeii, to cite an analogy he would have found more congenial, Spengler remained at his post when the heavens fell, dour, stubborn, disgruntled as ever. He may have been reckless, perverse, diabolical, even crazy; but he was neither a lackey nor a crook. Like Thomas Mann and other defenders of Kultur against Civilization, Spengler may, in some small degree, have prepared the way for Nazism. But he was an Heroic Vitalist, not a Nazi.

CHAPTER X. Stefan George and His Circle

> ". . . Liebe
> *Gebar die Welt, Liebe gebiert sie neu.*"
> STEFAN GEORGE, "Hyperion." [1]

> "*Wer niemals am bruder den fleck für den dolchstoss bemass*
> *Wie leicht ist sein leben. . . .*"
> —STEFAN GEORGE, "Der Täter." [2]

1

Early in 1889 Friedrich Nietzsche, hitherto the greatest mind
in Europe, left Turin, a mental corpse. Just at this time there
entered Turin a young German who was to continue Nietzsche's
work, though as yet he did not know it. This was Stefan George,
who had already written not a little, planned much more, and
published nothing. He took up Nietzsche's idea of an elite and
formed his Circle (*Georgekreis*). Nietzsche's first editor, Fritz
Koegel, was for a time a member. Another Nietzschean, Kurt
Breysig, a Berlin professor who spoke at Nietzsche's funeral, was
also a friend of George. In the early years of the twentieth
century, the historian of the movement tells us, some members
of the Circle studied naturalism, some Tolstoy, some Ibsen. But
all, he emphasizes, were bewitched (*hingerissen*) by Nietzsche.

The influence of Nietzsche was of course felt at this time in
many directions, but the influence he exerted on George was
purely in the direction of Heroic Vitalism. For the same social
and psychological forces were at work in the George Circle as in
Carlyle and Nietzsche. George is characterized by the same
ambivalence, that is, just like Carlyle and Nietzsche, he has an

---

[1] "Love gave birth to the world; love gives birth to her again."
[2] "Who never calculated the place for the dagger on his brother's body,
how easy is his life. . . ."

authoritarian side and a liberal side, and thus becomes a subject of endless partisan controversy. He wrote a poem about Nietzsche which indicates the way in which he wished to lead Nietzsche's teaching, namely, towards his doctrine of New Love:

> *Der kam zu spät der flehend zu dir sagte:*
> *Dort ist kein weg mehr über eisige felsen*
> *Und horste grauser vögel—nun ist not:*
> *Sich bannen in den kreis den liebe schliesst. . . .*[3]

On the one hand, George transferred the Nietzschean philosophy to the spiritual plane, and the tone of George Circle writings is much more lofty and remote from worldly affairs. On the other hand, it is the boast of Georgeans that George put into effect what Nietzsche merely thought. For George actually brought together such a group of believers in Heroic Vitalism as Nietzsche had often dreamed of, and the superman who was never more than a glimmer for Nietzsche was for the Circle incarnate in the boy they called Maximin. Furthermore George wrote specifically of the heroic rebirth of Germany after the First World War. In "Der Krieg" ("The War," 1917) he praised Hindenburg who, he said, had saved from destruction what the parliamentary prattlers had disgraced—the Reich. In "Der Dichter in Zeiten der Wirren" (The Poet in Times of Confusion) George sees a new Reich arising from the deeds of a hero who marches under a "folkish banner" (*voelkisch* is a word associated peculiarly with the Nazis): "he bursts the chains, refurbishes order on the ruins, whips the decadents home to eternal justice where greatness is once more greatness, master once more master, discipline once more discipline. He fastens the true symbol on the folkish banner. Through storm and terrible signals of dawn he leads the troop of his followers to the task of the bright day and plants the new Reich."

The pattern of the George movement is sinister, for is not George a sort of a literary Hitler, with Nietzsche as his Houston

---

[3] "He came too late who imploring said to you [*Nietzsche*]: there is no road any more over icy crags and eyries of terrible birds—now it is necessary to confine oneself in the circle closed by love. . . ."

Chamberlain, Maximin as his Horst Wessel, and Gundolf as his Rosenberg? The subject is worth investigating since George is a first-rate poet, and a poet peculiarly of our time. In that he bases his work not upon an accepted system of values but upon a subjective myth, in that he inclines more to nuance than to irony, in that he has more virtuosity than imagination, in that, like Richard Strauss, he prefers splendid orchestration to Mozartian economy, George is the greatest of all decadents. In his mastery and presentation of one small tract of experience, in his superb control over the dialectic of the short poem, he is the greatest of minor poets. If he is also one of the most meretricious of minor prophets, he none the less achieves through his prophetic pose the quality which of all moral and æsthetic qualities is most remote from the present age: grandeur.

There is an instructive parallel between the careers of George and the Irish poet, W. B. Yeats. Both began as æsthetes, both were interested in the occult, both yearned after past ages and consequently after aristocratic friends, both discarded their singing robes for the nakedness of their later poems, which are among the most powerful of our time, poems which express a philosophy of courage, austere, noble, anti-democratic, and somewhat perverse.

The story of Stefan George should be told from the beginning —a formidable task, for at present no complete or concise account is available. The short books on George are hopelessly fragmentary, the long ones—with one exception—non-biographical. The exception is Friedrich Wolters' *Stefan George und die Blätter für die Kunst: deutsche Geistesgeschichte seit 1890* (Stefan George and the *Blätter für die Kunst:* German intellectual history since 1890). This preposterous book is the official life. George was no lover of biography, and the book was put out to stifle rumors; Wolters' information, emanating from the Master, as he calls George, was to be regarded as final. His book was to be a life to end lives. It is the chief source book, but an enormous haystack has to be searched for a mere handful of needles. Wolters' pretentiousness outcrops in excessive generalizations and abstractions. Moreover he regarded George as a god, or at least as the high-priest of the church of his own god, Maximin. One of the few conversations in the book inevitably suggests Jesus talking to the rich young ruler. "What shall I do?" asks a young man who is inquiring about his own and the world's salvation; "Put yourself in my place, and I will do what you say." "I cannot tell," George replies. "If a man does not know of himself what he can do for me, I cannot enlighten him." When Wolters condescends to give details he is usually silly. In a description of the Master he writes: "As far as physiognomy is concerned I might add that George's ears are of especially beautiful construction."

2

Stefan George, born in 1868, was the son of a wine-dealer at Büdesheim, near Bingen. His ancestry was either French or German or Walloon or a mixture. While his parents were not rich enough to provide George with an aristocratic home, they were not poor enough to deny him a more or less aristocratic education, first at the *Realschule* at Bingen, later at the *Ludwig-Georg Gymnasium* at Darmstadt. George's lifelong hatred of the small bourgeoise (*Kleinbürgertum*) was a masochistic attempt to flee his own heritage and early environment. The modern philosopher of aristocracy is seldom an aristocrat.

George later made a grand tour of Europe. In the late eighties and early nineties, he learned a lesson from each major European country. England, which he knew as much from his friendship in Germany with Cyril Scott as from his two visits to London, made him feel the value of a national culture as against the hitherto municipal culture of Germany. France brought him into contact with many modern poets. He attended the celebrated Tuesday evening gatherings at Stephane Mallarmé's; impressed by the example of Mallarmé and Verlaine, George wished to give laws to his own little senate. The impact of Italy and Spain was less direct. Italy was always for George as for Goethe, Nietzsche, and Thomas Mann, of symbolic importance. Spain, it is said, filled him with a longing for leadership.

This longing is the mainspring of George's career. We shall see that D. H. Lawrence, vainly seeking equality in love, concluded in despair that equality was undesirable, and that lordship and slavery were the terms of human relationship. A spiritual son of Nietzsche, George reached this conclusion without preliminaries. *Herrschaft und Dienst* (lordship and service), these were the prime necessities of the spirit. George was not imbued with mere lust for power. His urge to lead was ambivalent. It carried with it the urge toward abasement before a greater leader.

If George's life was a pursuit of incarnate deity, it was also a flight, a long flight from the middle-class home and the philistine, commercial society to which it belonged. Reverse the values of *Kleinbürgertum* and you will have the values of Nietzsche and George. Seeking refinement, nobility, and religion, Nietzsche and George were of necessity very lonely men. They yearned for stronger bonds than the love of women. They yearned to lead men and to be led.

George was a supreme egotist. As a boy he sketched a language of his own and a kingdom. As a man he established himself as a literary dictator. One critic relates that when he visited George thirty years ago, the poet was wearing a toga. The table was covered with ivy. Even George's posture was Roman: he was reclining propped on his elbow. The room was sparsely but carefully appointed. The books were few: Plato's *Phædrus* in Kassner's translation, Shakespeare's Sonnets, Goethe's *Winckelmann*. On the wall was a picture of a beautiful boy in the scanty dress of a Greek shepherd. It was Maximin.

The scene is typical. Nearly all those who have set down their memories of George—Herbert Steiner, Friedrich von der Leyen, Cyril Scott, Sabine Lepsius—report strange evenings when by candlelight the poet-priest-prophet intoned his poems to the hushed and reverent disciples. The sprightly Maria von Reventlow wrote a delightful satire about George and his *entourage* in which the chief scene is a party where the Master appears dressed as Julius Cæsar.[4] Sabine Lepsius reports alternative rumors that the book at one poetry reading was held by two naked boys

[4] *Herrn Dames Aufzeichnungen* (*Mr. Lady's Observations*). München, 1913.

or that girls carrying lilies read the poems in a room with violet walls.

George wore his Bohemianism with a difference. While he was a middle-class German of the solemn, humorless sort, he was also homosexual. The doctrine of the New Love—*Das neue heil kommt nur aus neuer liebe*[5]—is the product of a homosexual mind. Whether George (or, for that matter, Walt Whitman who preached the New Love in *Calamus*) would confess to homosexuality is irrelevant except in so far as unconscious homosexuality is subtler in its manifestations than the conscious sort.

George may have considered his attachments to men in terms of religion and philosophy and have claimed his was in the proper sense Platonic love, such love as Socrates felt for Alcibiades. His choice among Shakespeare's Sonnets (those which give weight to Oscar Wilde's theory were published in the *Blätter*) seems to bear this out. So—more obviously—does his choice of the *Phædrus* among Plato's dialogues. *Winckelmann*—from a literary standpoint—is a more dubious choice, for Winckelmann is the prototype of the schoolmaster dreaming of the ghosts of Greek boys. The George Circle was a group of Platonic philosopher-kings.

George's life from 1898 to 1919 has with some reason been identified with his magazine *Die Blätter für die Kunst,* which appeared in twelve series between those dates. The George Circle was his little world, and the record is one of the exits and entrances of the members. A list of them is not uninformative. It contains many nonentities, several conscientious scholars, one brilliant critic. Wolters' seeming belief that their history is "the intellectual history of Germany" is, of course, monstrous, but it shows how the group thought of itself. The Circle was a closed one. Among German contemporaries, the only important poet whom they were ever interested in, aside from the Master, was Hugo von Hofmannsthal who at first was a leading contributor to the *Blätter* but later refused to be dominated by George, and quit.

Die Blätter für die Kunst—its title taken from *Ecrits pour l'art,*

---

[5] "The new salvation comes only from new love."

a French symbolist periodical—was founded by George and one of his first recruits, Carl August Klein, chosen by George because, it seems, he was easy to manage. George's magazine lived twenty-one years because he allowed no brother near the throne. In the nineties a nucleus was formed: it included Ludwig Klages, Alfred Schuler, Karl Wolfskehl, Leopold Andrian, and a George Edward who was subsequently a professor in America. Andrian was an Austrian aristocrat and writer of the Viennese decadent variety. Wolfskehl, being a Jew, was a somewhat precarious ally of the anti-Semitic Schuler and his friend Klages. Schuler was an amazing person, full of ancient lore and superstition, much of which he believed. He and Klages introduced their comrades to the work of Bachofen, who found matriarchy to be the first state of society. Our three *Cosmiker*, as Wolters calls them, discuss Eros and make free with the prefix *ur*. Wolters announces that around 1902 their theories—which attributed primacy to the feminine principle—proved so offensive to the Master that he broke with two of them. Wolfskehl remained after the purge.

The first Georgean group was composed of men about the Meister's age. Melchior Lechter, a pretentious pre-Raphaelitish painter who designed the extant editions of George, was indeed three years older than George. But elders and coevals did not provide the inspiration and leadership which George needed. Increasingly he turned to the young. In 1896 an English boy, Cyril Scott, brilliant and learned beyond his years, entered the Circle. Any Englishman who wishes to judge the extent of Wolters' exaggerations should read the section on Cyril Scott: one would think that this minor disciple of Debussy was as celebrated in England as Elgar or Delius. Anyway, Scott lacked Teutonic solemnity and was dropped by the Circle.[6]

In 1899 George met Friedrich Gundolf, the one first-rate intellect actually produced by the Circle. This young Jew, the son of a famous mathematician at Darmstadt, and later a celebrated

---

[6] Mr. Scott expressed the hope of supplementing his *Years of Indiscretion* with a whole book on George.

Heidelberg professor at whose feet Josef Goebbels sat,[7] was to George what Sterling was to Carlyle: the unquestioning yet amiable and gifted hero-worshiper. George was *Herrschaft*, Gundolf was *Dienst*. Gundolf wrote many historical studies, and on one occasion revealed what was to him their meaning. He had been drawing for an hour or so on a large piece of paper. Then he said: "Here are the heroes I have written about." The paper showed a series of small portraits—of Cæsar, Dante, Shakespeare, Goethe and so forth. But the face of each was the face of Stefan George.

Because Gundolf was so completely his creation George could not find in him the godhead his heart craved. The arrogance which his enemies condemn appears in George's remark when he pointed out Gundolf to a visitor: "Look what I have made of him."

3

About the time of the break with the *Cosmiker* occurred the central event of George's life. This was his meeting with Maximilian Kronberger, a Munich lad who died at the age of sixteen on April 15, 1904. His name was stylized to Maximin, which was thought to be more godlike, more comparable to Beatrice and Diotima. In 1906 a handsome *Maximingedenkbuch*, designed by Melchior Lechter, gave to the Circle the poems of young Kronberger, some by George and his friends, and an overwrought piece of prose by George. In 1907 appeared what is perhaps George's greatest work, *Der Siebente Ring*, which contains a splendid section entitled *Maximin*. Kronberger had by now become recognized by the Circle as the god of the new age. It was thought neither blasphemy nor hyperbole to call him a Christ.

The real identity of Maximin is revealed by his modest literary remains which were privately printed a few years ago (there is no date in the booklet) at Zurich. Here is the story. One day, as Kronberger was walking down the street, a stranger asked leave

[7] See: "Goebbels's Jewish Teacher," by Alfred Werner, *Jewish Frontier*, March, 1942.

to sketch his head. Leave was granted, and at a later date the
boy discovered that his new acquaintance, Stefan George, was
the subject of a book by Ludwig Klages, and a poet. The boy
had already composed some verses, and the surprising thing is
that they deal with the favorite subject of Hölderlin and Nietzsche: the rebirth of manhood out of catastrophe, the victory of
semi-divine youth. Henceforward this was George's subject.
Here are some lines of Kronberger's which George used as an
epigraph for his poem "Die Winke":

> *Jezt naht nach tausenden von jahren*
> *Ein einziger freier augenblick:*
> *Da brechen endlich alle ketten*
> *Und aus der weitgeborstnen erde*
> *Steigt jung und schön ein neuer halbgott auf.*[8]

Kronberger's journal is an unincriminating account of trivial
incidents. We have a glimpse of the all-too-human George whom
Wolters conceals with his screen of pretentiousness, a moody,
unhappy, unstable man, maladjusted to others and perhaps to
himself. His moodiness on one occasion resulted in a temporary
estrangement from Kronberger; the boy was hurt but uncom-
prehending. On other occasions there was mutual satisfaction.
Once George said: "Max, do you believe that there exists a friendship higher than love?" And Max answered "Yes."

Of George's later life little has yet been written. He lived
always in seclusion from the great world, in the company of a
few friends. He never worked for his living, but inherited a little
money and lived a good deal on his friends. His name was never
in his lifetime bruited among the vulgar, though some of his
followers, such as Lothar Treuge and Ludwig Derleth, sought to
give his life-view wider currency. The Master frowned upon
these attempts. He died at Locarno in 1933. The last famous
photograph of him taken in 1928 shows him obdurate as ever,
handsome and ascetic, magnificent and forbidding.

[8] "Now after thousands of years draws near a single free moment: finally
all chains are breaking—from the earth, burst wide open, rises a new demigod, young and fair."

4

What was George's attitude to the events of 1914-33? Progressively he and his friends shifted away from their æstheticism. In fact they claimed never to have been æsthetes but to have avoided both Zola's naturalism and Wilde's æstheticism in their obvious superiority to both. That they avoided naturalism is obvious. That they avoided æstheticism has to be argued by reference to their *Männerbund.*[9] The æsthete is devoted to abstract Beauty, to art for its own sake; George is devoted to manhood, to art for *his own* sake. Art for Art's sake was a religion, but George's religion was different, a strange compound of *Calamus* and *Thus Spake Zarathustra,* a religion of man and, specifically, of Maximin, man, artist, hero, and god.

Sometimes Wolters writes as if George were a social poet, an anti-democratic political leader. George himself never wrote on politics, but Wolters, Gundolf, and the others were merely their master's mouthpiece in their frequent sallies against the "modern idols" of technological progress, feminism, the masses, and permanent peace. This Georgean philosophy is not that of Hitler and Rosenberg, for it has little to say of race; many of the Circle (Wolfskehl, Morwitz, Gundolf, Kantorowicz) were Jews; so were many friends of the movement such as Georg Simmel. If Rosenberg's key term is Race, George's is the Hero. If Hitler's most individual contribution in *Mein Kampf* is his analysis of propaganda and mass politics, George's attitude is contempt for all such concerns. It is true that he combines a hatred of the masses qua mob with a love of them qua *Volk,* but his love of the German *Volk,* while no Christian charity, was not always exclusive or bloodthirsty.

> *Erzvater grub, erzmutter molk*
> *Das schicksal nährend für ein ganzes volk.*[10]

[9] "Male league": German youth organizations, sometimes boy-scoutish, sometimes æsthetic, sometimes nazistic, are a social phenomenon of first-rate importance.

[10] "The patriarch delved, the matriarch did her milking, fostering destiny itself for a whole people" ("Urlandschaft" in *Teppich des Lebens*).

This is regional love of soil, not political love of nation.

But sometimes George was closer to politics. The Messianic Hope of Germany, the expectation of a national awakening out of the spirit of youth, Hölderlin's vision of a German Hellas, which we have seen to lie at the root of Nietzsche's faith, was also the dominant image of George's life after the death of Kronberger. The Master's changes are reflected in the works of the disciples. Younger members of the Circle wrote on Napoleon and Frederick II of Hohenstaufen; in 1924 Gundolf began his biggest historical work with the remark that the crying need of the age was for a Cæsar; Wolters made nationalistic speeches at the universities. "When the First World War was in the offing," writes a spokesman of the Circle, "the best of Germany's younger generation tried to shape the pattern of their lives to the ideas they had abstracted from his [George's] poems; when it had begun, soldiers carried his books in their packs, and after it was over, his influence grew from year to year. His younger friends, schooled in his thought, held important posts in almost all of the leading German universities, and members of the spreading youth movements declaimed his poems at their reunions." If not a Nazi, was George the leader of a rival anti-democratic movement? The question can only be answered after a careful perusal of George's political pronouncements.

Several years before the First World War a petition protesting against the drift to war was signed by intellectuals of England and Germany. Hofmannsthal, who was not averse to the reactionary pacifism of the Anglo-German aristocracy, wrote to George soliciting a signature. George did not answer, but we have the reply which he never mailed. It is sardonic and sad. There was, George said, no such simple method of preventing wars. Wars were the result of a long *but meaningless* drifting on both sides. No botching (*Verklebmittel*) was any use. George is closer to the melancholy defeatism of Spengler than to the chauvinism of Adolf Hitler, who, when war was declared in 1914, passionately gave thanks to God.

Modern war is meaningless. Such was George's considered opinion. Again like D. H. Lawrence, he was in favor of struggle

and heroism but opposed to meaningless slaughter. Not of course
that he opposed the war when it came—Wolfskehl defended
Germany against Romain Rolland in the newspapers—but he was
agonized by the slaughter of the youth. After the war George
wrote "To a Young Leader in the First World War" (he knew it
was not the last). An American editor has pointed out that here
George adopts the German view than in 1918 the army, un-
defeated, was betrayed by its leaders. This is true enough, but
not the point of the poem. Here is the passage where the German
myth is expounded:

> *Jähe erhebung und zug*
> > *bis an die pforte des siegs*
> *Sturz unter drückendes joch*
> > *bergen in sich einen sinn*
> *Sinn in dir selber.*[11]

That is to say, the conclusion drawn from the theory is not an
argument of hatred or a plan for revenge, but the simple reflection that the trials of the defeat have ennobled the young men
submitted to them. Events have meaning not in themselves—his
letter to Hofmannsthal described events as meaningless—but
only in persons, only in heroes. The poem ends with a picture of
the young leader crowned with the gold of a sinking sun. A
symbolic picture of George's Heroic Vitalism. The hero is
crowned; but the sun is sinking.

What were the relations of Stefan George and the Nazis? The
question has been much discussed, and Germanophobes have, as
usual, gone too far. Aurel Kolnai, in *The War against the West*
—a prime source for publicists in this field—attributes to George
the prime responsibility for the invention and dissemination of
Nazi philosophy. Yet though his index reads "George, Stefan:
passim," Kolnai nowhere shows an intimate knowledge of the
poet or his work. *The New Republic* (October 28, 1940) published a somewhat ill-informed article on the subject by Paul
Rosenfeld. The truth is not easy to come by. There are stories,

[11] "Sudden uprising and advance right to the portal of victory; fall under
oppressive yoke: (*both*) conceal a meaning, meaning in you yourself."

contradicted by many non-Nazis, that George not only ignored the overtures of Goebbels and Rust, who offered him money and a laureateship, but swore he would never live in Germany after 1933 nor would he be buried there. Another story is that George insulted Goebbels by having a reply sent to him by Morwitz, a Jew. Morwitz says he told the German government that George "did not wish to discuss the boundaries between art and politics."

What did the Nazis say? One of them, Hans Naumann, dedicated the sixth edition of his book on modern German poetry (1933) to Our Leaders, i.e., Hitler and George. Both, he says, are of German peasant stock, both without wife or kinsfolk, both have the same ideal of race and leadership, both have developed organically in their literary productions, both live for others. A book was written by one Margarete Klein who elaborated the theme. But evidently we have false ideas about Nazi unanimity, for the same year—1938—which produced Miss Klein's book produced a denunciation of George by another Nazi named Hans Rössner. Rössner correctly observed that the *Georgekreis* was not Nazi in that (1) George did not understand the philosophy of race; (2) George did not understand the role of woman as creator. (Ludwig Klages scored here and became Nazi candidate for the Nobel Peace Prize, presumably because though in theory opposed to peace he showed his real hatred of war by poisoning himself as much as was compatible with survival to avoid the draft in the First World War.)

George, Rössner says, was not the founder of a new humanism, but the last relic of an old order. He was a nineteenth-century decadent who by his strength of will gathered round him the parasites of the West—Jews. Rössner is not hard on George's homosexuality except in so far as it implies misogyny; the strongest argument he advances is *à propos* of the Wolters-Gundolf *Jahrbuch für die Geistige Bewegung* (1910-12) in which there appeared an essay by Berthold Vallentin (a Jew, to Rössner's joy), entitled: *Napoleon und die geistige Bewegung.* Rössner seizes upon the phrase *geistige Bewegung* ("spiritual activity," or, more roughly, "intellectual history") and demonstrates that for all their anti-democratic realism the *Georgekreis* are interested in Napoleon and other heroes only as an influence upon "intellectual history."

This is acute, true, and crucial. George is no sort of a politician; his interest is centered in the intellect and the individual. The only conclusion he draws from the 1918 disaster is that a youth is now more beautiful and brave. He is as unaware of Ludendorff and Ebert as he is of Liebknecht and Rosa Luxemburg. Stefan George's New Empire is of the mind, and any impression we may have to the contrary is due either to George's occasional inconsistency, to the richness in suggestion of his verse which is relevant on so many planes of reality, or to statements of other members of the Circle. Ernst Bertram, one of the cleverest, became a prosperous Nazi Professor at Cologne; Ludwig Thormaehlen, the sculptor, was a friend of the Nazis even before 1933; Max Kommerell lived also in Nazi Germany writing trivial novels in the escapist manner which became a vogue among those who were uncomfortable under the Nazis. But the new day did not dawn for the Jewish section of the Circle.

In 1909 Wolters called George's proposed empire: *das geistige Reich* (the spiritual Reich). He was right, and George has himself clarified the matter:

> *Dies ist reich des geistes: abglanz*
> *Meines reiches hof und hain.*
> *Neugestaltet umgeboren*
> *Wird hier jeder: ort der wiege*
> *Heimat bleibt ein märchenklang.*
> *Durch die sendung durch den segen*
> *Tauscht ihr sippe stand und namen*
> *Väter mütter sind nicht mehr.*
> *Aus der sohnschaft der erlosten*
> *Kür ich meine herrn der welt.*[12]

[12] "This is a realm [*Reich*] of the spirit: court and sacred grove are reflections of my realm. Here every man is reborn in a new shape: the place of his birth and his homeland are now but a tinkling sound out of a fairy tale. Because you have a mission, because you are consecrated, you change kin, rank, and name. Mothers and fathers are no more. From the brotherhood [*literally* "sonship"] of the men of destiny, I choose my world rulers." (From *Der Stern des Bundes*.)

The use here of the phrase *herrn der welt*—reminiscent of Nietzsche's *Herrn der Erde*—helps us to understand Gundolf's remark that Stefan George was the most powerful man in the world.

5

Many of Stefan George's beliefs and attitudes are Carlyle and Nietzsche all over again. The total rejection of the bourgeois world, the desire to recruit a new class of leaders, the worship of heroic life as exemplified in certain epochs of the past— these are familiar traits. But whereas we see Carlyle groping after Heroic Vitalism and Nietzsche defiantly brandishing it, we find George taking it up in a tired, melancholy, and bitter way. He is an Heroic Vitalist of a later generation.

One of the special symptoms of George's Heroic Vitalism is the peculiar twist he gives to the Bohemianism which was already the culture pattern of the artist, especially in France and Germany. George's Bohemianism is not gay but austere, not carefree but deliberate, not disreputable but pretentious. Previous Bohemianism was a frivolous protest against Puritan propriety; George's Bohemianism was quasi-religious. He habitually wore a clergyman's frock coat and tried hard to look like Dante. It is a form of Bohemianism which at once reflects the mind of the German middle class and is a flight from it.

In studies of George one reads of two cults: the cult of technique and the cult of the self. Their meaning is interlocked. That technique, the least secret of things, should become a cult is a symptom of decadence in art and nihilism in culture. The modern world is rejected, external nature is regarded as alien and hostile now that the gods have fled from thence, the poet is alone. How can he find value and meaning in life? Paradoxically he does it by surrendering to the disvalued, alien, external world. He abandons himself to sensations, and by so doing claims to restore value and meaning to the world. Such is æstheticism, the basis of the cult of technique.

The cult of the self—the phrase is that of the French reactionary, Maurice Barrès—is its inevitable complement. The poet, in his enormous superiority, in his immoralist espousal of good and evil alike, in his unique capacity to feel sensations and create values, is "the most powerful man in the world." He therefore believes in himself. As one critic put it: the difference between George and Jesus, when they call on men to leave all and follow them, is this: Jesus points with one hand to himself, with the other to heaven; George points with one hand to himself, and with the other to himself. Such a conclusion is, we have seen, implicit in *Thus Spake Zarathustra*; in Stefan George's life and work it is explicit.

George was an outsider. His sexual constitution, reinforced by his position as an artist, made him so. He called on his disciples to leave house and home. He hated the mores. He made Gundolf learn to forge his signature and, when the bank refused to accept Gundolf's version of "Stefan George," he refused to have a bank account at all. His hatred of bourgeois life is at the root of his linguistic theory and practice. He hated nineteenth-century speech, and *a fortiori* its imitations by the naturalists. Therefore he invented an entire language of his own; loved to speak and read foreign languages which did not for him have everyday associations; finally, forged an hieratic German of his own at the opposite pole from colloquialism. In the era of monopoly capital he not only repudiated capitalist civilization and "escaped" to a dream-world, he constructed a model of capitalist civilization in the cultural sphere. As a supermagnate and dictator of culture, he established himself as the monopolist of poetry; all the other poets and schools were decried or, worse, ignored. Wagner had promoted the habit of discovering *the* style of the future and of slandering all potential and real rivals; by the subtler method of snobbery and ostracism, George transformed Wagner's crude tactics to a fine art. No poet—not even Milton—ever made higher claims for himself. Nietzsche had thought it a privilege to be the John the Baptist of the superman; after Kronberger, George was the superman's St. Paul.

Yet Stefan George is Nietzsche simplified and distorted. Not only is he a smaller mind but a much less flexible one. Some of Nietzsche's vitalistic philosophy is taken over, but the pragmatic

attitude to truth gives place in George to an Hellenic cult of the
Whole and to an Hellenic assumption of fixed and eternal verities.
George came of Catholic stock and appealed to Catholic words
and symbols much as Carlyle appealed to Presbyterian words
and symbols. As with Carlyle the result is contradiction. On
the one hand George keeps up an appearance of austere and
orthodox virtue. On the other he follows Carlyle, Baudelaire,
and Nietzsche into diabolism, as for instance in a poem called
"Der Täter," where the man of action expresses his contempt for
those who have never looked their brother over with a view to
stabbing him, and in "Der Gehenkte," where criminality is found
to be the prerequisite of virtue and culture. At this point the
ascetic George is not far from the voluptuary, D'Annunzio, or
from the æsthetic diabolism of intellectual fascists generally.

Catholicism, Hellenism, nobility, pride, egotism, Bohemianism,
illiberalism, homosexuality, diabolism—the mind and art of
George is a strange compound. In its willful inconsistencies, its
arrogant gestures, and its antisocial attitudes, it bears witness to
the failure of nerve in European culture which weakened the
intelligentsia and postponed or undermined democracy. The
George Circle is one of the many cultured groups which developed authoritarian tendencies at a time when authoritarianism
threatened their very existence. One need not seek a theoretical
refutation of their position. The hero with the folkish banner
swept them away and thereby closed a curious chapter in cultural
history.

CHAPTER XI

D. H. Lawrence, John Thomas,
and Dionysos

*"Let us submit to the knowledge that there are aristocrats and
plebeians born, not made. . . . Some amongst us are born
fit to govern and some are born only to be governed."*
—D. H. LAWRENCE.

*"The hero is obsolete and the leader of men is a backnumber.
. . . The leader-cum-follower relationship is a bore. And
the new relationship will be some sort of tenderness, sensitive,
between men and men and men and women, and not the
one up one down, lead and I follow,* ich dien *sort of business."*
—D. H. LAWRENCE.

1

Critics of D. H. Lawrence's thoughts have been either scornful
or soulful. Some early evaluators of Lawrence's "message" were
so blind with zeal that they did not trouble to think out the
social implications at all. Other critics have been content to
show that Lawrence was a fascist, on the assumption that this
discovery disposed of him once for all. Others thought the merit
or the modernity of Lawrence's work sufficient proof that he was
not a fascist. But, in truth, Lawrence's thought is sufficiently
clear in 1944, and, if it is often illiberal, readers of today will not
be so surprised at the fact as were the reviewers of the twenties.

Since the Christian religion ceased to be accepted automatically
by all men of imagination, many myths have been devised, some
of which have already been described in this book. *The Four
Zoas* was Blake's attempt to interpret the creation of man in the
light of his own awareness. In the twentieth century the two
greatest mythopœic geniuses have been W. B. Yeats and D. H.

Lawrence. (T. S. Eliot and James Joyce have employed old myths rather than created new ones.) Despite its kinship with Spengler, Yeats's *A Vision* does not come within the scope of my subject, but the myth that is set forth in Lawrence's *Psychoanalysis and the Unconscious, Fantasia of the Unconscious,* and *Apocalypse* is a pure emanation of Heroic Vitalism.

D. H. Lawrence was born in 1885 in a mining village near Nottingham, England. The son of a good-for-nothing miner and an earnest Congregationalist mother, he was from the first cramped in circumstances, steeped in religion, and confronted at close quarters with an unhappily married man and wife. The father threw things at his wife, and the son sided with the mother so persistently that Lawrence's disguised autobiography, *Sons and Lovers,* is a case history of an Œdipus complex. In 1910 the mother died, and two years later Lawrence eloped with the wife of one of his professors at Nottingham University, Frieda Weekley, the daughter of a German aristocrat named Baron von Richthofen. This lady was a tower of strength to Lawrence and guarded his shrine at Taos, New Mexico, till her dying day. During the First World War, Lawrence definitely took writing as a profession and made friends with the then important editor, Middleton Murry, and his wife, Katherine Mansfield. Irritated by the censorship of his work and by government agents who kept an eye on his German wife, Lawrence grew to hate England and left as soon as the war was over. The last years of his life were spent in wanderings which ranged over four continents. He was buried in the south of France in 1930.

As a personality Lawrence was as remarkable in his own way as Stefan George in his. Although the adoring women who followed him around have probably done as much harm to his reputation as the adoring Circle has done to George's, we can accept the verdict of all of them that Lawrence was a man of astonishing and magical vitality. Despite his thin, stooping figure and his receding chin, his presence was electric and unforgettable. Though in his foibles he is obviously quarry for Stracheyan biographers, he arrests our attention as a supremely "representative man." (That he was also a great writer I take for granted though it is not the greatness of the writing that concerns me here. My theme compels me, on the contrary, to stress the less great and non-great works.)

His career affords some interesting parallels. Like Carlyle and Nietzsche, Lawrence was born into a very religious home where the mother ruled. Like Carlyle and Nietzsche, he was taken out of the warm bath of his early evangelicalism and plunged into the rationalist and scientific skepticism of his time. Carlyle's life was a battle against the eighteenth century, Lawrence's against the nineteenth. Born in 1795, Carlyle had his roots in the eighteenth century, was more widely read in that period than in any other, was early "emancipated" by Gibbon and Hume, and lived to hate them for their pains. Born in 1885, Lawrence had his roots in the nineteenth century, was more widely read in that period than in any other, was converted to the attitudes of Huxley and Hæckel and later revolted against these attitudes. Science rendered a wholly negative service to Carlyle and Lawrence. It stripped them of their Christianity and left them, as far as religion is concerned, a *tabula rasa*. Carlyle ended with a religion of his own that was neither Christian nor eighteenth-century. Lawrence ended with a religion of his own that was neither Christian nor Victorian.[1]

It was Lawrence's friend, E. T., the Miriam of *Sons and Lovers,* who told us, in her charming *D. H. Lawrence: A Personal Record,* about Lawrence's period of scientific skepticism. It was she too who revealed the fact that the greater part of Lawrence's formative reading was in the literature of the nineteenth century. E. T. mentions close upon fifty nineteenth-century writers whom Lawrence read in late adolescence. The only others mentioned are (significantly enough) Swift and Blake. E. T. mentions Bacon only to add that Lawrence preferred Charles Lamb. Carlyle is mentioned, though no more conspicuously than many others. Lawrence read Nietzsche, but somewhat furtively and without encouraging E. T. to read him. Nietzsche is mentioned by Lawrence half a dozen times but these allusions are never very significant. For the most part Lawrence covered up his traces.

[1] For a further Lawrence-Nietzsche parallel see note on p. 111 above.

The dichotomy of religion and politics, the eternal and the temporal, the metaphysical and the historical has been at the back of this study of Heroic Vitalism. In Lawrence the dichotomy is clarified into that of Love and Power. All his endeavors, personal and literary, are attempts to discover more fully the meaning of these two words. On Lawrence's investigation of Love there has been a spate of comment. His life and his works have been the subject of chit-chat, scandal, and psychoanalysis. The focus is chiefly on love in *Sons and Lovers, Women in Love,* and *Lady Chatterley's Lover,* which are of all Lawrence's works the most widely read. But in *Kangaroo, The Plumed Serpent, Reflections on the Death of a Porcupine, Psychoanalysis and the Unconscious, Fantasia of the Unconscious, Apocalypse,* in many of the letters and in many of the essays in *Phœnix,* it is the relation between Love and Power that Lawrence examines.

Lawrence has told us that "this pseudo-philosophy of mine . . . is deduced from the novels and poems, not the reverse."[2] Let us, therefore, look for a moment at Lawrence's two chief novels about power, *Kangaroo* and *The Plumed Serpent.*

2

Kangaroo is a version of Lawrence's life during the years 1916-22. It described a conflict and an attempt at resolution; and ends with departure to fresh woods. The conflict began (in England in 1916) with Lawrence's questionings about the meaning of the war. He had no conscientious objection to warfare, for he believed with Carlyle and Nietzsche in the necessity of struggle. Nietzsche lived to regard the victory of 1870 as worthless and Carlyle thought all the wars of his lifetime futile. Lawrence, in like manner, disapproved the particular war under his nose while not disapproving war in general. Physically vast, the war seemed to him spiritually trivial. It would settle nothing. If only men could have fought it out cleanly that would have been something, but trench warfare was a blasphemy against life itself. The war did three things for Lawrence besides shattering his nerves.

[2] *Fantasia of the Unconscious,* Foreword.

It made him into an opponent of democracy. It tore him up from
his roots in English society. It emptied the universe of all meaning for him.[3] That he went in search of a new anti-democratic
religion only emphasizes the obvious similarity between this stage
of his career and that of many others in his generation, of whom
Adolf Hitler is the best known.

Giving up Europe for lost, Somers (Lawrence's hero) sails—
as Lawrence himself had done—for Australia, hoping to find a
meaning in human life and a solution of the social problem. He
encounters there two political movements, the communist and the
nationalist, which aim at replacing the old Christian-democratic
world with a new way of life. Somers, like Nietzsche, finds the
motive of communism to be envy and the denial of authority.
The Victorian bourgeoisie have idealized work and now the cult
of work has been taken over by workers' movements, which make
service, not the gift of leadership, the test of authority. But this
is to reverse the natural and necessary order of things. The Communist leader, Willie Struthers, is represented as lean and covet-
ous. He embodies mere *lust* for Power.

The Nationalist leader, Kangaroo, appeals to Somers more
strongly. Kangaroo believes in the omnipotence of Love, and
Somers' problem is whether to accept the personal love of Kangaroo for himself and with it the gospel of love for the world.
The crisis in this conflict is reached when the wounded Kangaroo
tells Somers that he can recover only through the knowledge that
his love is reciprocated. The words "I love you" stick in Somers'
throat and Kangaroo dies. It should be added that the love of
the Nationalists suggests the *Kameradschaft* of the fascists, not the
universal benevolence of the older liberals, much less the *caritas*
of Christianity. One of the Nationalists talks this way: "Now
I hate the thought of being bossed and messed about by the Old
Country, or by Jew capitalists and bankers, by a lot of labor
bullies, or a Soviet" (Chapter X). Kangaroo himself has studied
Somers' anti-democratic essays, and his movement works through
athletic clubs in which the demobilized, discontented men of the
post-war slump gathered together. It is agreed that parliamentary

[3] *Kangaroo,* Ch. XII.

democracy is an anachronism. A new principle is needed for men to live by.

The real sense of liberty only goes with white blood. And the ideal of democratic liberty is an exploded ideal. You've got to have wisdom and authority somewhere. . . .

The secret of all life is in obedience. . . . Life is cruel—and above all things man needs to be reassured and suggested into his new issues. And he needs to be relieved from this terrible responsibility of governing himself. . . . Man again needs a father. . . .

The demobilized soldiery and disillusioned intelligentsia of the post-war years have much to answer for; it is they who laid the foundations of "the revolution of nihilism."

Somers repudiated Kangaroo not for his authoritarianism, but for three interlocked reasons: because Kangaroo believed exclusively in the power of love, because he did not comprehend the sinister nature of the mob, and because Somers himself was incapable of faithful partisan allegiance. This last point is important in the history of Heroic Vitalism. Many of the advocates of aristocratic principles in the past century have been too skeptical or too squeamish to give active support to the political movements which espouse their doctrines. Stefan George held aloof from National Socialism, and it is a serious criticism of aristocratic theorists that their revulsion from bourgeois industrialism and bourgeois religion is far stronger than their practical programs. The leaders Heroic Vitalism produces are not always more attractive than democratic leaders. Ramsay MacDonald was an unfortunate spectacle, but was Goering any more aristocratic? Furthermore, the advocates of hierarchy and social solidarity have frequently tended to an anarchistic extreme of individualism. According to his sister, Nietzsche stated his disinclination to marriage in the following terms: "Why, I should have to become a citizen in some European community, exercise a vote, take account of wife and child, of my wife's family, of the place I live in, of the people I had intercourse with! Such a state of bondage would be the ruin of me." The First World War reduced Somers, in *Kangaroo,* to a similar anarchism. "Never

while he lived again would he be at the disposal of society"
(Chapter XIII). Protestantism, the religion of individual conscience, reaches its extreme in Lawrence's nonconformity. "So he
discovered the great secret: to stand alone as his own judge
of himself, absolutely. He took his stand absolutely on his own
judgment of himself. Then the mongrel-mouthed world would
say and do what it liked. This is the greatest secret of behaviour:
to stand alone . . ." (Chapter XII). Like other Heroic Vitalists,
Lawrence can drop his defense of relativism when he comes to
his favorite absolute. He can drop his collectivism when he comes
to the favored individual: himself.

Somers was incapable of allegiance to a political cause. When
he ought to have been fired with enthusiasm, he was bored, self-
pitying, or self-despising. Like Carlyle and Nietzsche, Lawrence
was always a spectator, slightly jealous, but more enamored of
real leaders. As Carlyle's critics have found him politically ambitious, so Mr. Middleton Murry has found in Lawrence ca-
pacities for leading men.[4] An American fascist, Mr. Stebelton
H. Nulle,[5] considers Lawrence an unfulfilled Hitler, the hero as
politician, "dark, brooding, inward-looking, both of them, with
the same capacity for attracting loyalty and the same disdain for
intellectuals and æsthetes." Perhaps Lawrence had hoped to
enter politics under the patronage of Asquith, whose wife he
cultivated, as Carlyle had hoped to be patronized by Sir Robert
Peel. At the period when *Kangaroo* was written, Lawrence wrote
elsewhere that he longed personally to save the common man from
mechanization. "I would like him to give me back the responsibility for general affairs, a responsibility which he can't acquit,
and which saps his life. I would like him to give me back the
responsibility for thought, for direction. I wish we could take
hope and belief together. I would undertake my share of the
responsibility, if he gave me his belief." [6] Belief from the hero-
worshiper, responsibility from the hero: the prescription is

[4] *Son of Woman*, New York, 1931, p. 158.
[5] "D. H. Lawrence and the Fascist Movement," in *The New Mexico Quar-
terly*, February, 1940.
[6] *Fantasia*, Ch. IX.

Carlylean. So is the personal ambition. So is the disappointment: for Carlyle and Lawrence were both outside politics.
Their love of nonconformity for its own sake prevented both of
them from being politicians. It was also inconsistent with their
view of society as an organism.

Somers had, therefore, to repudiate active reform, personified
in Kangaroo, and follow his destiny as a Flying Dutchman searching the world for perfect love. As has been said, he repudiated
Kangaroo partly because Kangaroo believed exclusively in love
and did not despise the mob. It was the mob-mind, operating
through Horatio Bottomley and the bellicose cheap press, that
made Lawrence an enemy of democracy. The Christian democratic ideal of Love was inadequate. Kangaroo got a bullet in
the belly, and that was the end of him. In place of the self-
indulgent, expansive emotion of Love, Somers proposed the
aristocratic virtue of courage. Never was Somers a better Heroic
Vitalist than when he wrote: "It is not the love, but the *Muth*
(courage) that I believe in" (Chapter VIII). As for love, it is
to be wedded to power. The two great telepathic vibrations of
love and power rule all the vertebrates, man and beast.

"Man, whether in a savage tribe or in a complex modern
society, is held in unison by these two great vibrations emitted
unconsciously from the leader, the leaders, the governing classes,
the authorities. First, the great influence or shadow of power,
causing trust, fear, and obedience; second, the great influence
of protective love, causing protectivity and the sense of safety.
These two powerful influences are emitted by men like Gladstone
or Abraham Lincoln" (Chapter XVI).

Most leaders, it seems, fail by leaning too much to the side of
power or too much to the side of love. Cæsar and Napoleon
leaned too much to the side of power, and Lawrence is against
them. Lincoln and Woodrow Wilson leaned to the side of love.
Wilson is for Lawrence the archetype of the good man whose
goodness makes for bad politics. We have to get on the other
side of Wilson's good and evil. As for Lenin, the anti-leader, he
is the embodiment of mob-mind, sheer envy, and insurrectionism.

3

Not finding what he sought in Australia, Lawrence left in 1922 for the New World. The fruit of his visits to Mexico was *The Plumed Serpent*. This book Lawrence meant to be his greatest, and he insisted that he agreed with the opinions of the chief hero, Don Ramon, who represents the marriage of love and power.

The book tells of an Irish *émancipée,* Kate, through whose eyes most of the story is viewed. She goes to Mexico and finds in progress a religious and social movement for national regenera- tion. The leaders of the movement are Don Cipriano, an Indian soldier, and Don Ramon, whose wife, Doña Carlota, symbolizes Christianity. The sexual problem, which also depends on the balance of love and power, is solved when Kate learns to forego her feminist independence and submit to a servitude that is perfect freedom as wife of Don Cipriano. Kate's final view of marriage is Milton's: "He for God only, she for God in him."

If we read: "He for God only, *they* for God in him," where *they* are the people, we have Lawrence's account of the relation of the masses to the hero and of the hero to "God," the life-force, the cosmos. Don Ramon is the model hero. After the death of Doña Carlota, he solves the sexual problem by marrying Teresa, a simple girl who finds her fulfilment in her husband and learns not to ask questions; this solution has a wider application. The nationalist movement offers the people a new religion whose emblem is not the cross but the serpent and the eagle. This, of course, is the emblem not only of ancient Mexico but of Nietz- sche's Zarathustra. And Don Ramon communes with the sun— another Nietzschean touch.

The new vitalistic religion which preaches that life is cruel and holy is opposed by Doña Carlota, whose Christianity had removed from life the holiness and the cruelty. Doña Carlota attends a service of the religion of Quetzalcoatl. (The word means bird- serpent. A dragon is of course a combination of the bird and the serpent, a primordial version of Zarathustra's emblem.) In her efforts to protest, she has convulsions and dies. It is thus that

Don Ramon breaks free of Christianity and subsequently marries a woman who knows her place. *The Plumed Serpent* ends with the personal and social success of all the main characters.

It is Lawrence's worst novel: a grotesque mixture, as Hugh Kingsmill suggests, of Rider Haggard's *She* and *Also Sprach Zarathustra*.[7] The type of badness that is most relevant here is the use of symbolism. It is ponderous and *voulu*. The cult of Quetzalcoatl is hocus-pocus. The regular symbols of Heroic Vitalism are frequent. "I wish the Teutonic world would once more think in terms of Thor and Wotan and the tree Igdrasil," says Don Ramon (Chapter XVII). Dionysos appears as Pan: "The God-demon Pan, who can never perish, but ever returns upon mankind from the shadows" (Chapter XX).

Since Carlyle, Heroic Vitalism has involved an enthusiasm for human flesh and blood. Carlyle wondered what the members of parliament would look like without clothes. Lawrence takes up the challenge and Cipriano shouts to his soldiers: "I am a man naked inside my clothes as you are" (Chapter XXII). Lawrence has not Carlyle's sense of feature and physiognomy. He imparts a sense of the physical presence and potency of a man without giving a description of his face. In *The Plumed Serpent*, Lawrence's physical awareness is at its most intense. The word *naked* occurs hundreds of times. An arm cannot be bare without Lawrence calling attention to a "naked arm." A man cannot be clothed without Lawrence's mentioning that he is "naked under his clothes." Carlyle took up the cry of Novalis that the body is holy and Lawrence is obsessed with the thought. He looks through the eyes of Kate, as in *Lady Chatterley* he looks through the eyes of Connie, in order that he may describe male beauty the more passionately.

Don Ramon might have come out of Byron or P. C. Wren. At this point Lawrence's is the Heroic Vitalism—is it not the most widely disseminated brand?—of boys' adventure stories and of Hollywood. "Don Ramon was flashing his knowing Spanish eyes and a little sardonic smile lurked under his moustache" (Chapter II). Sometimes, there is a sadistic touch. "The soft,

[7] *The Life of D. H. Lawrence.* New York, 1938, p. 216.

cream-brown skin of his back, of a smooth, pure sensuality, made
her shudder. The broad, square, rather high shoulders with neck
and head rising steep, proudly. The full-fleshed, deep-chested,
rich body of the man made her feel dizzy. In spite of herself,
she could not help imagining a knife stuck between those pure,
male shoulders. His nakedness was so aloof" (Chapter XII).

Ramon's political philosophy is not new. "'There is no such
thing as liberty,' she heard the quiet, deep, dangerous voice of
Don Ramon repeating. 'There is no such thing as liberty. . . .
You only change one sort of domination for another. All we can
do is to choose our master'" (Chapter IV). Ramon explains that
a man is led by an appetite, an ideal, or by an inspiration. The
categories are Lawrentian. Among the men of appetite are the
egoists, among whom he numbers Alexander, Napoleon, Cæsar,
Sardanapalus, and Saul. Shelley and Woodrow Wilson are men
with an ideal. ("Has President Wilson, or Karl Marx, or Bernard
Shaw ever felt one hot blood-pulse of love for the working-man,
the half-conscious, deluded working-man? Never."[8]) Who are
the men of inspiration? Lawrence offers Don Ramon.

4

All these ideas are so far in the tradition of Heroic Vitalism that
it is absurd to dismiss them as mere whimsies. It is hard to say
anything about Lawrence's faith that has not already been said
about one or other of the writers discussed on a previous page.
Lawrence pretends to accept a destiny without repining, yet in
fact he is forever complaining of his lot (cf. Nietzsche). Lawrence sometimes seems to admire nature more uncompromisingly
than he admires men. He finds animals more agreeable than
people (cf. Nietzsche and Wagner's Siegfried). He derives much
of his pungency from a certain immoralism "on the other side
of good and evil," yet he is himself persistently didactic. He was
born poor but rose to the heights of Bloomsbury, where he was
not at home. He loved to play the part of the fish out of water;
it is Nietzsche's anti-present-day-ism. He planned Utopian set-

[8] *Fantasia*, Ch. IX.

tlements in Florida and New Mexico; they were to be stocked,
like Nietzsche's projected Swiss château, with a select party of his
friends and disciples. Everyone noticed the analogy between his
farewell party in London (1923) and the Last Supper.

The detailed similarities of Lawrence to his predecessors are
innumerable. What Lady Ashburton was to Carlyle, Lady
Ottoline Morrell was to Lawrence: his combination of an ill
temper and a soft heart suited a patroness because it argued
genius. Lawrence's political views, summarized in the essays
"Blessed are the Powerful" and "Aristocracy," are: that authority
and obedience are the basis; that everyone is either a born aristocrat or a born democrat, a master or a slave; that the present
aristocracy has something to be said for it, but that aristocracy
is not necessarily hereditary; that regionalism is preferable to
internationalism;[9] that it is foolish to try to abolish suffering[10] and
that therefore the hero must rule "as he can";[11] that history is
cyclical, consisting of alternating periods of peace which palls
and of war which releases pent-up energies, and, finally, that the
unity which good Europeans desire will only be achieved when
Europe unites round a single figure, a hero responsible only to
"God," a hero who can lead a great war as well as administer a
wide peace.[12] But the Heroic Vitalist has a final card to play.
Ignorant of economics (only Carlyle among Heroic Vitalists even
toyed with the subject), he makes a merit of his ignorance by
representing Money, along with Christianity, as the great foe.
His enemies, in psychological terms, are appetites and ideals.
The corresponding material enemies are money and the churches.
Heroic Vitalism is anti-bourgeois and therefore against capitalism. It is anti-proletarian and therefore against Christianity.

Lawrence maintained with Stefan George that a new aristocracy
was needed to combat the commercial spirit and to inaugurate a
new age. The whole effort of Heroic Vitalists is towards excel-

[9] *Sea and Sardinia*, V.
[10] *The Crown*, III.
[11] *The Plumed Serpent* (Ch. XXV).
[12] *Movements in European History*. Written by D. H. L. under the pseu-
donym of Lawrence H. Davison. Oxford, 1922, p. 306.

lence in an age of mediocrity, dignity in an age of vulgarity, courage in an age of fear or complacency, honor in an age of chicanery. Lawrence's desire for aristocracy was no mere wish for a ruling caste. It was a desire for a renewal of manhood and of vitality. Lawrence came to regard the need which he had felt for absolute friendship with his peers to be misguided. It was a legacy of the era of universal benevolence, the "man of feeling," and the myth of perfectibility. In the new age, all equalitarianism must go. The place of friendship will be taken by lordship, even as the place of cash-nexus will be taken by mastership and servantship. "Lordship" means the relation between men which was encouraged by Carlyle. Lawrence defines it as "the other mystic relationship between men, which democracy and equality try to deny and obliterate. Not any arbitrary caste or birth aristocracy. But the mystic recognition of difference and innate priority, the joy of obedience and the sacred responsibility of authority." [13] A whole view of life is implied in these opinions and an attempt should be made to outline it.

Heroic Vitalists have tended, since Carlyle, to regard history in terms of spiritual epochs and cycles. They have never shrunk from large generalizations about these cycles, although they are not always clear about the motive-forces of history. They are unwilling to grant much efficacy to everyday cause and effect. They hate mechanical determinism. Heroic Vitalism is a protest against the machine, and therefore, Heroic Vitalists substitute a Higher Causality such as fate or destiny, or they assert free-will through the living power of the hero. The tap-root of their sociology is the concept Power, which they interpret broadly. "There is physical strength like Samson's. There is racial power, like David's, or Mahomet's. There is mental power, like that of Socrates, and ethical power, like that of Moses, and spiritual power, like Jesus' or Buddha's, and mechanical power like that of Stephenson, or military power, like Napoleon's, or political power, like Pitt's." Lawrence says that destructive power is also valid, if it is the old divine power and not the new, pas-

[13] *Kangaroo*, Ch. VI.

sionless power. The power of Napoleon and George Washington was right. So was Attila's, for "he was the scourge of *God:* not the scourge of the League of Nations, hired and paid in cash." As for Lloyd George, Wilson, and Lenin, "they never had the right smell."

Blessed are the powerful, says Lawrence, for this world is the greatest kingdom and it is theirs.

"The reign of love is passing, and the reign of power is coming again.

"The day of popular democracy is nearly done. Already we are entering the twilight, towards the night that is at hand.

". . . If you want a dictator, whether it is Lenin, or Mussolini, or Primo de Rivera, ask, not whether he can set money in circulation, but if he can set life in motion by dictating to his people." All this was published in 1925.[14] When one hears it said that writers of the twenties were liberal utopians, one can only smile. So many of Lawrence's generation spent their lifetime complaining of liberalism that a few years later—1930, 1940—we had all the illiberalism we needed.

Lawrence's view of history is expounded in *Twilight in Italy.* Its conclusions are often contrary to those of Nietzsche and Stefan George, and more akin to Carlyle's. The Middle Ages were healthy because of the tension set up between man's animal nature and Christian spirituality, the lion and the unicorn. The Renaissance was unhealthy because the spiritual and mental powers exceeded the Dionysian. The modern epoch (here Lawrence comes close to Nietzsche) has tried to annihilate the ego and its legitimate self-regard in an orgy of sympathy, emancipation, and insurrection. "When they beheaded Charles the First, the King by Divine Right, they destroyed symbolically forever the supremacy of the Me." This method of picking out a single figure and a scene to enforce a view of life is characteristic of intuitional historiography in general. Carlyle exhibits Luther at Worms, and Spengler, Jesus before Pilate.

---

[14] The quotations are all from "Blessed Are the Powerful" in *Reflections on the Death of a Porcupine.*

5

Christianity, Lawrence maintains, has been the greatest thing in the world so far. But history (as for all Heroic Vitalists) is organic. The flower blooms and fades, and so does Christianity. Or, to use Lawrence's favorite symbol, the phœnix dies but a new one arises from the ashes. Heroic Vitalists, and Lawrence among them, wish to assist at the birth of a new phœnix. Lawrence's criticism of Christianity is substantially that of Nietzsche. There are two Christianities. The first is that of Jesus, and its ethic is to render good for evil and to submit to the aggressor's violence. The second, according to Nietzsche, is that of Paul, and its motive is resentment and pride. This second kind of Christianity D. H. Lawrence attributes not to Paul but to John of the Apocalypse.

After his sharp criticisms of Christianity in *Twilight in Italy,* Lawrence was overcome by "the absolute need which one has for some sort of satisfactory mental attitude towards oneself and things in general." The two little books on the Unconscious provide myths for the new order. There is a myth of creation, involving a whole cosmology, and, more especially, there is a physiological myth of man. These myths are necessary because, as Carlyle knew, science and industry have taken the kernel out of the universe and Christianity stands by helpless. It is as absurd to say that the sun is gas as to say that it is toasted cheese. It is absurd to regard man biologically. These scientific computations forget Life. Where Carlyle attacks Bentham and vindicates the soul, Lawrence attacks Freud and vindicates the unconscious.

The basis of the argument is the idea of polarized duality. Heroic Vitalists had always replaced the uniformities of liberalism with the clash of opposites and Lawrence reiterates their doctrine. "The Infinite is twofold," he wrote, "the Father and the Son, the Dark and the Light, the Senses and the Mind, the Soul and the Spirit, the self and the not-self, the Eagle and the Dove, the Tiger and the Lamb." But the opposites in Lawrence are polar-

ized. He has contented himself with *rapport* between himself
and the beloved, the complete identity for which lovers strive
being attainable only in the womb and at the breast. Lawrence's
love poetry indicates a tremendous yearning for the love which
is to come to him through the philosophy of courage which is
Heroic Vitalism.

The body, according to Lawrence's theosophical myth, original
only in the interpretation he puts upon it, has four primary
centers of consciousness in polarized relationship. Two are
located in the thorax, two in the abdomen: the point of this being
that the brain or mind is not primary. The electrical circuits
which constitute life are not all completed within the individual.
There are three groups of circuits: those which run between one
center and another within the individual; those which run between individuals; and those which run between an individual
and the non-human cosmos. The Lawrentian theory of the hero
should now be more exactly comprehended. The hero is a necessity because most people lack the third kind of circuit, that which
runs between a man and the cosmos. The hero is the man who is
most fully alive because he possesses all three groups of circuits.
He is necessary because other people do not. Carlyle said that
while the law of master and man is inexorable, every man may be
in his degree heroic. The act of worshiping a master puts a man
in a vital *rapport* with the heart of the cosmos. "Give homage
and allegiance to a hero," says Lawrence, "and you become yourself heroic, it is the law of men."

6

So much for the need of heroes at all times. The need is especially acute today, says Lawrence, because of a steady decline in
human vitality and impulse; though many little serpents sting
us, the great divine dragon of vitality is inert. Lindbergh and
Dempsey, says Lawrence in *Apocalypse*, are lifted for a while to a
certain level of heroism. "But on the higher planes, there is no
glimpse or gleam of the great dragon." A new phœnix-hour is
awaited.

"Leaders—this is what mankind is craving for." The leader, Lawrence's *Fantasia* reveals, will bring in the year that is to be. In this age there will be no newspapers, because the people will not be taught to read and write. There will be no feminism, for women, tied to their husbands for life, will descend from the garret of intellect to the warm cellar of phallic consciousness. Children will not be taught about sex, and when they ask, "Why is grass green?" father will reply, "Because it is." No one will allow science to limit his horizon. Let a man believe, not that the sun creates human life, but that the sun was originally a piece of a primordial animal and is even now kept alive *by* human life. Here are a few sentences from Lawrence's blueprint for the new Heroic Age:

All schools will shortly be converted either into public workshops or into gymnasia. . . . Active training in primitive modes of fighting and gymnastics will be compulsory for all boys over ten years of age.

The great mass of humanity should never learn to read and write— never.

First and foremost establish a rule over them, a proud, harsh, manly rule.

There are wars in the future, great wars, which not machines will finally decide, but the free indomitable life spirit. No more wars under the banners of the ideal, or in the spirit of sacrifice, but wars in the strength of individual men.

Is it beside the point to recall that the advocate of the permanence of marriage ran away with the mother of three children, that the advocate of harsh rule was goaded to fury because the State interfered with him to the extent of stripping him for a medical examination, that the advocate of fighting gladly avoided military service in the only war for which he was eligible, that the advocate of gymnasia was himself a self-conscious weakling? The subjective element in the Heroic Vitalist has been important in three ways. First, Heroic Vitalism has been a projection of his own sense of vitality and superiority. Second, Heroic Vitalists have made an implied exception of themselves when advocating harsh discipline and immediate action. Third, they have all retained the right of the man in perpetual opposition to oppose in any and every way without regard to consistency. Nietzsche's attacks on the State, for instance, he contradicts elsewhere, and the chief interest of Lawrence's disclaimers of political intentions and of George's aloofness is that they prove the literary Heroic Vitalist's bark to be worse than his bite. He is not *really* in favor of the violence he appears to countenance. But this is to say that there is an element of irresponsibility in Heroic Vitalists. Many people protest against utopian liberalism and are later shocked at the result of their own protests. If you have talked like a man in perpetual opposition it is embarrassing to find yourself in office. Hence Stefan George's embarrassment at the Nazi victory of 1933. Death spared Lawrence a similar shock. It was better that his political disciples restricted their activities to folk-dancing.[15]

The ambivalence of Lawrence's character, his tenderness offset by violence of temper, is paralleled in Carlyle and Nietzsche and is equivalent on the psychological plane to the mixture of mysticism and militarism that characterizes Heroic Vitalists. Because Lawrence was more religious and less violent than some others, charity is more conspicuous in his social philosophy. In the essay on Whitman called "Democracy" he longs for the abolition of politics because the problem of love and life cannot be faced until the problem of food is disposed of. Heroic Vitalism is the æsthete's attempt to get beyond politics with its parties and economics and its businessmen. In his letters, Lawrence longs for a time when, through a correct relationship of leaders and followers, society will be founded on a reciprocity of tenderness. The world will be overwhelmed either by a wave of death or by a wave of love. Love is the desideratum, but it must be balanced and ensured by power.

[15] See *D. H. Lawrence and Susan his Cow,* by W. Y. Tindall (New York, 1939) for an account (Ch. VI) of Lawrence's (tenuous) connection with National Socialism.

7

So much for Lawrence's philosophy of love and power in its personal and social aspects. Lawrence had also a theory of time. His hunger for immortality was as strong as Carlyle's or Nietzsche's and like them he was haunted by Jesus of Nazareth. *Apocalypse,* his last work, exactly parallels Nietzsche's last work, *Antichrist.* Both books are a sharp assault on Christianity. The criticisms are substantially the same, and so is the animus. Yet much as they hated Jesus' indifference to power, Nietzsche and Lawrence were never fully convinced of the untruth of Christianity. Suppose the rich young ruler, when told to give his wealth to the poor, had given it to Jesus, suggests Lawrence and looks elsewhere for the immortality which the half-hearted Heroic Vitalist requires. Lawrence embarked on the same quest for a new immortality as Carlyle and Nietzsche.

In the volume of poems entitled *Look! We Have Come Through,* the idea of resurrection was used to support Lawrence's faith in the renewal of the phœnix-life of mankind. There is *Selbsttödtung* (self-killing), followed by new life as in *Sartor Resartus.* Heroic Vitalism attracts the twice-born. But there is a further point to Lawrence's two essays entitled "The Risen Lord" and "Resurrection," and to the story, "The Man Who Died," in which, following George Moore and Frank Harris, Lawrence has the crucified Jesus nursed back to health to live a new life according to the ethics of the modern writer.

The idea of Eternal Recurrence is not easily reconciled with Nietzsche's pragmatism, and I have made much of this irreconcilability. Nevertheless, Nietzsche contrived to make himself stronger by his idea of Eternal Recurrence. Heroic Vitalism is a philosophy of courage. The Heroic Vitalists are men who have the courage of their historical imagination, the courage to abandon morals and metaphysics, the courage to accept life. So far their view is consistently in terms of time. But they strained so hard at the leash of time that it snapped, and, if we are to believe what they say, they found themselves in a preternatural timeless world. Instead of repudiating this world of eternity, as would have befitted them, they drew from it energies with which they attacked those philosophies which asserted the importance of the eternal. They betrayed their own experience. They found in their mystical experience not an argument against vitalism but a fund of strength to uphold vitalism, not an impersonal doctrine of atonement but an added devotion to the hero. They strained at the leash of time and they strained at the leash of intellect. The leash of intellect broke, too, and Nietzsche, despite his sporadic encomia on the critical brain, described the mind of man, with everything else, in terms of power, while Lawrence thought complete mindlessness the necessary prelude to correct living. Don Ramon's prayer consisted of standing rigid with arm upraised until he became mindless, a column of dark blood.

8

It is easy to end with the vague conclusion that Lawrence preached regeneration, and not much harder to comb his life and works for activities and remarks which prove him a fascist. But the present analysis, if it proves anything, proves that Lawrence belongs not with the Nazis—even if he unwittingly strengthened the Nazi cause—but with the artists who in longing for perfection attacked democracy for its record of venality and vulgarity. Because Lawrence could not find the perfect democracy which he speaks of in his essay on Whitman, he rejected democracy altogether.

That is, sometimes. Consistency is not a Lawrentian virtue, and one finds in his anarchism, in his unwillingness to kill a fellow man, in his emphasis on tenderness, a rejection of fascist theory and practice. Lawrence esteemed the individual above everything else, and he hoped that workmen, not simply a few supermen, would become true individuals: hence he incited the miners to stand on their own feet.

An inconsistent author can be cited in support of anything. If Lawrence's portrait of Don Ramon convinces the fascist, his repudiation of Don Ramon ("The hero is obsolete . . .") convinces the democrat. The critic of Lawrence must recognize both sides of him. Don Ramon is the symbol of a great deal in Lawrentian thought, a symbol that cannot be canceled by a contemptuous remark in a letter. On the other hand, the recantation reveals Lawrence's uneasiness. Is inconsistency the best word? Oscillation would be a better description of Lawrence's changes from a philosophy of love to a philosophy of power. It might at first seem that in the late twenties Lawrence finally exorcised the fascist demon, and that *Lady Chatterley's Lover* represents a solution through John Thomas (as Lawrence called his hero's sexual organ) alone. But *Lady Chatterley's Lover* was followed by *Apocalypse*, the most fascistic of Lawrence's works. The conflict of Lawrence's life, like Nietzsche's, was unresolved at his death.

"The new relationship," says Lawrence, in his momentary rejection of heroes and hero-worship, "will be some sort of tenderness, sensitive, between men and men and men and women." The basis of this statement, beyond the stock charges of the æsthete that money, industrialism, and democracy have annihilated humanity, is the æsthete's itch for new sensations. Everything old is to be destroyed, and a whole world of *new* sensations is to be created. A new love will be created—this is the hope of many proto-fascists—in which all the pleasures of Christian *caritas,* tribal solidarity, homo and heterosexual passion, will be combined. Mr. Nulle has written of Lawrence and Hitler: "Both are adventurers who point the way to a quality of experience other than any yet achieved, knowing full well that the destruction of what exists is necessary to that which is to supersede it." The comment brings to mind the dictum of one of Lawrence's heroes whose first name is Dionys and whose second is Psanek (the outlaw): "I shall be king in Hades when I am dead." Lawrence's Dionysos professes belief in "the blessed god of destruction . . . the god of anger, who throws down the steeples and the factory chimneys. Ah, Lady Daphne, he is a man's god, a man's god."

An outlawed Dionysos! It is almost a definition of the Heroic Vitalist. One trembles at the conception of manhood implied in this "man's god," or the conception of godhead either. One has of course to hunt for passages as sinister as this in Lawrence, but their existence is none the less remarkable. Lawrence started with all the great artists of the past one hundred years from a sense of disvalue in a mechanized world. Nihilism is always close to diabolism, and Lawrence sometimes overstepped the boundary. He is not a Hitler, for he never recognized the exigencies of mass politics such as trickery and meanness. He is comparable rather to such a man as that apostate from the George Circle, Ludwig Klages, who has championed a "biocentric" philosophy, a philosophy rooted in life, against the "logocentric" or merely cerebral philosophies of the democrats and Christians. Klages' vitalism ends like Lawrence's in blasphemy against life itself, and *Lady Chatterley's Lover* is rather a shocking book, not for what it mentions but for what it preaches; it is the complement, not the rebuttal, of *Apocalypse.* The romantic quest for a life of sensations rather than thoughts reaches its culmination in a religion of sex and power, of Lawrence's own John Thomas and Nietzsche's Dionysos.

Aldous Huxley was right when he asserted that Lawrence could only be understood as an artist. His faults at least are those of the Bohemian, the artist who achieves individuality by desperate means. Mr. Nulle genially suggests that Lawrence stands to Hitler as Rousseau to Robespierre. If one could accept the popular conception of Rousseau, this would be true. The brilliant, undisciplined, self-indulgent, anarchistic authoritarian, with all his sophisticated primitivism, emotional naïveté, and utter impracticality, precedes the practical fanatic who makes not dreams but nightmares come true. Lawrence is to be understood as an artist, but the artist's function in recent times has been a peculiar one.

Part Four. The Meaning of Heroic Vitalism

". . . *In picking out from history our heroes, and communing with their kindred spirits,—in imagining as strongly as possible what differences their individualities brought about in this world, while its surface was still plastic in their hands, and what whilom feasibilities they made impossible,—each one of us may best fortify and inspire what creative energy may lie in his own soul. This is the lasting justification of hero-worship, and the pooh-poohing of it by 'sociologists' is the everlasting excuse for popular indifference to their general laws and averages. The difference between an America rescued by a Washington or by a 'Jenkins' may, as Mr. [Grant] Allen says, be 'little,' but it is, in the words of my carpenter friend, 'important.'*"

—WILLIAM JAMES, 1890.

"*We are waiting for another intuition, one more birth of ideas beyond Nietzsche, who already superseded Carlyle; a synthesis that must reconcile life with the idealism of thought. . . . Fortunately the pragmatists, professing a philosophy harmonious with Carlyle's influence, came to correct in good time the most evident of its weaknesses.*"

—LOUIS CAZAMIAN, 1913.

"Or all day they sit with their fishing rods besides swamps and therefore think themselves profound. But the man who angles where there are no fish—I don't even call him superficial."—Thus Spake Zarathustra.

1

It has not been the purpose of this book to formulate a single system of philosophy which is approved by Carlyle, Nietzsche, Wagner, Spengler, Lawrence, and George. What they have in common in general tendency must by now be as clear as the fact that they differ in very many ways. There is no creed of Heroic Vitalism. Heroic Vitalism is a faith, a dynamic *Weltanschauung*. In the details of application it adapts itself to the need of the moment. Its roots are in despair, therefore it despises all optimistic systems. But it respects the fact and the masters of fact, and thereby surpasses pessimism. Its roots are in evolutionism and therefore it is aloof from the static thought of the eighteenth century. But it is less a science of biology than a religion of metabiology, a religion of Dionysian life and energy. Its roots are in the deep sense of individuality which has been growing since the Renaissance. But it assails the idea of human equality and issues a warning against the belief that the crew should control the captain. Its roots are in the classical sociology of the Greeks, the Middle Ages, and the Renaissance, a sociology which regards society as a vital organism and which compares a culture to harmonious music, a human body, a ship, or a cosmic system. But it announces an end to ideals, to the prescription of otherworldly ends, to the creation of double (Christian and Machiavellian) standards, and seeks to conclude the enmity in ethics of power and wisdom by locating wisdom precisely in the seizure and exercise of power itself. Naturally, therefore, the idealist who expects immorality to be covert is shocked by Heroic Vitalism.

The great ideas of the older liberalism were gradualness and regularity. The great idea of Heroic Vitalism is difference. Where the old liberalism depicted uniformity, smoothness, rectilinear progression, Heroic Vitalism depicts difference, uneven leaps, and recurring cycles. The liberal stressed equality, gradualness, and the perfectibility of an improving mankind. The Heroic Vitalist stresses inequality, and evolution for him is saltatory, history is cyclical. The liberal professed fraternity. The Heroic Vitalist believes this profession to be a pious aspiration which the course of history does not support. Men kill each other. Most men are stupid. A few rule. These are the facts on which Heroic Vitalists insist.

We have seen how the principle of difference and variety results in an Heraclitean view of life as a contest. Man struggles for existence, the fittest survive, nature is red in tooth and claw, the army is the prototype of the State, politics are the continuation of war by other means, action is preferable to thought, suffering is ineradicable, happiness is incompatible with greatness: these are the truisms of Heroic Vitalism. Since, however, one of the chief intentions of the philosophy is to create the splendid and the beautiful, it does not rest content with description of man's estate. Out of the process of living it claims to extract a cosmic force, Destiny, and an aristocratic code which exalts valor above all other virtues. Where the liberal finds unity, the Heroic Vitalist finds duality: mankind consists of two groups, the many fools and the few wise, the shiftless majority and the energetic minority. From this duality of commanders and obeyers arises the aristocratic morality of Heroic Vitalism. While Christianity opposes the loving to the hard-hearted, the humble to the arrogant, Heroic Vitalism opposes the bold to the cowardly and the noble to the vulgar. In their hearts many people prefer courage to humility, and Heroic Vitalism legitimizes their preference.

Wherever the Heroic Vitalist touches on Destiny and Heroism he makes up in emotion for what he feels cannot be provided by argument. It is not at all clear, for instance, how the aristocratic code is dictated by the historical process. It seems more like a simple preference of some people who are or would like to be aristocrats. Galahad also is part of the historical process, but Nietzsche prefers Launcelot.

Heroic Vitalists do little to extricate themselves from very old philosophical tangles. On the question of free-will and necessity, they comfort themselves, like many Marxists, with the thought that historical necessity renders the success of their views inevitable, yet they anxiously try to influence history as if by volition. Success and survival are made the test of right, yet its extraordinary "survival-value" did nothing to reconcile Nietzsche to ecclesiasticism. The idea that the man of Fact is somehow more a part of history than the man of Truth is an arbitrary value judgment like the idea that a man in a Dionysian orgy is more alive than a man meditating. At one point it is implied that value is in the process, in *growth* towards superman. At another it is implied that the life of a Cæsar or of a Cesare Borgia is valuable in itself. As to the Destiny which informs history, it is a much less defended and perhaps much less defensible concept than any metaphysician's God. The belief of Nietzsche and Lawrence that Destiny directed their steps, like a celestial travel agency, is an extreme example of preference of magic to common sense and science. The myths and metaphors which Heroic Vitalists utilize or invent—the created myths of Lawrence, the reliance upon the Prometheus and *Götterdämmerung* patterns, the image of the tree of life—are more comprehensible as a solace to the author than as an explanation to the reader.

So much for the ideas in themselves. Since, however, the Heroic Vitalist prefers historical interpretation and criticism which bears on action, it will be interesting to apply these methods to Heroic Vitalism itself.

2

It is one of the clichés of historiography that modern culture reached its height in the seventeenth century, declined in the eighteenth to rationalism and rococo, and fell in the nineteenth, the century of chaos and industry. For Marx the curve of these centuries is the rise and fall of modern economy; for Spengler, the summer, autumn, and winter of modern culture; for Egon Friedell, noon, evening, and night of the modern soul.

What is the validity of these large generalizations? Can one— to take the case in hand—justifiably maintain that the nineteenth century is inferior to the eighteenth? Such blanket assertions surely result from the too easy acceptance of Spenglerian or other patterns which are snap judgments upon whole epochs. History has of course known periods of decline and fall—of which the decline and fall of Rome has remained an archetype to fascinate the mind. But the idea of decadence which has pre-occupied historians since Nietzsche tends to lead to an underesti-mation of less catastrophic change and the gross oversimplification of difficult and complex phenomena. "Decadence" is a term to use warily. It may be one of many aspects of an age, it may characterize this author or this book or that, it is not necessarily an adequate description of the whole culture, for autumn, to fol-low Spengler's metaphor, is also seed-time, and in so-called ages of decadence the seeds of the future are sown. One might even suggest that history is constant and simultaneous growth and decay and that the rigid separation of the two processes into distinct periods is a misleading distortion of the truth.

For society is not a vital organism, as Heroic Vitalists assume. A vital organism and a society are radically distinguished by the fact that the individual components of a vital organism, namely, the cells, are morphologically as well as functionally differentiated, whereas the individuals which compose a society are morphologically homogeneous and only functionally differen-tiated. Hence, for example, the Heroic Vitalist belief that a master differs from a slave as a queen-bee differs from a drone (i.e., morphologically) is a result of an inexact equation of society and organism. As to function, the equation is more plausible. There seems to be some truth in the figurative assertion that a stage has been reached in European culture at which some individual cells have acquired so complete an individuality that the health of the organism itself has been impaired. Romanticism, scientific analysis, and liberal nationalism, though all creative movements, have also their disruptive side.

The Marquis de Sade is an extreme but significant type. He was among the first to deny not only Christian theology but Christian ethics and to "transvaluate" these values into a diabolonian and dionysian creed that would give the released human animal his emancipation. The divine Marquis, as Swinburne called him, thought that natural law ought to hold unrestricted sway, but, unlike most thinkers of his day, he was not prepared to overlook the bar of black across the shield of man. Nature was queen, but she was evil. "Evil, be thou my good" was a valid principle not only for a fallen Satan but for fallen man. The algolagnia[1] for which the Marquis is more celebrated than for his general ethics is on all fours with these ethics. He was an artist exiled from the salon, an artist born into a new individuality. He had been torn from the maternal breast of society and from the protective bosom of God. He was isolated but not free of the complaint of Œdipus. The artist of the new age—Byron is the classic instance—is an outcast.

The Marquis was a rebel against order in every sphere. That is why he is the acknowledged patron of the surrealists, who believe that, as a moralist, he stands supreme.[2] Surrealism marks the point at which the individual cuts the last rope that binds him to society and leaps into unabashed irresponsibility. Like the Marquis, the surrealists are revolutionary in politics and in morals. Like him they are much more preoccupied with the nocturnal side of man, with the irrational, with the Dionysian, than with daylight, reason, and Apollo. They too are algolagnic and, therefore, the pictures of Salvador Dali are characterized by distortions of shape and size, cruelty, and mutilation. It is not that the experiences portrayed by surrealists are unusual but that they are *tabu* in the art of our culture: Dali's *Le Grand Masturbateur* is an instance. The dadaists, from whom the surrealists sprang, gave people an axe instead of a program at

[1] Pleasure in inflicting or suffering pain.
[2] *A Short Survey of Surrealism*, by David Gascoyne. London, 1935, p. 2.

one of their exhibitions. It has been debated whether their lack of principle does not require that the Surrealist Movement should begin by disbanding. As Sade advocated sin, the surrealists advocate neurosis. M. René Crevel defends paranoia in the following terms: *"Le droit de la pensée à la paranoia quoi qu'en puissent dire nos Mussolini de l'hygiène mentale est le même que celui d'un sexe à l'éjaculation. Donc plus de housses sur les objets, ni de capote anglaise sur les idées."* [3]

What Sade is in psychology, Max Stirner is in political philosophy. He is a minor writer who tells us more about the times than many a greater thinker. Sade and Stirner had neither the discretion nor the modesty to conceal their decadent souls; they are, therefore, more revealing than many of their contemporaries; they are the exhibitionists of decadence. Max Stirner pointed out, in *Der Einzige und sein Eigentum,* that Feuerbach had traveled only a part of the way in denying the supernatural sanctions of Christianity. The natural sanctions of European custom had also to be denied. Stirner wished to reject all general principles whatsoever. They were mere abstractions. All that a man can be certain of is himself. The only valid moral philosophy is a philosophy of egotism. Stirner's book is a melancholy reminder that the nineteenth century gave us the word nihilism. It is rebellion chemically pure. Every alloy of previous prejudice has been strained off. But an egotist cannot justifiably recommend egotism to others, and Stirner is no more than a symptom.

3

The Heroic Vitalists consider themselves an answer to the problem, but they sometimes forget that they are themselves a part of the processes they describe. The oversight is important because they have not been able to decide whether to be rebels or authoritarians. It might be objected that this question solves itself pragmatically: rebellion is to be regarded as right until the Heroic Vitalists are in a position of authority; afterwards

[3] *Dali ou l'anti-obscurantisme.* Paris, 1931, p. 23.

it is to be regarded as wrong. This is authentic Carlylean reasoning, but there is a snag.

Of all the social forces that serve to integrate a community, *mana* and *tabu* have customarily been among the most prominent. *Mana* is the positive force that man tries to acquire from his totem animal or his god, *tabu* is the negative of this positive: the Forbidden, the Thing Feared. *Mana*, therefore, is the complement of *tabu*. Now the position of the Heroic Vitalist is precisely this: that he wishes to increase the power of *mana*, through the *mana* personality of the hero, while simultaneously breaking every existing *tabu*. But by thus weakening respect for the very notion of *tabu* he is bound indirectly to weaken respect for *mana* too. Hence, the stability for which Heroic Vitalists work is not likely to be attained by their methods. We have seen how Nietzsche could not bear to be married, because marriage implies a prescribed pattern of social behavior, and how D. H. Lawrence declared he would be free of every social tie. A lifelong warrior, Nietzsche said that the first principle of his war tactics was that he attacked only things which were triumphant; the second principle was that he chose enemies against whom he fought alone, without allies.[4] What could be further from authoritarianism as we know it? To the negation of authoritarianism Nietzsche adds the bravado of the anarchist. The sheer anarchism of Lawrence's remark, "The result of taboo is insanity,"[5] is close to surrealist irresponsibility. But the surrealists are at least consistently irreverent. When Lawrence tries at the same time to decry *tabu* and exalt *mana* he is cutting off his nose to spite his face. And the mixture of anarchism and authoritarianism is characteristic of all the great Heroic Vitalists.

Of course, when "the mythos of the twentieth century" has eliminated every trace of former *tabu*, it will establish *tabus* of its own. There will be no practical difficulty about it. But I am not objecting here to the practitioners of Heroic Vitalism but to those prophets of Heroic Vitalism whose anarchism was

[4] *Ecce Homo*, "Warum ich so klug bin."
[5] *Phœnix*, p. 282.

genuine, who did not mean to be inhumane and who would weep at the events of the nineteen-forties. With the exception of the great self-flagellator Nietzsche—and even he had misgivings—none of the literary Heroic Vitalists whom we have considered was quite honest with himself. Because the world seemed so incurably democratic, at least in tendency, they forced themselves into fiercely anti-democratic postures. If we say that some of them might like to return to earth and recant, we do not mean that their philosophy was sheer bluff. But one and all yearned primarily for genuine excellence.

The intention behind their philosophy of power was that power should guarantee the security of beautiful things which otherwise would fall a prey to vulgarity and commercialism. The great Heroic Vitalists were literary men, inheriting the attitude of the literary man as critic of the age and devil's advocate. With the best of intentions they used arguments which today come too pat to the lips of demagogues. Unconsciously, they were a part of a movement in human history which passed the boundaries of the intelligentsia. Their attack on democracy was cogent, but they expected too much of the enemies of democracy. For all their harsh realism, they expected too much of human nature; not, it is true, of the common man, but of superior castes and heroes. They expected too highly of *super*human nature. What practical suggestion is there in any of their writings for the union which they desiderated of philosophic and political power? Unless a Heroic Vitalist can propose as rulers somebody more prepossessing than himself and friendly intellectuals we shall remain unconvinced.

Nietzsche tried to follow Socrates and Callicles (Plato's representative of the Napoleonic idea) at the same time. He took his conception of the complete man and of the ordered, hierarchical society from Plato's Socrates and from Aristotle despite the fact that, as Socrates knew, Callicles' admiration of the iconoclast and Thrasymachus' devotion to strength cannot be reconciled with Socratic doctrine, according to which harmony and synthesis are the true form of the psyche, the community, and the cosmos. Heroic Vitalism is an attempt to reconcile Socrates and Callicles.

Socrates was "right," but materially ineffectual and emotionally tame. Callicles was "wrong," but his doctrine is a challenge and a lure; it has appeal and is therefore, psychologically "right." Nietzsche insisted on retaining the psychological wisdom of Callicles without forfeiting his right to defend the order and hierarchy which Callicles' heroes would shatter. Though far from purely destructive in intention, the great Heroic Vitalists retained too much of the rebellious spirit of Callicles to be convincing when they spoke of order and organism.

In the nineteenth century, there was current on the one hand a spirit of pure rebelliousness and insubordination and on the other a spirit of pure authoritarianism and repression. Byron is the prototype of the former. Hegel's reputation suggests that he is the prototype of the latter; but there is a tinge of liberalism in Hegel; his English disciple, F. H. Bradley, is a better example of pure authoritarianism. In his essay, "My Station and its Duties," [6] Bradley advanced the view that, since society is an organism, Protestantism and its offshoots are a disease of over-developed individual cells; that skepticism is the fruit of an egotistic effort of the part to be wiser than the whole; that conscience itself is a device for exalting yourself above the wisdom of the community; that to encourage difference of opinion is to encourage self-conceit; that a man should do his duty without reflection. If it be asked what should be done if there is a conflict of duties, Bradley replies that such conflicts arise very seldom, once habits of inquisitiveness have been destroyed. . . .

We have seen that Heroic Vitalists incorporate a good deal of this authoritarianism in their philosophy. But being men of the nineteenth or early twentieth century, they belonged to the decadence they depicted. The spirit of sheer rebellion, of Byron and Sade and Stirner, was in them too. One recalls the self-conscious "realism" of *Latter-Day Pamphlets*, the bravado of *Götterdämmerung*, the sardonic smile and diabolism of Lawrence's Don Ramon. The sadistic streak in Lawrence is foreshadowed in Nietzsche's: "You are visiting women? Don't forget your whip!" Nietzsche's society of destroyers announced

[6] In *Ethical Studies* (London, 1876).

that they did not know whether reconstruction would be possible, and Wagner's Siegfried is so purely the destroyer that one might be tempted to regard Ibsen's *Peer Gynt* as a satirical comment on him.

Nietzsche's dichotomy of master-morality and slave-morality is a brilliant idea according to which the masses live by Bradley's code and the ruling caste by Byron's. Brilliant but Byronic. Nietzsche is the most serious of all critics of democracy but in his positive aspirations he is "romantic" in the bad sense. These aspirations are either nostalgic yearnings like Zarathustra's yearnings for the superman or they are Byronic posturing like Nietzsche's pretended admiration of Cesare Borgia and Cagliostro. Nietzsche is like his own heroes in that his energy overflows the measure. His *gaya scienza* is the sheer exuberance of carnival, and not sober criticism. He recommended the whip for women, but Lou Salome, whom he worshiped, was an intellectual with a will of her own. He said that the good war justifies any cause, but when war actually occurred in his lifetime he was disgusted.

4

Aside from this major confusion of attitude, there are at least two practical objections to Heroic Vitalism. The first is the Marxist objection that no amount of education or eugenic selection is enough unless the hero has control of the commercial and industrial machine which is the modern state. It is true that Hitler and Mussolini secured control of commerce and industry, but their methods in doing so savored of the Mammonism which Heroic Vitalist philosophers condemn. If Marxist writers overrate the economic factor, Heroic Vitalist writers underrate it. They assume that economics can be transcended by being ignored. In this respect, Nietzsche is much more naïve than Hitler.

The second practical objection to Heroic Vitalism is that there is a sheer lack of any class of higher men who are as wise as they are effective. Heroic Vitalists claim to unite wisdom with power, yet since this union is effected by declaring that the powerful is the wise, morals, like economics, are not so much transcended as ignored. In our time we have been witnesses of dictators of immense power and dexterity: but where is the nobility and magnanimity of Nietzsche's ideal? We listen for the sound of Dionysian revels and to our ears comes only the noise of the pogrom. Union of wisdom with power is still as far off as ever, and the upshot of Nietzsche's brave efforts is in practice the capitulation of the wise to the strong.

The æsthetic movement of the nineteenth century was a revulsion against the machine age, and the unconstructive nausea of the æsthetes has been the core of Heroic Vitalism. Heroic Vitalists have sought new knights and new priests to oust forever the despised third estate, the burgesses. Hence, for all their professions of futurism, they have not been practical men creating the future but worshipers of past heroic ages. This worship was their deepest emotion. Any honest reader must have noticed that hope for present and future heroism is much weaker in Carlyle than love of Cromwell, much weaker in Wagner than love of Siegfried, much weaker in Gundolf than love of Cæsar, much weaker in Lawrence than love of Etruscan remains. Nietzsche is not in the list because his longing for the superman probably *was* even greater than his admiration of dead heroes; Nietzsche is always too lithe to be easily caught in the net of generalization. Yet the generalization stands, and even Nietzsche's idea of the Renaissance is escapist. He makes his favorite ages far too exciting and, if he luxuriates in their violence, that is only because he wore his escapism with a difference. Did Nietzsche ever realize, for example, that the invention of gunpowder rendered bodily strength and the Herculean ideal practically null in the struggle for power?

Heroic Vitalists have been a prey to regressive fantasy. Lawrence's poetry evinces a recurring wish to return to the womb and the breast and, enlarging the horizon, it would be true to say that Heroic Vitalists long for the days before the people entered politics, when "the masses" were like the sea, that is, more plentiful than the land and also less important. They regard the democratic epoch as a mere tempest, an inundation of the land

by the sea. Because they take this tendentious view of democracy, they do not look to an adjustment of democracy or to an
evolution from democracy for a solution, but to seismic eruptions
that will push up unpredictable new peaks above all reach of the
angry waves.

In an epoch of vulgarity and journalism, Heroic Vitalists have
sought excellence and individuality. They have envied the individuality that was attained in ages when few individuals had
emerged from the undifferentiated mass. Hence their hostility
to Christianity, which teaches the equality of men before God,
and to Rousseauism which is, in many respects, secularized
Christianity. Their envy of the Greeks and the Romans has not
been happy in its results. Some have written glibly that Heroic
Vitalism is a break with the Græco-Christian tradition, but, in
truth, Heroic Vitalism owes more to Greece and Rome, or, more
precisely, to the classical education of many of its adherents, than
do most other philosophies.

But the time has come when one doubts the value of classical
education. The classical education that was fastened on the ruling
classes of England and Germany in the nineteenth century was a
contrivance for breeding rigid, snobbish minds aloof from the
society they ruled and ignorant of the world they lived in. Every
cult of Greece and Rome that has been formed since the Renaissance has served to exalt the go-getting, destructive type with
all his overstimulated ambition and vanity. One thinks of the
Girondins.

One form of Hellenism, moreover, is as false as another.
Winckelmann and Goethe formulated one Hellenic myth, Nietzsche a different one. Nietzsche has won higher praise from
scientific historians, but one may doubt whether Athenian life
was always as bracing and magnificent as Nietzsche would have
it. The idealization of youth, a perennial characteristic of Hellenism and an important aspect of Nietzsche, George, Lawrence, and
the rest, is one of the most morbid products of regressive fantasy.
The idealization of youth, outcropping in a hundred youth movements, is an attempt to find sufficiency and inspiration in the
sporting life. It is highbrow boy-scoutism.

And one doubts whether the schools of classical learning before Nietzsche, who is credited with the rediscovery of the real charac-- ter of the Greeks, were really so ignorant of the brute violence and recklessness which anyone can find recorded by Thucydides. When Sir John Seeley, for example, was defending the British Empire before his classes over half a century ago, he suggested the analogy of Athenian hegemony in Greece. "Much would be gained if the student of history would look at modern Europe *as he has already the habit of looking at ancient Greece.*"[7] Let no one say that classical education has not served a purpose. Nietz- sche was a classical scholar, and Alfred Rosenberg, with his praise of youthful beauty, has not missed his cue.

This is very academic criticism. But the argument is precisely that the philosophy of Heroic Vitalism has its origin in the literary and academic mind, a mind which, however much it pretends to be unacademic and practical, however much it pretends to repudiate itself, regards itself, when all comes to all, as *spectator ab extra:* even Nietzsche's tragic participation in the process was a solitary one. Ever since Carlyle declared that to be heroic is to be competent in all realms of activity, Heroic Vitalists have pretended to be men of action while retaining all the merits, in intelligence and understanding, of the man of thought. This is the weakness of their case for Heroic Vitalism. The strength of Heroic Vitalism is that it points to pent-up energies and acknowl- edges sentiments that were overlooked by the early liberals. The doctrines of Heroic Vitalism are often false. But the problems which called them forth are real, the impulse which created them was genuine. Heroic Vitalism has failed and its failure is part of a larger failure in modern history. The revival of hero- worship in the modern, industrial epoch is a symptom of the failure of plutocracy, and unless the rational and fruitful element in it can be assimilated by a more rational and fruitful phi losophy than that of Hitler and Mussolini, Heroic Vitalism will go down in history as no more than a portion of European nihil- ism, a mere segment of the great shadow which the machine age cast over the mind.

[7] *The Expansion of England.* New York, 1931, p. 114. (My italics.)

"Our wills and fates do so contrary run
That our devices still are overthrown,
Our thoughts are ours, their ends none of our own."
—SHAKESPEARE.

1

Much has been written on the influence of Heroic Vitalists,
and it will be well to mention at least the influence of the two
ringleaders, Carlyle and Nietzsche.

How much can safely be said of Carlyle's influence on history?
He has been praised by several eminent Germans. Goethe told
Eckermann (October 11, 1828) that Carlyle was almost more at
home with German literature than were the Germans themselves. Bismarck doubly and trebly underlined the passages in
Carlyle which concerned political genius, and gave Carlyle assur-
ances of respect which he never gave to any German man of
genius.[1] In his *History of Germany in the Nineteenth Century,*
Heinrich von Treitschke described Carlyle as the only Briton who
ever fully understood Germany.

There is little evidence of anything more than stray statements
such as these. It is true that editions of translated excerpts from
Carlyle's works in 1920, 1921, and 1922 accompanied the rise of
fascism to power in Italy and that three hundred thousand copies
of translated Carlyle selections were sold in Germany between
1926 and 1931. It is true also that *Heroes and Hero-Worship* has
been widely prescribed in American schools for a long time now.
But such facts do not tell us to what extent Carlyle is read and
relished. Nor, in Nietzsche's case, is it clear how far he has
swayed the minds of men. In 1908 Benito Mussolini wrote an
article on Nietzsche praising his criticism of democracy and his

[1] *Bismarck,* by Emil Ludwig. Boston, 1927, p. 473.

forecast of the twentieth century. Mussolini and his friend D'Annunzio have sometimes seemed to be related to Nietzsche as Lenin was related to Marx; yet more often they seem to be influenced by no doctrine but opportunism. In 1917 alone, one hundred and forty thousand copies of the pocket edition of *Thus Spake Zarathustra* were sold in Germany. Of recent years Nietzsche has been widely publicized by the Nazis, who have placed Nietzscheans in important chairs of political philosophy.

Carlyle and Nietzsche in twentieth-century politics have been useful to German Governments in search of authorities to impress their intelligentsia with. They have been useful also to anti-German propagandists as Aunt Sallies, and my guess is that in so far as Nietzsche has influenced the general public he has influenced them *against* Nazism through the agency of anti-Nazi propaganda. If Hitler himself is indebted to literature it is more probably to the paranoiac wild-west stories of Karl May, known to every German lad of his generation, than to the rather more advanced thought of Carlyle and Nietzsche. Alfred Rosenberg has, of course, been close to Hitler, but *his* debt to Carlyle and Nietzsche is almost *nil.*

America has produced a Karl May *for adults* in the shape of a series of stories told in colored pictures of the adventures of Superman, a hero of superlative strength, swiftness, chivalry, and beauty, who teaches his readers that the *coup d'état* (a modern name for the *deus ex machina*) is preferable to workaday reform. Featured in seventy-seven daily papers and thirty-six Sunday papers, "Superman" has been running to a million and a half copies as a pulp-paper magazine. Yet how can Nietzsche be held responsible for a conception he would have despised, presented through a press he would have despised to a public he would have despised?

There is more to be learned by regarding Carlyle and Nietzsche as symptom than as cause. In those astonishing prophecies, for instance, which come so much nearer the truth than the prophecies of liberal optimists like Macaulay, Carlyle and Nietzsche typify an attitude uncommon in their day but less uncommon in ours. Asked about the future in 1856, Carlyle said: "I see terrible calamities impending, a total severing of every tie and bond of the world as it exists—blood-shedding and destruction." In 1871, he wrote to his brother: "In fact, I apprehend before many years the huge abominable boil will *burst*, and the British Empire fall into convulsions, perhaps into horrors and confusions which nobody is yet counting on. All Europe, indeed the whole civilized world, is in weltering and confused struggle and mutiny. . . ." We have seen how, in *Frederick*, Carlyle contemplates two to ten centuries of barbarism.

Nietzsche's prophecies are similar. He says that socialistic experiments will entail a vast expenditure of lives, but that this expenditure will be a salutary proof that socialism is a denial of life and evolution. The Paris Commune will be a slight indigestion beside the convulsions of the twentieth century. "There will be wars such as have never before happened on earth. Great politics date from me."

Carlyle and Nietzsche shared the view that they lived at the phœnix-hour of civilization. Fire was surging but there was hope of rebirth. The agent of rebirth was the Prussian State, according to Carlyle. Nietzsche, on the other hand, notoriously ridiculed the *Reich* and, in the end, hated Bismarck; yet he did not retract his statement that the future rests with the sons of Prussian officers, whose character he had definite ideas about. Looking into the future of government, he asks: "Where are the barbarians of the twentieth century?" In the twentieth century, there will be, on the one hand, the chaos of disintegrating democracy, on the other, a new barbarism and a new hardness ending in a new discipline. It will be, Nietzsche forecasts, an era of conscription and total war.

2

The influence of Carlyle and Nietzsche is one thing. The way they and their work have been exploited is another.

In the past seventy years three great wars have been initiated by the German Empire. In the first, Friedrich Nietzsche served the Reich as an ambulance man and Thomas Carlyle supported the

German cause in the columns of *The Times*. The second was known in some quarters as "the Nietzschean War" and many professors and parsons chose the period 1914-18 to write denunciations of Nietzsche and of German philosophy generally. These writings make melancholy reading today, nor do they form a consistent body of doctrine. J. H. Muirhead's *German Philosophy in Relation to the War* (London, 1915), which attributes bellicosity to German materialism, is canceled out by George Santayana's *Egotism in German Philosophy*, first published in 1916 and reissued for the next war in 1939, where the blame is laid on German idealism.

Nietzsche was for some a militarist and for others a harmless visionary. So was Carlyle. An Englishman, M. Kelly, declared that Carlyle had proved for him that the German cause was the right one. Mr. Kelly accordingly repudiated the government of his own country and addressed a tract to the American people: *Carlyle and the War* (New York, 1915). An enemy of Prussianism, Norwood Young, thought that the war might not have occurred had Carlyle's *Frederick the Great* never been written.[2] But Carlyle's biographer, D. A. Wilson, tried to prove Carlyle a peace-lover (*The Faith of All Sensible People*, London, 1913). A Cambridge professor, A. Wolf, made a similar attempt on Nietzsche's behalf (*The Philosophy of Nietzsche*, London, 1915).

The rise of fascism and National Socialism brought Carlyle and Nietzsche back into the news, but critics did not agree as to which side they were on. Nietzsche's sister told Hitler that he was her brother's superman (*Der Montag*, July 7, 1935). Another member of the Nietzsche family, Richard Oehler, identified Nietzsche with National Socialism and prefaced his book—*Nietzsche und die deutsche Zukunft* (Leipzig, 1935)—with a portrait of Hitler looking at Nietzsche's bust. Sir Herbert Samuel told the House of Commons (March 20, 1935) that the cause of present discontents was Germany and the philosophy of Nietzsche. The Boston *Evening Transcript* (April 24, 1940) carried the headline: HITLER WAR URGE BLAMED ON INSANE PHILOSOPHER; NIETZSCHE NAZI CHIEF'S FAVORITE AUTHOR. The

[2] *Carlyle, his Rise and Fall.* London, 1927, Ch. XXIX.

Nazi appointee to the chair of political philosophy in Berlin was Alfred Bäumler, one of Nietzsche's editors. On the other hand, M. P. Nicolas, a Frenchman, indignantly denied any similarity between Nietzsche's views and Hitler's (*De Nietzsche à Hitler*, Paris, 1936).

Some years ago Sir Herbert Grierson drew a comparison between Carlyle's political philosophy and the regimes of Hitler and Roosevelt.[3] Signor Mario Palmieri said that Italy had added a type of hero to the six classic types of Carlyle: the hero as Leader. Mussolini, he wrote, "is fulfilling for instance the prophecy of Nietzsche . . . he is fulfilling also the words of Carlyle." [4] Baron Ernest Seillière devoted a volume to the study of Carlyle's fascism: *L'Actualité de Carlyle*. In 1937 the Nazis handed out the party line on Carlyle and Nietzsche in two books: *Carlyle und der Nationalsozialismus*, by Theodore Deimel, and *Nietzsche und der Nationalsozialismus*, by Heinrich Haertle. Although they were born too early for racial science, we are told, Carlyle and Nietzsche are genuine ancestors of Nazism. Yet Mr. Emery Neff, a staunch American democrat, was commending the political philosophy of Carlyle in this same decade.

Carlyle and Nietzsche have been uncommonly good copy. But there has been no agreement as to the role of either in the history of the past hundred years, and consequently there could be no agreement as to their relationship to each other. Was Nietzsche, like Bismarck, a pupil of Carlyle's? Was he working in the same direction, on behalf of the same interests? Bertrand Russell has placed one above the other in the genealogy of fascism,[5] others have as confidently declared that there is no significant similarity.[6] We have seen that there has been a like disagreement about all the men discussed in this book. Each has been called a fascist or proto-Nazi both by supporters and opponents of fascism and Nazism. None is so, yet those who suggested a connection with fascism were wiser than those who

[3] "Carlyle and Hitler," republished in *Essays and Addresses*. London, 1940.
[4] *The Philosophy of Fascism*. Chicago, 1936, pp. 236-37.
[5] "The Ancestry of Fascism," in *In Praise of Idleness*. New York, 1936.
[6] E.g., B. H. Lehman, *Carlyle's Theory of the Hero*, p. 92.

denied all such allegations. Unfortunately the whole discussion was polemical. The critics have tried either to prove a man a fascist or to prove him the reverse. It would have been better to separate out fascist and non-fascist elements and draw conclusions, better to paint the portrait of Janus and speculate on his significance than to be indignant or enthusiastic about one face on the assumption that the other does not exist.

And it would have been advisable to view Heroic Vitalism in broader perspective.

3

A hundred years ago men were already aware that a process of rapid change was transforming the world. The human side of the change might be called Democracy, embodying as the word does the idea of government by the people and the idea of possible progress. The non-human side of the process might be called Industrialism, meaning the economic and technological changes which destroyed the agrarian economies and gave to man an infinitely greater control over nature. There were two main schools of thought about the whole process. The optimist school saw an imminent Utopia in universal suffrage, universal literacy, and the progress of applied science, and took heart at the construction of every new factory chimney. The pessimist school saw in the political change the handing-over of power to the ill-bred, the immoral, and the unintelligent, while in the technological change they saw the mechanization of life, the extinction of the soul of man, and the destruction of beauty and values generally.

Since the days of the Benthamites and the Utopian socialists the optimist philosophy has taken many hard knocks. Europe met with revolution after revolution, yet each revolution created not a New Harmony but a new group of disillusioned intellectuals. Almost all intellectuals of modern times are disillusioned—if not in 1848 then in 1870, if not in 1919 then in 1939. Optimism is of all discredited philosophies the most discredited; aspersions upon the decadence of modern times are of all critical routines the most regularly performed. Hence a great deal of modern thought is rationalization or even open expression of disenchantment. Our contemporary pessimists are only minor followers in the train of Schopenhauer, Wagner, Nietzsche, Gobineau, Kierkegaard, Dostoevski, or another of the bizarre enemies of the post-industrial world. Not all of these had personally ever entertained any hope for democracy, but out of disgust at a world which strives after democracy despite repeated failure, they propose the alternative of aristocratic privilege, racial superiority, dictatorship, and the like.

We do not have to choose between the extremes of optimism and pessimism, yet it is evident that the pessimist school is the anti-democratic side and the optimist view only a too naïve, unqualified statement of our own democratic beliefs. The implication of anti-democratic writing today is that democratic thinkers have not moved very far from Bentham and James Mill in a hundred years. Doubtless this is a just criticism of some liberal idealists, but it is no fair account of the history of the democratic ideas generally. It ignores the influence of Marxism with its emphasis on hostile economic interests, the necessity of struggle, the power basis of politics. And among the many other factors it ignores is the nature of historical Romanticism.

The negative function of the Romantic Revolt was to discredit the Classicism of the previous epoch, a Classicism which meant the Newtonian universe, Newtonian physics, pleasure-and-pain psychology, in fine an outlook that had grown increasingly rationalist but which remained narrowly mechanistic. The positive function of Romanticism was to fill the gaps which Classicism had always ignored and also the gaps created by the destruction of Classicism. It is natural that the Romanticists were themselves much more aware of the negative than of the positive side of their task. It is natural too that some interpreted their tasks as more restorative than creative, that others used the new freedom from prescribed correctness and dogma to set up their own private correctness and dogma—this response is still common in our time. But the mistake is to imagine that Romanticism stopped with the first generation of Romanticists or only lingered on in Celtic or Maeterlinckian twilights. In the second half of the nineteenth century came a renewal of intellectual activity so vast that it is just as much entitled as Romanticism to be regarded as the beginning of a new era. I refer to the generation that produced—among so many others—Nietzsche, Tolstoy, Dostoevski, Strindberg, Manet, Cézanne, Bergson, and Shaw. Perhaps the best symbol and example of this renewed activity, its meaning, and its relation to Romanticism is William James.

It is some time now since A. N. Whitehead suggested that as Descartes opened the epoch of Classicism, William James has opened a new epoch, as yet unnamed, in human thinking. That is a brilliant and original formulation. But an alternative way of looking at the same phenomena is to take James as the culmination of Romanticism, as the man who made articulate what the earlier Romantics were groping after, as the man who built into a philosophy and a method what had previously been a series of hints, images, symbols, and intuitions. It is not simply that James translates into the terms of ratiocination what Goethe's *Faust* had symbolically said. In his attitude we find fully articulated an attitude as fully expressive of modern life as was Descartes' of the century of Louis XIV.

In the matter of Heroic Vitalism, James represents a position between the two contemporary extremes, the respective extremes reached by Tolstoy and Nietzsche who found the new world disgusting and saw only, one might say, the alternative of outright paganism or outright Christianity—activity without values or values without activity. James united activity with values. He represents what is positive in science but not what is hampered by hard and fast categories and narrow determinism. He was "positivistic" in a broad sense but utterly opposed to mechanistic explanations of non-mechanical phenomena. He gave status alike to Baconian experiment and to reason but transcended the earlier rationalism and empiricism in the firm yet elastic method of pragmatism. His theory of truth is relativistic, but he knew that what is relatively true is not necessarily mere subjective fantasy but can be objective and worthy of a fiery faith. He attacked the narrower science of an earlier period, but he did not therefore assume that science is neutral to values. He distinguished between the conclusions of a particular science, which may well have no broader bearing, and the experimental method itself, a method just as necessary in human behavior as elsewhere.

He was a militant democrat, though he has been looked askance at because he knew the value of superior brains. James knew that whole peoples do not rise up and start governing themselves. That leaders may *mis*lead is no reason for assuming that leaders may be dispensed with or that leadership must necessarily be bad. James knew, moreover, that democracy must have certain ends in view toward which political and economic equality are only means. He found value in men; and the better the man, the greater his value. Like most great thoughts, this one sounds trite enough once it is formulated. But, in the nineteenth century, the formulation had to be hammered out between the upper grindstone of nihilistic determinism and the nether grindstone of Heroic Vitalism.

4

Heroic Vitalism has been criticized in this book. But it is not the worst of all alternatives.

Our Heroic Vitalists strove towards the future. They were less interested in preserving and pickling an old system than in sowing the seeds of a new one. Otherwise, they clearly saw, a new one would grow of itself, undetermined by human volition. Further, we have seen that Heroic Vitalists have helped to shake off outworn beliefs. Unhampered by beliefs suited to the days of the stagecoach, we are enabled to let beliefs emerge from the environment which creates them, in order that in turn they might react upon the environment. Our literary Heroic Vitalists were not whole-hearted haters of mankind, not sadists, not racists, not simply "reactionaries." They saw the necessity of culture, the "study of perfection."

Carlyle, Nietzsche, Wagner, Lawrence, Spengler, George—

their faults and foibles, their frustrations, and shortcomings, their agonies and their fumblings, all speak eloquently to us. Perhaps I have over-stressed the negative side. Their merits, their ecstasies, their energy, their tenderness, their vision are eloquent too. It is sentimental to respect a great man more because he fails; but one cannot respect a failure less because he is great. Erratic, perverse, unbalanced, or wilful, these men bore the stamp of greatness. As heirs of the common lot they suffered; as artists they transmuted their sufferings into the rich strangeness of word or sound; as great writers, though involved in a general decadence, they made grandeur even out of decay, and their own magnificence is itself the refutation of their belittlement of mankind. There is hope in the very cogency of their pessimism.

The Heroic Vitalist has much to say against modern society and the inevitable immaturity of liberal thought; for the liberal experiment—the great experiment of our epoch, man's greatest fight for mastery through practical reason—is barely two hundred years old. However much its more callow advocates prate of "democratic tradition," it is the baby of world history. Of this immaturity their advocacy is testimony strong enough. We should be thankful to the Heroic Vitalists for stressing the difficulties in rearing the child, and for reminding us that he cannot grow to maturity in a day, though their half-sincere proposal to hit him over the head and have done is an error, since their own candidate for his office is not present at all; their dream-hero belongs to the distant past or the distant future.

Heroic Vitalism does not have all the answers, yet the Heroic Vitalists, if we interpret them wisely, may be tonic and astringent to us. Perhaps their contribution is less to our polity than to our private selves. "I do esteem the individual above everything else," said Lawrence, speaking for Carlyle, Nietzsche, and Stefan George, the greatest enemies of modern individualism. Their intellectual performances were all desperate shifts in a search for freedom from the cash-nexus. They often head in precisely the wrong direction. Does not dialectic imply the interaction of opposites? Would not freedom spring from its contrary, and the individual from the awakened sense of community? At least these searchers after the hero, after the individual who is master of his fate, have much to say to the modern separate individual. And despite themselves they contribute to the liberal movement, a movement which began with the writers of the eighteenth century whom they despise, a movement which aims precisely at making man master of his fate, at establishing the ascendancy of man's mind.

Idealists since William Godwin, the once famous father-in-law of Shelley, have made of reason a sort of autonomous, autotelic power which can overcome brute nature by ignoring it. This is lunacy: the polar opposite of Nietzsche's intermittent lunacy and Hitler's persistent lunacy, namely, the belief that power is autotelic and that reason might, without much loss, become as extinct as the brontosaurus. Hitler's philosophy, or anti-philosophy, refutes itself; but so does Godwin's, for it is not reasonable to refuse to recognize the non-reasonable elements in man and in nature. Godwin is an eccentric. Recognition of the facts of power, willingness to be involved in conflict, ability to discern the direction in which history is moving—these are things which Heroic Vitalists advocate and which some foolishly condemn as "success-worship," "historicism," "barbarism." Riveted to social purposes these things are desirable because they are necessary.

Heroic Vitalism was many things, but outstandingly it was an attempt to fix the place of the superior man in civilization, the place not only of the great soldier but of the man of intellect. Nazism meant intellectuals in uniform, intellectuals in the padded cell, intellectuals in graves. Much as they worshiped heroes, preached power, turned diabolist, the Heroic Vitalists did not want this. They wanted the opposite. What they hated was the mechanization of life, and Nazism, for all its lip-service to vitalism, heroism, and the like, is the highest degree of mechanization yet attained. Nazi economics, for all the lip-service to collectivism and community, are the highest degree of exploitation yet attained. When Carlyle said the cash-nexus was the only bond between men, he exaggerated; among the Nazis he would be near to literal truth. Nazism is the apotheosis of all that the Heroic

Vitalists loathed, and it drew support mainly from that class whose values Heroic Vitalists sought to invert: the lower middle class.

The Heroic Vitalists proposed unacceptable philosophies of politics, but the impulse that produced them was a good one. It was the impulse to seek the excellent in an age of the average, the individual in an age of masses, the organic in an age of mechanism, in fine, quality in an age of quantity. In many respects they failed in their quest, or found only personal solutions. But the problems they faced remained. What is the place of superior ability in society? What is the place of the intellectual? What is the status of heroes and hero-worship?

No one would now suggest that all these topics are empty and futile. The hero is a fact. He is a man to whom things do not merely happen but who makes them, or some of them, happen. The environment can accept or reject him, and a democratic people—which would be a very decisive part of the environment—can accept or reject him. Indeed this is probably the greatest problem of democratic politics: to find peoples who can wisely accept or reject the leaders who come forward.

But at the root of the Heroic Vitalist's ferment is his uneasiness about himself, the intellectual, and his status. To be sure, he sometimes shouted that the intellectual was of no importance and that all should bow before a Cæsar. But that was only in times of discouragement over the prime issue. Carlyle began by praising the poet and elevating him to the status of prophet; he ended praising Frederick and Bismarck. By the time Spengler arrived, the world, and especially Germany, was ready for the pronouncement: the sword is mightier than the pen. The wheel had come full circle. The Heroic Vitalist philosophy, which had begun as a defense of the intellectual, as an attempt to find an honorable place for him in the modern world, ended as Spenglerian anti-intellectualism.

In our time the status of the intellectual has remained low. Where he is not the tool, willing or unwilling, of a political machine, he is an outsider. He is either at party headquarters or on a rock in California; either orating from a soap-box or taking his ease in Axel's Castle. What is wrong? Primarily that

we have not learned from Romanticism and early Heroic Vitalism
that the intellectual need not be either hireling or hermit, that
he can be political without loss of integrity, and broad in his
interests without vulgarity, above all that his calling is a high
one which he has no right to be ashamed of, either overtly or
secretly. The modern intellectual is ashamed of his existence.
He takes it for granted that other groups should act in their own
interest, but he makes an exception of his own group. He is
a friend of the worker, the party, the nation, of mankind. The
only group to which his benevolence does not extend is the
intelligentsia. Of them he speaks with caution or with sarcasm,
in a word, with embarrassment.

The least of the ill effects of his attitude is his own unhappiness.
A more important weakness of the position is its neutralization
of the intellectual as a distinct force in society. The intellectual
may be a force as soldier or agitator, even as journalist, though
he is not likely to do these jobs better than the next man. But,
as an intellectual, he is no longer a force.

Carlyle, on the other hand, took himself seriously, regarded
himself as a leader and a prophet. The words *leader* and *prophet*
are invoked today chiefly by the champions of the second-rate
literature of Uplift. Few have seen their way to a position between blind hero-worship and the opposite extreme—impersonal
determinism, the denial of individuality. Yet blind hero-worship,
as Hitlerism has shown, is actually accompanied by a denial of
individuality. Conversely: to accept individuality, to glory in it,
is to accept the hero, the superior man, and to glory in him.
Democracy is paradoxical: democratic equality means to respect
the individual and thus to notice individuality, to welcome
variety, to revere superiority—which implies inequality. If this
were not so, what would be the ultimate worth of democracy?
What is more basic to democracy than "careers open to talent,"
a doctrine which so evidently implies that talent is of supreme
value? Democracy, to justify itself, must *include* aristocracy. It
is partly because democracy alone *can* produce aristocracy, because democracy alone can offer careers open to talent, that we
are democrats.

Anti-democratic philosophies of aristocracy, namely, Heroic Vitalism and kindred attitudes, are part æstheticism, part fascism. When the hour strikes, if he cannot swing to democracy, the Heroic Vitalist becomes either pure æsthete or pure fascist. In neither case does he help to equalize opportunities. Democracy does; or, more precisely, democracy can. It can help the best men, the *aristoi,* to the front; and when it has done so it will have produced the first real aristocracy in history, for all previous "aristocracies" were formed either by accident of birth or by expropriation. Aristocracy is one of the goals of democracy. That is the truth which the Heroic Vitalists, who did not see it, help us to understand.

Index